*Amazing Grace in John Newton*

*Slave-Ship Captain,*
*Hymnwriter,*
*and Abolitionist*

MW00777866

John Newton, 1725–1807

# Amazing Grace in John Newton

## Slave-Ship Captain,
## Hymnwriter,
## and Abolitionist

by William E. Phipps

MERCER UNIVERSITY PRESS
Macon, Georgia USA / 2001

ISBN 0-86554-716-5                                                    MUP/H536

The paper used in this publication meets the minimum requirements
of American National Standard for Information Sciences—
Permanence of Paper for Printed Library Materials, ANSI Z39.48-1984.

*Library of Congress Cataloging-in-Publication Data*

Phipps, William E., 1930–
Amazing grace in John Newton : slave-ship captain, hymnwriter,
and abolitionist / by William E. Phipps.
      p.   cm.
Includes bibliographical references and index.
ISBN 0-86554-716-5 (alk. paper) 1. Newton, John, 1725–1807.
2. Church of England—England—Clergy—Biography.
I. Title.
BX5199.N55.P45 2001
283'.092—dc21

                                                            2001004148

# Contents

*To my sister, Margie Lee Shick,*
*who, as did John Newton,*
*combines evangelical joyfulness*
*with concern for the needy.*

# Significant Dates for John Newton

| | |
|---|---|
| 1725 | Born in London |
| 1732 | Death of his mother |
| 1733–1735 | Attends school in Stratford, Essex |
| 1736–1742 | Sails with his father on Mediterranean voyages |
| 1743 | Falls in love with Mary Catlett |
| 1744 | Midshipman on HMS *Harwich* |
| 1745 | Illness and servitude in Africa |
| 1747 | Rescued from Guinea |
| 1748 | Survives a violent storm at sea |
| 1749 | First officer on slave ship |
| 1750 | Weds Mary in Chatham |
| 1750–1754 | Captain of slave ships |
| 1755 | Customs supervisor at Liverpool |
| 1756 | Becomes disciple of George Whitefield |
| 1757 | Friendship with John Wesley begins |
| 1758 | Theological study intensifies |
| 1760–1763 | Lay preaching experiences |
| 1763 | Writes narrative of his life |
| 1764 | Ordained Church of England priest in Olney |
| 1767 | Friendship with William Cowper begins |
| 1779 | *Olney Hymns* published |
| 1780 | Becomes rector of St. Mary Woolnoth Church in London |
| 1782 | Friendship with Hannah More begins |
| 1785 | Friendship with William Wilberforce begins |
| 1788 | *Thoughts upon the African Slave Trade* published |
| 1790 | Mary dies of cancer |
| 1793 | *Letters to a Wife* published |
| 1807 | Britain makes slave trade illegal; Newton dies |

# Foreword

*Amazing grace! (how sweet the sound)*
*That saved a wretch like me!*
*I once was lost, but now am found—*
*Was blind, but now I see.*

This hymn by John Newton has become the most popular hymn in America.[1] *Our Spiritual National Anthem* is the appropriate subtitle of *Amazing Grace in America*, a 1996 book by Mary Rourke and Emily Gwathmey. The editors of *The Hymn* journal give evidence that it also has top ranking in Europe.[2] Calling it "the world's most beloved hymn," *Roots* author Alex Haley observed from his intercontinental visits that the "hymn has traveled the world, bringing a message of hope and forgiveness to all people of faith."[3] The "Amazing Grace" television special produced by Bill Moyers not only presented versions of this song by American folk musicians—such as Judy Collins and Johnny Cash—but also illustrated the song's global appeal from South Africa to Japan.

The hymn "Amazing Grace" portrays Newton's life in cameo, so chapter headings below are taken from its stanzas. It affirms Newton's awareness of being divinely rescued from "many dangers" as well as from a wretched life, and alludes to the blindness that prevented his seeing the anti-Christian nature of the slave business. His life span was coterminous with the period when England dominated the most colossal, lucrative, and inhumane slave trade the world has ever known. And Newton had the dubious distinction of becoming an Anglican priest after having served as the captain of slave ships.

During the second half of his life, Newton became prominent among those who favored a Methodist type of revival in the Church of England. That movement stressed personal conversion, simple worship, emotional enthusiasm, and social justice. Looking into Newton's ties with outstand-

---

[1]According to a survey of more than 10,000 newspaper readers by religion columnist George Plagenz, "Amazing Grace" is the most popular hymn in America. *Presbyterian Outlook* (14 May 1990).

[2]*The Hymn* (July 1972): 93.

[3]*Reader's Digest* (October 1986): 138, 142.

ing clerical and lay evangelicals helps us discern the movement's auspicious beginnings. His camaraderie with George Whitefield, John Wesley, Lord Dartmouth, William Cowper, John Thornton, Hannah More, and William Wilberforce is worth examining closely. Newton used his pulpit in London as one means for raising British consciousness of the immorality of the slave trade. The accounts he gave to parliamentary committees of atrocities he had witnessed assisted significantly in the passage of legislation during his lifetime to abolish the British slave trade.

David Jeffrey, an English literature professor and noted author, claims that "the life of John Newton offers some of the most interesting reading in eighteenth-century biography."[4] "His life story might have formed the background for a Defoe to work upon had it not been even stranger than the strangest fiction," suggests Marcus Loane.[5] Newton's account of his life relates numerous near-death experiences, some suffered when he himself was forced into slavery. Leonard Binns, in an incisive study of Newton, calls him a historical standout because "few men have managed to crowd into their lives so much of sin" and still become admirable persons.[6] Erik Routley sums up Newton's life in this way: "He moved in the lowest and vilest circles and sank to the depths of vice, and yet there emerges from this stormy story a man who not only commands the affection of any humane soul, but who showed himself then and afterwards capable of the highest Christian graces."[7] Moreover, there are romantic adventures in Newton's saga, including seven years of unrequited passion for his sweetheart, followed by their lifelong mutual affection in marriage. Michael Hennell claims that there are "few romances either in fiction or history whose intensity and beauty surpass that of John Newton and Mary Catlett."[8]

Even though he lived two centuries ago, a *well-documented* biography of Newton has never been published. Much reliable data can be found in Bernard Martin's out-of-print biography, written fifty years ago for a British literary audience, yet most of those who have written extensively about him have interjected much fiction, resulting in pious treatments intended less for historical information than for reinforcing notions of

---

[4]David Jeffrey, ed., *A Burning and a Shining Light* (Grand Rapids MI: Eerdmans, 1987) 388.

[5]Marcus Loane, *Oxford and the Evangelical Succession* (London: Lutterworth, 1950) 128.

[6]Leonard Binns, *The Early Evangelicals* (Greenwich CT: Seabury, 1953) 257.

[7]Erik Routley, *I'll Praise My Maker* (London: Independent, 1951) 146.

[8]*Theology* (October 1948): 378.

evangelicalism current in their time. For example, nineteenth-century biographers of Newton say little or nothing about his being an abolitionist. Nor do they tell of the horrors he inflicted as a slave ship captain, which Newton carefully logged. In writing definitively about the Atlantic slave trade several decades ago, historian Roger Anstey relied heavily on Newton's log, recognizing it to be virtually the only record of day-to-day activities on board an eighteenth-century slave ship.[9]

Unlike previous studies of Newton that have given little attention to historical context, this biography will examine the tribes from which Newton obtained slaves and the Caribbean and Carolina plantation societies, as well as the Protestant, literary, economic, and political culture of eighteenth-century England. Hopefully, this biography will correct some widespread errors about Newton. The main misunderstanding is that he was first a slave ship captain, and then a religious experience during a tumultuous storm at sea caused him to change his vocation. Some recent writers—understandably assuming that getting religion causes someone to turn from doing evil to doing good—have reversed the sequence of Newton's marine activities. Thus, the dramatic shipboard spiritual awakening *follows* a description of his harsh treatment of Africans during his years as ship commander.[10] At the other extreme, many otherwise well-researched books state that Newton composed "How Sweet the Name of Jesus Sounds" in his comfortable cabin while captured Africans were in agony below deck.[11] For example, Robin Furneaux charges, "When faced with the contrast between the gentle beauty of this hymn and the abominable background against which it was written, one can only regard its author as being among the most insensitive men who ever lived."[12] Newton did engage in devotional practices while a slave ship captain, but all of his famous hymns were written many years later when, as a parish minister, he was ashamed of his involvement with slavery.

---

[9]Roger Anstey, *The Atlantic Slave Trade and British Abolition 1760–1810* (London: Macmillan, 1975) 13-32.

[10]Lindo Jo McKim, *The Presbyterian Hymnal Companion* (Louisville: Westminster/John Knox, 1993) 280; Henry Gariepy, *Songs in the Night* (Grand Rapids MI: Eerdmans, 1996) 106; Linda Granfield, *Amazing Grace* (Toronto: Tundra, 1997).

[11]Albert Belden, *George Whitefield* (New York: Macmillan, 1953) 254; Daniel Mannix, *Black Cargoes* (New York: Viking, 1962) 133; Jack Gratus, *The Great White Lie* (New York: Monthly Review, 1973) 63; Hugh Thomas, *The Slave Trade* (New York: Simon & Schuster, 1997) 309; Terence Brady and Evan Jones, *The Fight against Slavery* (London: British Broadcasting Corporation, 1975) 11.

[12]Robin Furneaux, *William Wilberforce* (London: Hamilton, 1974) 38.

But the aim of this study is wider than providing an accurate under-standing of a pivotal figure in eighteenth-century England. Newton's life story luminously depicts unauthentic as well as authentic ways that Christians practice the gospel in everyday life. His close involvement with both capitalism and evangelicalism, the main economic and spiritual forces of his culture, provides a fascinating case study of the relationship of religious persons to their social environment.

During my career as a writer, religious biography has been a special interest. While working on my doctoral dissertation, "Paul's Use of Jewish Scriptures," I became aware of the central importance of an indi-vidual's earliest environment on his or her religious orientation for life. Subsequently I have examined, among others, the lives of Mary Magda-lene, Augustine of Hippo, John Knox, John Donne, Muhammad, William Sheppard, and Mark Twain.[13]

When "Amazing Grace" was achieving fame a generation ago in the wake of America's Vietnam debacle, I began researching Newton. My his-torical imagination was stimulated by studying precolonial African cultures and by traveling to places in West Africa where Newton had been, for example, the island of Madeira and castles along the coast that had served as slave stations. In England, I visited sites where he lived, and had the privilege of perusing documents at the Cowper and Newton Museum in Olney. More recently, I have spent several days reading Newton's unpublished diary and other Newtonian materials in the Firestone Library at Princeton University.

My interest in Newton has been enhanced by a similar upbringing. With my Calvinist mother's encouragement, I learned hymns by heart as a child, as well as the Westminster Shorter Catechism, and chapters from the Bible. She later financed my studies at the Scottish university that Newton's mother hoped her son would attend. Also, I was reared in a community that presumed WASPs to be God's elect. Both of my grand-fathers fought in the Confederate army for the preservation of slavery, and I was an adult before I fully realized that the presumption of the in-ferior status of any ethnic group could not be reconciled with the gospel.

---

[13]William E. Phipps, *Influential Theologians on Wo/Men* (Washington DC: Uni-versity Press of America, 1980); idem, *Muhammad and Jesus: A Comparison of the Prophets and Their Teachings* (New York: Continuum, 1996; idem, *The Sexuality of Jesus* (Cleveland: Pilgrim Press, 1996); *William Sheppard: African-American Living-stone* (Louisville: Geneva Press, 2002).

# A Newton Album

*Memorial window, Olney parish church.*
Photo by William E. Phipps.

*Slave ships and boats off the Sierra Leone coast.*
A 1750 sketch by slave trader Nicholas Owen.

*Standard equipment for slave ships from Liverpool.*

<u>*Top*</u>*: Handcuffs in which the wrist of one slave was padlocked to the wrist of another.*

<u>*Center*</u>*: Leg irons, also for two slaves.*

<u>*Bottom*</u>*: A thumbscrew, an instrument of torture.*

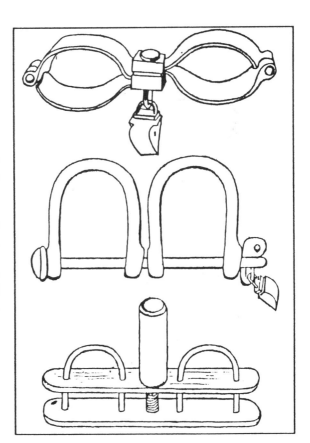

Medallion made by potter
Josiah Wedgwood (1730–
1795) that became the seal
of the Committee for the
Abolition of the Slave
Trade, formed in 1787.

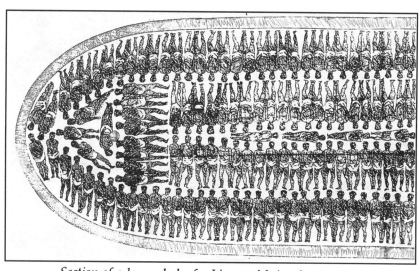

*Section of a lower deck of a Liverpool brig, showing how
124 of the 450 total slaves were stuffed aboard.*

*Olney parish church house, established in 1325,*
*along the Ouse River in Buckinghamshire.*

*The Olney vicarage where the Newtons resided. The study was on the third floor.* Photo by Martha Phipps (1987).

*The author stands in the pulpit used by Newton
from 1764 to 1779 while Newton was pastor
of the Olney parish church.*
Photo by Martha Phipps (1987).

*Window in the nave of the Olney Anglican Church,
featuring Newton writing the Omicron (his pen
name) letters while he served that parish.
Below is represented his slave ship
and a person liberated from bondage.*
Photo by the author (1987).

*St. Mary Woolnoth Church in the grimy center of London,
where Newton was rector from 1780 to 1807.
The bodies of John and Mary Newton were interred beneath the sanctuary.*

*Young member of Parliament
William Wilberforce (1759–
1833) consulting with John
Wesley (1703–1791) about
abolishing the slave trade.
Wesley was a mentor to Newton, and Newton was a mentor
to Wilberforce.*

*An engraving of
George Whitefield (1714–1770),
whose evangelicalism
was an inspiration to Newton.*

*Poet William Cowper (1731–1800), who
worked with Newton to compose the
selections in* Olney Hymns.

*A 1786 engraving of Hannah More (1745–1833). This leading English writer and educator was a close friend of Newton during his London years.*

*An engraving of Olaudah Equiano (aka Gustavus Vassa, ca. 1750–1797), who published in 1789 his story of his years as a slave, to aid the abolition movement. Equiano's* The Interesting Narrative of the Life of Olaudah Equiano, or Gustavus Vassa, the African *reinforced Newton's* Thoughts upon the African Slave Trade *(1788).*

# 1

## Through Many Dangers

### European Adventures

John Newton began the memoirs of his youth by telling about the influence of his mother Elizabeth. Most of her attention was devoted to him during the six years they had together before she died of tuberculosis. She was "a dissenter," meaning she belonged to a Protestant denomination that was independent of the established Church of England, such as Congregational, Presbyterian, or Baptist. In particular, she was a devout Congregationalist, and would have been called a "Puritan" in an earlier century. Newton was baptized by David Jennings, a learned pastor of the Gravel Lane Chapel of Wapping, in the dock area of London alongside the Thames River. After the 1689 Act of Toleration was approved, dissenters could practice their religion without persecution but they could not study at English universities. Jennings had connections with the University of St. Andrews, from which he received an honorary degree. He was a friend of Rev. Isaac Watts and later edited some of his works for publication.

Due to his mother's intense nurture, Newton acknowledged that he loved learning more than playing:

> As I was her only child, she made it the chief business and pleasure of her life to instruct me, and bring me up in the nurture and admonition of the Lord. I have been told that from my birth she had in her mind devoted me to the ministry; and that, had she lived till I was of a proper age, I was to have been sent to St. Andrews, in Scotland, to be educated.[1]

---

[1]Richard Cecil, "Memoirs of John Newton," in *The Works of the Rev. John Newton Containing an Authentic Narrative, etc., Letters on Religious Subjects, Cardiphonia, Discourses Intended for the Pulpit, Sermons Preached in the Parish Church of Olney, a Review of Ecclesiastical History, Olney Hymns, Poems, Messiah, Occasional Sermons, and Tracts, to Which Are Prefixed Memoirs of His Life, &c.,* 2 vols., ed. Richard Cecil (Philadelphia: Uriah Hunt, 1831) 1:7.

When I was four years old I could read with propriety in any
common book that offered. She stored my memory, which was
then very retentive, with many valuable pieces, chapters, and
portions of Scripture, catechisms, hymns and poems. . . . I had
little inclination to the noisy sports of children, but was best
pleased when in her company, and always as willing to learn as
she was to teach me. . . . Though in process of time I sinned
away all the advantages of these early impressions, yet they were
for a great while a restraint upon me; . . . and when the Lord at
length opened my eyes, I found a great benefit from the recollection of them. . . . In my sixth year I began to learn Latin.[2]

A precocious child, Newton memorized the Westminster Shorter
Catechism and Watts's little book of hymns for children. His mother was
especially attached to Watts because he also was an English Congregationalist. Watts composed Psalm paraphrases, such as "Our God Our
Help in Ages Past" and "Joy to the World," as well as hymns, such as
"When I Survey the Wondrous Cross." Memorizing many such lines with
simple and vivid imagery would have an impact on John Newton as he
matured. One selection he learned from Watts's children hymns is now
sung by all ages. Two of the stanzas stress God's basic attributes:

I sing the mighty power of God,
That made the mountains rise;
That spread the flowing seas abroad,
And built the lofty skies.

I sing the goodness of the Lord,
That filled the earth with food;
He formed the creatures with his word,
And then pronounced them good.[3]

From the Calvinist Shorter Catechism, Newton internalized its central
opening declaration: "Man's chief end is to glorify God, and to enjoy him
forever." He also committed to memory another affirmation that would
have more meaning as experiences in life deepened: "Faith in Jesus Christ

---

[2]John Newton, *The Works of the Rev. John Newton . . . from the Last london
Edition*, 4 vols. (New Haven: Nathan Whiting, 1828) 1:12; hereafter cited as
Newton, *Works*.
[3]Isaac Watts, "I Sing the Mighty Power of God," *Divine Songs: Attempted in
Easy Language for the Use of Children* (London: Printed for M. Lawrence, 1715) 3.

is a saving grace, whereby we receive and rest upon him alone for salvation, as he is offered to us in the gospel."

The nurture that Newton received from his pompous father, a skipper on merchant ships, was of a different quality. He wrote concerning his later childhood:

> Though my father left me much to run about the streets, yet, when under his eye, he kept me at a great distance. I am persuaded he loved me, but he seemed not willing that I should know it. I was with him in a state of fear and bondage. His sternness, together with the severity of my schoolmaster, broke and overawed my spirit, and almost made me a dolt.[4]

Captain Newton remarried soon after Elizabeth died; his young wife neglected her stepson as she attended to propagating new Newtons. John recalled that neither was concerned with his Christian education: "My father was a very sensible and a moral man . . . but neither he nor my stepmother was under the impressions of religion."[5] John was sent for two years to a boarding school at Stratford in Essex, for what was to be his only exposure to formal education. English grammar schools were modeled after those of the classical era: severe environment, spartan discipline, and autocratic headmaster. The English proverb "Spare the rod and spoil the child" was operative. Even so, John liked one Latin teacher at the school and excelled in reading Cicero and Virgil.[6]

Between the ages of eleven and seventeen, Captain Newton took John on five Mediterranean voyages. By sharing his father's cabin, his accommodations were more pleasant than the crew's tasteless hardtack and hammocks on deck. When he was fifteen, Captain Newton arranged with a merchant friend in Alicante, Spain, for John to acquire skills that might assist him in entering the merchant marine. The captain had been educated at a Jesuit college near Seville, and he decided that being an apprentice in Spain would be good discipline for his son. John went to the port city of Alicante but, because of misbehavior, remained only several months.

Brushes with death during this period, such as a dangerous fall from a horse or arriving too late to take a boat that overturned, causing several to drown, temporarily caused John to take religion seriously. During his

---

[4]Cecil, "Memoirs of John Newton" 1:7.
[5]Cecil, "Memoirs of John Newton" 1:7.
[6]Cecil, "Memoirs of John Newton" 1:8.

adolescent cycle of moral resolution and failure, "profane practices" were interspersed with periods of praying, reading Christian literature, and self-denial. Because of the encouragement of his mother, his fondness for reading had become habitual. One book that made an impression on him then was Benjamin Bennet's instructional manual for private devotions. Its theme is that the holy life is found by withdrawal from social contacts. Appeal is made to the psalmist who exhorted, "Commune with your own heart upon your bed," to the practice of Jesus who "continued all night in prayer," to Pythagoras who advised his students to ask themselves at the end of the day, "Wherein have I transgressed?" and to a maxim of Francis Bacon, "Friends are robbers of our time."[7] Bennet's advice "appeared very desirable" to John and he "was inclined to accept it."

Newton wrote about his manner of life while on a ship in the Mediterranean:

> I often saw a necessity of religion as a means of escaping hell. . . . Of this period, at least of some part of it, I may say in the apostle's words, "After the strictest sect of our religion I lived a Pharisee." . . . I spent the greatest part of every day in reading the Scriptures, meditation, and prayer. I fasted often; I even abstained from all animal food for three months; I would hardly answer a question for fear of speaking an idle word. . . . In short, I became an ascetic, and endeavoured, so far as my situation would permit, to renounce society, that I might avoid temptation. I continued in this serious mood for more than two years.[8]

While at a port visited by his father's ship, John purchased an ethics text by the Earl of Shaftesbury entitled *Characteristics*. He became fascinated by the content and style of a large section of the book entitled "A Rhapsody." John commented:

> I thought the author a most religious person, and that I had only to follow him and be happy. . . . This book was always in my hand; I read it till I could very nearly repeat the Rhapsody verbatim from beginning to end. . . . I so much admired the pictures of virtue and benevolence as drawn by Lord Shaftesbury.[9]

---

[7]Benjamin Bennet, *Christian Oratory* (Norristown PA: Winnard, 1819) 3, 14, 27.
[8]Newton, *Works* 1:14.
[9]Newton, *Works* 1:15-16.

Shaftesbury had studied under the eminent philosopher John Locke, but was not his disciple. Founding the "moral sense" school of philosophy, Shaftesbury posited that true virtue requires a harmonization of internal feelings with reason. A book of sermons he edited conveyed his outlook that humans should focus on God's goodness rather than on God's power to punish or reward as they pursue the moral value of religion.[10] The excellence of religion, Shaftesbury argued, was that it provides an anchor for objective standards of morality. He wrote: "Nothing can more highly contribute to the . . . sense of right and wrong than to believe a God who is . . . a true model and example of the most exact justice and highest goodness and worth."[11] He stressed patient endurance and discovering inner tranquility by balancing self-love and benevolence.[12]

Captain Newton attempted to find British employment for John through a close friend, Joseph Manesty. That Liverpool ship owner had an opening for an agent in Jamaica, which was then Britain's most important island for the production of sugar. The slaves there were many times more numerous than the Europeans, but white men were in demand for handling the exchange of goods and for slave control. Not finding the notion of vigorous work as a merchant appealing, John acknowledged: "I was fond of a visionary scheme of a contemplative life, a medley of religion, philosophy, and indolence; and was quite averse to the thoughts of an industrious application to business."[13]

In spite of his reluctance, John had promised to take a long-term job in the British colony. Then, in December 1742, he received a letter from Mrs. Catlett, a cousin of his mother. Having lost touch with John for many years, she invited him to her home in Chatham, where his mother had died. Recognizing that he would soon be traveling near there while in Kent on business, he dropped by for a visit. The warmth of the Catlett home relieved John of the loneliness that had long troubled him. While there he fell in love with Mary, the older Catlett daughter. Two decades later, he stated, "Almost at the first sight of this girl (for she was then

---

[10]Basil Willey, *The Eighteenth-Century Background* (London: Chatto, 1940) 58-61.

[11]Shaftesbury, Anthony Ashley Cooper, Earl of, *Characteristics of Men, Manners, Opinions, Times,* 2 vols., ed. J. M. Robertson (New York: Bobbs-Merrill, 1964; orig. 1711) 1:264.

[12]Frederick Copleston, *A History of Philosophy* (Westminster MD: Newman, 1959) 5:176.

[13]Newton, *Works* 1:15.

under fourteen) I was impressed with an affection for her, which never abated or lost its influence a single moment in my heart from that hour."[14] John transferred to her the undying love he had for his mother, and she ever represented all that was good and tender. The two mothers long ago had wistfully thought that John and Mary would someday be an appropriate match for one another.[15] John later recalled to Mary the first time they met: "When you were present I scarcely durst look at you. If I attempted to speak, I trembled and was confused."[16]

Newton described the way his "tormenting passion" for Mary came to dominate his life:

> It remained as a dark fire, locked up in my own breast, which gave me a constant uneasiness. By introducing an idolatrous regard to a creature, it greatly weakened my sense of religion. . . . My heart being now fixed and rivetted to a particular object, I considered everything I was concerned with in a new light. I concluded it would be absolutely impossible to live at such a distance as Jamaica for a term of four or five years; and therefore determined, at all events, that I would not go. I could not bear either to acquaint my father with the true reason, or to invent a false one; therefore without sending any notice to him why I did so, I stayed three weeks instead of three days in Kent, till I thought, (as it proved) the opportunity would be lost, and the ship sailed.[17]

Captain Newton, chagrined but forgiving, again arranged with another friend for John to find work on a ship to the Mediterranean. He did follow through and lived in the cramped sailors' quarters. In the company of those crude fellows, his religious and intellectual interests diminished, and he delighted in fouling the pious language his mother taught him.

After visiting Venice, John had a haunting dream with its setting in that harbor. During his watch on deck, a stranger appeared and gave him a ring. John was cautioned that he would be happy and successful only if he preserved it. Then, in the dream, a second person came to him and John proudly told him of the virtues of the ring he was wearing. That person scorned John's naivete in believing the ring had magical powers

---

[14]Newton, *Works* 1:16.
[15]Newton, *Works* 4:102.
[16]Newton, *Works* 4:47.
[17]Newton, *Works* 1:17-18.

and convinced him to discard it. As soon as he tossed it overboard, a great fire burst out from a range of alpine mountains along the horizon. The tempter then informed John that the mercies God had reserved for him were associated with the ring he had deliberately thrown away and that the flames indicated his destruction. John agonized over all the misery his foolish doubt was causing, both for himself and his environment. Then someone approached him, who might have been the same person who had given him the ring, and blamed him for his rash action. The "unexpected friend" dived into the water and found the ring. As soon as he came aboard with it, the flames on the distant mountains were extinguished. Much relieved, John said:

> My fears were at an end, and with joy and gratitude I approached my kind deliverer to receive the ring again; but he refused to return it, and spoke to this effect: "If you should be entrusted with this ring again, you would very soon bring yourself into the same distress, you are not able to keep it, but I will preserve it for you, and whenever it is needful, will produce it in your behalf."[18]

For several days after this extraordinary dream, John could hardly eat, work, or sleep. But he eventually forgot about it and not until years later did he again remember it. He found in the haunting dream this meaning:

> Had the eyes of my mind been then opened, I should have seen my grand enemy, who had seduced me willfully to renounce and cast away my religious profession, and to involve myself in complicated crimes. . . . I should perhaps have seen likewise, that Jesus, whom I had persecuted and defied, rebuking the adversary, challenging me for his own, as a brand plucked out of the fire.[19]

At the end of this voyage in December 1743, John returned to the Catletts where, by protracting his visit, he again disappointed his father. After leaving Chatham, he wrote "Polly," his nickname for Mary: "No person living can so tenderly regard you as myself" and recalled, "The first day I saw you I began to love you."[20]

---

[18]Newton, *Works* 1:20.
[19]Newton, *Works* 1:20.
[20]Bernard Martin, *John Newton: A Biography* (London: Heinemann, 1950) 39.

Before John found any new work, he was "impressed" (forced to enlist) as a common sailor on HMS *Harwich*. The tyranny aboard ships, the terrible rations, and the high death rate was such that few youth volunteered for merchant or naval ships. In order to obtain crews, the British government permitted ship owners and captains to send out gangs to kidnap able-bodied men off the streets or from taverns after getting them drunk. Commenting on the inhumane treatment of English sailors, Dr. Samuel Johnson said "a man in jail has more room, better food, and commonly better company," as well as "better air" and less chance of perishing from disease.[21] Captain Newton was unable to procure John's release, because war with France was imminent, but he did persuade the captain, Philip Cartaret, to make him a midshipman so he could eventually become an officer in the royal navy. His cadet companions encouraged him to abandon further his moral principles.

On learning that the Harwich was preparing for a five-year voyage to the East Indies, John anxiously realized that Mary might be someone else's wife before he returned. When the ship was along the Thames, John took advantage of a one day shore liberty to go to Chatham to plea for a marriage commitment from his one and only. However, he found that Mary was unwilling to give him "a positive encouragement, or an absolute refusal." Her mother requested that he should cease seeing her until "a maturer age" and until his father consented to the relationship.[22] She also asked that John stop troubling Mary by writing to her. John's return to the ship many days late, in addition to other demerits, caused Captain Cartaret to be permanently displeased with him.

When the man-of-war put into Plymouth for repairs after a storm, John wanted to make contact with his father who was in the region. Knowing that he had a connection with the Royal Africa Company that had been established to exploit the black continent, John hoped he could get work with the company and avoid the long Harwich tour of duty. One day, when John was sent ashore in charge of a boatload of sailors, to see that none deserted, he himself acted on impulse and deserted. On the second day of travel to find his father, he was arrested near his destination and imprisoned like a felon. When he was returned to his ship, he was placed "in irons," publicly whipped with a cat-o'-nine-tails, and stripped of his midshipman status. Since he had previously been overbearing toward the common sailors, they joined with all the crew in treating him badly. Bereft of all friends, he admitted:

---

[21]G. B. Hill, ed., *Boswell's Life of Johnson* (Oxford: Clarendon, 1934) 1:348, 2:438.
[22]Newton, *Works* 1:24-25.

My breast was filled with the most excruciating passions, eager desire, bitter rage, and black despair. Every hour exposed me to some new insult and hardship, with no hope of relief or mitigation: no friend to take my part, or to listen to my complaint. . . . I was tempted to throw myself into the sea, which would put a period to all my sorrows at once.[23]

John's resentment of the punishments inflicted caused him to resolve that he would not commit suicide before murdering the captain who had humiliated him. He was convinced that there was no life after death when he would be held accountable for dastardly deeds. The only constraint upon his conduct was his love for Mary. He said, "Though I neither feared God, nor regarded men, I could not bear that she should think meanly of me when I was dead."[24] Also, he wrote:

The bare possibility of seeing her again was the only means of restraining me from the most horrid designs against myself and others. . . . I often formed mighty projects in my mind of what I would willingly do or suffer for the sake of her I loved; yet . . . it did not prevent me from engaging in a long train of excess and riot, utterly unworthy of the honorable pretensions I had formed.[25]

## African Sojourn

When the Harwich called at Madeira, an island off the coast of Africa, John learned of an exchange of sailors between his ship and one bound for Guinea. He requested that he be included in the exchange, and Cartalet welcomed the opportunity to be rid of him. The commander of his new ship was acquainted with Captain Newton and treated John kindly. As a result, he expressed this relief:

I now might be as abandoned as I pleased, without any control; and from this time I was exceedingly vile indeed, little if anything short of that animated description of an almost irrecoverable state, which we have in 2 Peter 2:14. . . . I had a little of that unlucky wit, which can do little more than multiply troubles and

---

[23]Newton, *Works* 1:23.
[24]Newton, *Works* 1:25.
[25]Newton, *Works* 1:17.

enemies to its possessor; and, upon some imagined affront, I made a song, in which I ridiculed his [the captain's] ship, his designs, and his person, and soon taught it to the whole ship's company.[26]

John added that if he were to give details of his wickedness, his account would be too shocking to be published.[27] When writing this account after marriage he probably realized that his wife would find a fuller description of his immorality embarrassing. In the 2 Peter 2:14 text, the wicked are described as "having eyes full of adultery." His belief as well as his conduct was unchristian, because six decades later, he confessed: "I fought against Jesus—I sometimes compared him with Mahomet, and gave the preference to the latter—no vice was too wretched or mean for me."[28]

While on the ship that was searching for slaves, John became acquainted with a Mr. Clow, an Englishman who was returning to West Africa. He was in the lucrative business of purchasing Africans from inland suppliers for resale to ship captains. These middlemen were typically poorly educated and unsuccessful at making a living in their country of origin. Stories of finding wealth and plenty of voluptuous women lured them to Africa. When John learned that Clow had moved rapidly from rags to riches, he imagined that he could do the same were he to enter the slave business. Then he could impress the Catletts by his ability to provide adequately for a wife. John asked Clow for permission to work with him and learn his trade. The health hazards in Guinea had given it the reputation of being "the white man's grave," so Clow was willing to use an able-bodied Englishman for as long as he survived. Wages were not discussed and John never received any compensation. Since Clow was a part owner of the ship, he obtained John's discharge on reaching Guinea.

The name "Guinea" was placed on maps by European geographers to designate a stretch of the largely unexplored coastal area from the Sierra Leone River eastwards for more than one thousand miles. The

---

[26]Newton, *Works* 1:27.

[27]Josiah Bull, compiler, *John Newton of Olney and St. Mary Woolnoth: An Autobiography and Narrative*, compiled from his diary and other unpublished documents by the Rev. Josiah Bull (London: Religious Tract Society, 1868) 197.

[28]John Newton, *Letters and Conversational Remarks by the Late Rev. John Newton*, ed. John Campbell (New York: S. Whiting & Co., Paul & Thomas, 1811) 159; henceforth cited as Newton, *Letters*.

name may have been derived from "Ghana," one of the earliest kingdoms of that region. From the gold found there, the British minted a coin they called a guinea, which was intended to be the equivalent of a pound sterling.

Until the nineteenth century, European powers had only toeholds on tropical Africa. A combination of factors limited their penetration to the coastal plain. The oppressive climate, the deadly diseases, and the few natural harbors of Guinea discouraged permanent settlements. The annual hundred inches of rainfall gave the area some of the densest jungles on the African continent. Insects were the main protector of the interior from outsiders, though no one then recognized their significance. High fever from a disease transmitted by the anopheles mosquito was attributed to "noxious vapors"; accordingly the Italians misnamed the illness malaria (literally, "bad air"). The tsetse fly carried sleeping sickness that was devastating to domestic animals as well as to humans. In addition, yellow fever, liver flukes, river blindness, yaws, and Guinea worm abounded. As a health precaution, European traders stayed on board their ships as much as they could, away from the fever-ridden swamps on the coast. Eighteenth-century records of the Royal Africa Company show that six out of every ten men sent to work in Guinea died in the first year. The mortality there explains this hyperbolic sea shanty:

> Beware and take care of the gulf of Benin,
> For the one that comes out there are forty goes in.

John went ashore in the Sierra Leone region to the largest of the Plantane (or Plantain) Islands. At the mouth of the Sherbro River there were three Plantanes—named for the banana-like fruit that grew there. Because they could more easily be defended, Coastal islands attracted slave traders, and slaves were less likely to escape from holding areas surrounded by surf. Clow was the first European to move to the island abounding with coconut palms, two miles in circumference, and John helped him construct a house there.

Clow had an African mistress who held high standing among the Bulom people living along the coast. His relationship combined business with pleasure, for she could effectively negotiate exchanges of slaves for European goods with her tribe. "P.I." was the way John wrote her name because "pee-eye" was the way her African name sounded. She immediately took a dislike to John, perhaps because he did not honor her as a princess. Also, she may have been envious that she could not converse with Clow as easily as John did. Treating a white man with contempt increased her sense of power.

P.I. displayed her loathing of John when he became severely ill, probably from malaria. Because of his sickness, he was left in her hands while Clow took a boat to go up a river to buy slaves. But no one took care of him, and he had difficulty obtaining even a drink of water when burning with fever. P.I. moved him from his hut to live in the slave quarter, where the furnishing was limited to a mat for a bed and a log for a pillow. After his appetite returned, she occasionally humiliated him and amused herself by sending him leftovers after she had dined. By way of illustrating his plight, he said:

> I was called to receive this bounty from her own hand; but being exceedingly weak and feeble, I dropped the plate. . . . She had the cruelty to laugh at my disappointment; and though the table was covered with dishes, (for she lived much in the European manner,) she refused to give me any more. My distress has been at times so great as to compel me to go by night and pull up roots in the plantation, which I have eaten raw upon the spot for fear of discovery.[29]

John identified with the Palestinian prodigal in a far country who "would gladly have fed on the pods that the swine ate." This was his first experience of deprivation of survival needs, for he had been physically well cared for as a child. The plant that helped to keep him alive was probably the tuber of the cassava that the Portuguese had introduced from Brazil.

P.I. treated John more harshly than slaves who were awaiting shipment to America. Occasionally, he said, his hunger was relieved by slaves "who secretly brought me victuals from their own slender pittance." He found that he was pitied by even the meanest of P.I.'s slaves. Her contempt was almost as devastating to John as his near starvation. He recalled being treated worse than a dog:

> When I was very slowly recovering, this woman would sometimes pay me a visit, not to pity or relieve, but to insult me. She would call me worthless and indolent, and compel me to walk; which, when I could hardly do, she would set her attendants to mimic my motion, to clap their hands, laugh, throw limes at me; or if they chose to throw stones, (as I think was the case once or twice,) they were not rebuked.

---

[29]Newton, *Works* 1:30.

John's situation did not improve when Clow returned to the isle. He complained of P.I.'s scorn and mistreatment, but his master preferred to believe her false report. On the next expedition in search of slaves, Clow took John far upriver where the prices were lower. A fellow trader on the trip told Clow that John stole his goods whenever he had the opportunity, and again Clow believed a false report. John said:

> This was almost the only vice I could not be justly charged with; the only remains of a good education I could boast of was what is commonly called honesty; and, as far as he had intrusted me, I had been always true; and though my great distress might in some measure have excused it, I never once thought of defrauding him in the smallest. However, the charge was believed, and I was condemned without evidence.[30]

Assuming John might attempt to flee when left behind on the sailboat, Clow had a blacksmith put ankle irons on him, connected by a chain. When Clow ventured into the interior, he locked John on deck and gave him a pint of rice no matter if he was to be gone for one day or for several days. Also John was left without protection from the blazing sun or from the continuous driving rain and strong gales. He averted starvation by devising a way to catch fish while in constraints.

Decades later, John thought that the violent pains he occasionally was feeling had been contracted from Clow's cruel treatment. He recognized that he had become "a captive and a slave," causing him to be "depressed to the lowest degree of human wretchedness."[31] He was here undergoing a unique experience for a European in learning firsthand the contempt and deprivation shown a slave. Inwardly he realized that his outward docility was that of "a tiger tamed by hunger."[32]

On returning to the Plantane Island, John kept his mind active by working out geometric proofs from the only book he brought with him. He went to a secluded beach and drew diagrams with a stick in the sand. "Thus I often beguiled my sorrows," he wrote; "without any other assistance, I made myself . . . master of the first six books of Euclid."[33]

A century later William Wordsworth heard of a shipwreck victim:

---

[30]Newton, *Works* 1:31.
[31]Newton, *Works* 4:525.
[32]Newton, *Works* 1:32.
[33]Newton, *Works* 1:32.

'Tis told by one whom stormy waters threw,
With fellow-sufferers by the shipwreck spared,
Upon a desert coast, that having brought
To land a single volume, saved by chance,
A treatise of Geometry, he wont,
Although of food and clothing destitute,
And beyond common wretchedness depressed,
To part from company and take this book
(Then first a self-taught pupil in its truths)
To spots remote, and draw his diagrams
With a long staff upon the sand, and thus
Did oft beguile his sorrow, and almost
Forget his feeling. . . .[34]

John was assigned the task of planting a lime orchard on the island, for limes were in demand by ship captains to deodorize slave compartments. When his "master and his mistress" inspected the completed work, Clow commented: "Who knows but by the time these trees grow up and bear, you may go home to England, obtain the command of a ship, and return to reap the fruit of your labors?" Pertaining to that sarcasm, John remarked, "I believe he thought it full as probable that I should live to be king of Poland."[35]

John managed to send a letter to his father, informing him of his predicament and beseeching his help. Meanwhile, another slave trader set up business on Plantane Island and wanted John as an apprentice. Since Clow had not acquired a liking for his servant, he agreed to release him. John began to work for someone who treated him as a companion and entrusted him with goods of great value. Soon he became an agent or "factor" in one of his employer's stockades, called a "factory." European goods used in trading were stored in such a place, and slaves were corralled there like cattle after being purchased from the interior until they were sold to a ship captain. John was sent to help manage a factory that was located along the coast a hundred miles from the Plantanes, where he made commissions on slave trading. Slaves were brought there from up to hundreds of miles away by "coffles," a long chain of captives who were kept secure by being paired in wooden yokes and were kept

---

[34]William Wordsworth, "Cambridge and the Alps" (1802), book 6 of *The Prelude, or, Growth of a Poet's Mind: An Autobiographical Poem* (London: Moxon, 1850) lines 142-54.
[35]Newton, *Works* 1:33.

moving by the use of the whip. Men, women, and children were marched down trails marked by the skeletons of captives who had dropped along the way, to trading post concentration camps. Even though John knew from personal experience better than any other Englishman how dehumanizing it was to be enslaved, he apparently had no qualms over inflicting the same treatment on Africans.

Having found profitable employment as a middleman between African and European buyers and sellers, John began to consider staying in Guinea indefinitely. To help in bartering, he no doubt made use of his linguistic abilities and learned to speak some words of the local African language. He said he had "entered into such connections with the natives" that he had lost interest in leaving Africa.[36] This, coupled with his acknowledgment that he was leading a "licentious life" and had "grown black,"[37] suggests that he had acquired an African mistress. In any case, his "infatuation" with African culture increased, and he became especially interested in local religious practices. Like the natives, he began to venerate the moon and remain awake when it was visible above the horizon.[38]

What religions were to be found in the area of Guinea where John resided? He was living in the midst of the Bulom tribe, whose members believed in a creator who made the world and all things therein, but they devoted more attention to lesser spirits.[39] The Buloms were subsequently dominated by the Mende people, who have similar religious practices; they continue to be a large tribe in Sierra Leone and Liberia. The festival of the new moon, accompanied by dancing at night, is associated with taboos that were believed to affect both human and agricultural fertility.[40] According to Mende mythology, the earth was created by Ngewo who began with things and ended with making a primal human pair. That creator-god once lived among humans, but they pestered him so much by their incessant requests for retributive justice that he withdrew to live in the sky. Consequently, Ngewo is often not prayed to directly but is reached by going through intermediaries. The Mende ask that their petitions "reach all our forefathers who are in Thy hands." Yet, on beginning an endeavor, they pray directly to the ruler of the world and end it with the phrase, "Ngewo willing." Then, on saying farewell to one

---

[36]Bull, comp., *John Newton*, 196.

[37]Newton, *Works* 1:33-34.

[38]Martin, *John Newton*, 62.

[39]Nicholas Owen, *Journal of a Slave-Dealer* (London: Routledge, 1930) 49.

[40]Harry Sawyer, *God: Ancestor or Creator?* (London: Longman, 1970) 67-79.

another, they say "Ngewo take care of you."[41] John probably recognized similarities in that African faith to the doctrine of providence he had learned from his mother.

John also encountered among the Africans a few devotees to the world's two main monotheistic faiths, Islam and Christianity. Muslim kingdoms for centuries had dominated the western Sahara area north of Guinea and their influence had penetrated into some areas near the coast. Also, from the opposite direction, Portuguese and Spanish missionaries had established beachheads on the Guinea coast in the seventeenth century and had had some effect in Sierra Leone. Jesuits had persuaded one chief there to become Christian,[42] but John found the Portuguese proselytes in Guinea "the most deceitful, malicious, and revengeful of all the inhabitants."[43]

## The Prodigal's Return

In time, John's letter to his father reached its destination and once again his father acted to express his steadfast concern for his son's welfare. The senior John Newton asked for Manesty's assistance in rescuing his son. Accordingly, that ship owner gave orders to the commander of the *Greyhound*, who was taking on supplies in Liverpool: he was told to search for the castaway while trading along the African coast, and to bring him home if found. Moreover, Manesty insisted that if John needed to be redeemed, payment should be made regardless of cost.

Since the Guinea coast lacked good harbors, "smoke trading" was the common mode. Those on shore having goods for sale would send a smoke signal, and a passing vessel, if interested, would fire a cannon. A canoe would then ply the surf between ship and shore to transact business. An associate of John followed those procedures and began trading with the *Greyhound*. The captain inquired about the whereabouts of a John Newton and was pleased to learn that his search was over. He went ashore to persuade John to leave his work and return to England on his ship. However, John could not conceive of finding a job in England that paid nearly as well as the one he now had; his longing to return had vanished. Having a reversal of fortune after more than a year

---

[41]John Mbiti, *African Religions and Philosophy* (Garden City NY: Anchor, 1970) 48, 82, 86, 120, 126.

[42]Kenneth Latourette Scott, *Three Centuries of Advance, A.D. 1500–A.D. 1800*, vol. 3 of *A History of the Expansion of Christianity* (New York: Harper, 1939) 242.

[43]William Barlass, *Sermons and Correspondence* (New York: Eastburn, 1818) 586.

of captivity, he was now being served by slaves on a lagoon and was beginning to enjoy his African adventure.

To satisfy Manesty, the captain realized he had to make John an offer that could not be refused. By way of overcoming his reluctance to leave his profitable job, he was assured that he could lodge and dine in the skipper's cabin and that no work would be expected from him. Also, the *Greyhound* captain fabricated an announcement that John was the recipient of an enormous bequest from a relative who had recently died. Without little hesitation, John decided to leave Guinea, even though he doubted a fortune awaited him in England. His main reason for embarking on the *Greyhound*, as well as his reason for going to Africa and averting years of sailing on the Harwich, was his hope of seeing Mary soon and gaining her hand in marriage.

The *Greyhound* was not being used for slave trading on this voyage, probably because the profitability of a previous voyage of this ship was ruined when 214 out of 339 slaves were lost. The captain was now seeking what the first Portuguese on the African coast had looked for: mineral and forest products, especially gold and ivory. Also he had orders to collect beeswax as well as camwood, which was used to make red dye. The *Greyhound* sailed more than a thousand miles farther down the coast—as far as the equator—over the course of the year 1747 to obtain a full cargo.[44]

Displaying the spirit of a riotous buccaneer, John gained the reputation among the crew as the most "profane" and "dissipated" person aboard. His wild talk and actions shocked even the hardened sailors who, in his words, came from "the refuse and dregs of the nation."[45] John later acknowledged, "The little instruction I had received in my youth I had renounced; I was an infidel in the strictest sense of the word." Also, he recalled that the captain found his blasphemy and behavior disgusting: "Not content with common oaths and imprecations, I daily invented new ones; so that I was often seriously reproved by the captain, who was himself a very passionate man, and not at all circumspect in his expressions." Once, during a binge-drinking contest, he "danced about the deck like a madman" to entertain his companions. When his hat blew overboard, he was about to plunge into the ocean at night to rescue it when someone caught hold of his clothes and pulled

---

[44]Newton, *Works* 1:37.

[45]John Newton, *The Journal of a Slave Trader*, ed. Bernard Martin and Mark Spurrell (London: Epworth, 1962) xiv; henceforth cited as Newton, *Journal*.

him back.[46] Had he jumped off the ship, he would probably have drowned because he did not know how to swim even when sober.

The *Greyhound* followed the tradewinds to return to Liverpool. In order to get into the Gulf Stream from Central Africa, the ship had to sail westward to Brazil and then head to England by way of Newfoundland for a total of seven thousand miles. In the North Atlantic, after fishing one day for cod, John killed time by reading Thomas à Kempis's *Imitation of Christ*, one of the few books aboard. (Thomas [1379/80–1471] was a medieval Dutch monk who belonged to the order of the Brethren of the Common Life, and his book—one of the first books ever printed on a printing press—had been widely translated.) John encountered passages such as this:

> O my Lord Jesus Christ, most loving spouse, most pure lover and governor of every creature! . . . Give me grace to know and to understand thy will, and with great reverence and diligent consideration to remember thy manifold benefits, that I may from henceforth yield to thee due thanks for them again.[47]

Even though John read that devotional classic "with indifference as if it was entirely romance," the question crossed his mind, "What if these things should be true?" He went on to say, "I could not bear the force of the inference as it related to myself, therefore shut the book presently." But reflection on quality books did much to keep him connected to human ideals.

The following night, March 21, 1748, John was awakened from a deep sleep by a violent storm that caused waves to crash over the deck and flood his cabin. It splintered the mast and caused the crew to cry out that the ship was sinking. As he struggled to reach the deck, the sailor on the ladder just above him was swept overboard and lost forever. John said: "We had no leisure to lament him, nor did we expect to survive him long, for we soon found the ship was filling with water very fast." The sea had torn away the upper timbers on one side, and made the ship a mere wreck in a few minutes. In spite of the frigid weather, some were bailing out with buckets, others were plugging leaks with clothing and bedding. John lashed himself to the deck because almost every wave crashed over his head. Although he pumped hard, he "expected that every time the vessel descended into the sea she would rise no more." In

---

[46]Newton, *Works* 1:38.
[47]Thomas à Kempis, *The Imitation of Christ* 3:21-22.

the midst of his Trojan efforts, he prayed, almost flippantly, for the first time in years: "If this will not do, the Lord have mercy on us!"[48] John was struck by his utterance, for he had not used "Lord" in a sincere, nonblasphemous way for years. The situation verifies the proverb: "When sailors are swearing, all is well; when they are praying, prepare to abandon ship."

John described his anxiety: "Death stared me in the face. . . . I began to fear and tremble."[49] Also, he said, "I dreaded death now, and my heart foreboded the worst. . . . I thought if the Christian religion were true, I could not be forgiven; and was therefore expecting, and almost at times wishing, to know the worst."[50] After nine hours, totally exhausted and numbed by the cold, he collapsed into a bunk, virtually indifferent as to whether he would rise again. But the lighter-than-water cargo of beeswax and dyers' wood kept the vessel from sinking.

After a brief rest, John was called to relieve the captain on deck. While trying to steer the helm of the battered *Greyhound* into the wind for the next ten hours, scenes of his past life flashed across his mind:

> I began to think of my former religious professions; the extraordinary turns in my life; the calls, warnings, and deliverances I had met with; the licentious course of my conversation, particularly my unparalleled effrontery in making the gospel history the constant subject of profane ridicule.[51]

On facing up to his past, John did not feel as though he had suddenly become converted. As the storm blew with less ferocity, he credited the Almighty for his deliverance, but felt too distant to call God "Father." He compared his plaintive cry to that of a soulless raven and assumed that his sins were unforgivable. One "awful passage" of the Bible that returned to his memory was this:

> It is impossible for those who were once enlightened . . . and have tasted the good word of God, . . . if they shall fall away, to renew them again unto repentance; seeing they crucify to themselves the Son of God afresh, and put him to an open shame. (Hebrews 6:4-6)

---

[48]Newton, *Works* 1:40-41.
[49]"Diary of John Newton," unpublished (Princeton University Library) 2:321; henceforth cited as "Diary."
[50]Newton, *Works* 1:41.
[51]Newton, *Works* 1:42.

John did begin to read the New Testament more carefully, in spite of his doubts about the factuality of its contents. What made sense to him was this logic of Jesus: "If ye then, being evil, know how to give good gifts unto your children: how much more shall your heavenly Father give the Holy Spirit to them that ask him?" (Luke 11:13).[52] John commented, "The Lord knows what is best for us all; . . . his pity exceeds that of the most tender parent; and though he cause grief he will have compassion."[53] In all probability, Newton reflected then on his relationship with his father. In spite of Captain Newton's haughtiness, he had repeatedly tried to find employment for his son and had done as much as he could to rescue him from bondage in a far country. According to Jesus, even more could be expected of the parent-like God.

Newton also found encouragement in some other words of Jesus: "If any man will do his will, he shall know of the doctrine, whether it be of God" (John 7:17). After pondering this test of time and practice, Newton said:

> Though I am not assured of the truth of the New Testament, yet I cannot be certain it is false; I will endeavour, therefore, that if I mistake, it shall be on the safe side. I will take its truth for granted; I will study the promises, and comply with the commands I find there; and if it did indeed proceed from God, . . . He undoubtedly will assist me and enable me to understand it by degrees, till at length I believe it from the bottom of my heart.[54]

After four days, the tempest passed but the sails were mostly shredded or blown away, and the *Greyhound* could do little more than drift. The violent motion of the ship had torn to pieces casks containing food, or they had floated away. The storm had washed the livestock overboard and little had been saved other than some cod and grain intended for the pigs. When they were near the coast of Britain, a gale arose that blew them off course northward for two weeks. The situation became desperate:

> Provisions now began to grow very short; the half of a salted cod was a day's subsistence for twelve people. We had plenty of fresh water, but not a drop of stronger liquor: no bread, hardly

---

[52]Newton, *Works* 1:43.
[53]Newton, *Works* 3:447.
[54]Bull, comp., *John Newton*, 52.

any clothes, and very cold weather. We had incessant labor with the pumps, to keep the ship above water. . . . We could not afford this bare allowance much longer, but had a terrible prospect of being either starved to death or reduced to feed upon one another.[55]

At that time the superstitious captain felt that his earlier suspicion had been confirmed, and that a cursed Jonah was aboard. "The captain," John said, "whose temper was quite soured by distress, was hourly reproaching me as the sole cause of the calamity." He was confident that God brought on the ship's disaster because of hearing John grossly profaning his name, and that God might be appeased by throwing John overboard. Consequently, John's suffering from lack of food was light in comparison to his mental torment from agreeing that "all that had befallen us" was due to his having been "at last found out by the powerful hand of God."

But then, a month after the initial storm, and as the last morsel of food was being consumed, the tattered ship limped to the north shore of Ireland. "About this time," John affirmed, "I began to know that there is a God who hears and answers prayer."[56] He felt that he had been "snatched, by a miracle, from sinking into the ocean and into hell."[57] At this point in his life he seemed to think that "man's chief end" was to avoid dying and sinking into the subterranean torments.

While in Ireland, John made this assessment of his spiritual situation:

> I stood in need of an Almighty Saviour, and such a one I found described in the New Testament. . . . I was no longer an infidel; I heartily renounced my former profaneness; I had taken up some right notions, was seriously disposed, and sincerely touched with a sense of the undeserved mercy I had received, in being brought safe through so many dangers. I was sorry for my past misspent life, and purposed an immediate reformation; I was quite freed from the habit of swearing, which seemed to have been deeply rooted in me as a second nature. Thus to all appearance, I was a new man; . . . yet still I was greatly deficient in many respects. . . . The hidden life of a Christian, as it consists in communion with God by Jesus Christ, and a continual

---

[55]Newton, *Works* 1:45.
[56]Newton, *Works* 1:46.
[57]*Twenty-five Letters of the Rev. John Newton* (Edinburgh: Johnstone, 1840) 69.

dependence on him for hourly supplies of wisdom, strength, and comfort, was a mystery of which I had as yet no knowledge. . . . I learnt them here a little, and there a little, by my own painful experience. . . . I consider this as the beginning of my return to God, or rather of his return to me; but I cannot consider myself to have been a believer (in the full sense of the word) till a considerable time afterwards.[58]

During the six weeks the *Greyhound* was undergoing repair in Londonderry to sail the short distance to Liverpool, John attended church for the first time in years. Having no Christian companionship among the ship's crew, he felt the need of a supportive community where his emerging faith could be nurtured. He found praying in the Church of England twice a day and participating in holy communion meaningful.

The precariousness of life was reinforced when John went hunting with the mayor of Londonderry. As the result of an accidental discharge of John's gun, shot passed so close to his face as to burn away a corner of his hat. He thought, "When we think ourselves in the greatest safety, we are no less exposed to danger than when all the elements seem conspiring to destroy us."[59] Even though that near fatal happening resulted from his own carelessness, John interpreted it in the manner he did for all subsequent situations of personal peril, that special providence was operative to discipline and preserve him.

Since Manesty had received no report about the *Greyhound* for eighteen months, Captain Newton presumed that the ship and John had perished. That anxiety was dispelled when the father, who was in London awaiting a new posiiton, received a letter from John. Heartened to learn that John was alive and safe, the elder Newton sent affectionate letters to his son. John wanted to visit him and ask forgiveness for the troubles he had caused over the years. But before this reconciliation could be completed, his father had to sail for Canada, where he had been appointed commander of Fort York. Captain Newton had hoped John could have worked with him during his three-year assignment there with the Hudson Bay Company. Before departing, he visited the Catletts and gave his blessing to a possible marriage between John and Mary.

At this time, John especially identified with one of Jesus' most noted parables. "In perusing the New Testament I was struck with . . . particularly the prodigal," he said; "I thought that had never been so nearly

---

[58]Newton, *Works* 1:47-48.
[59]Newton, *Works* 1:49.

exemplified as by myself."[60] The English prodigal had also engaged in "riotous living" and had been starving and demeaned in a foreign territory. "When he came to himself" he realized that he would be better off to return home and accept any harshness his father might give. However, when still some distance from home he found that his father was compassionate and eager to accept him even before he confessed his unworthiness. The father rejoiced and forgave his son who "was dead, and is alive again" Luke 15:11-24).

When John arrived in Liverpool, he met for the first time the ship owner who, five years earlier, had offered him a job in Jamaica and who had given the crucial assistance in bringing him back from Africa. He called Manesty a second father and told of his kindness:

> He received me with great tenderness, and the strongest expressions of friendship and assistance. . . . My friend immediately offered me the command of a ship, but upon mature consideration, I declined it for the present. I had been hitherto always unsettled and careless; and therefore thought I had better make another voyage first, and learn to obey, and acquire a further insight and experience in business before I ventured to undertake such a charge.[61]

John headed across England to visit Mary, and found that it was more difficult to obtain a consent of marriage from her than from his father. She was not charmed by his shyness, which surfaced whenever they were together. Being bolder and more expressive with his pen than with his lips, he wrote her from an inn where he stayed when walking more than two hundred miles back to Liverpool:

> I believe no one was ever engaged in an amour with such slender hopes in so long a time as I have been. If (as they say) living upon love itself is but thin diet, how do you imagine I have subsisted upon the shadow and idea of it all this time. . . . Bestow a little of your charity, one morsel for God's sake before I am quite starved. Were you willing you could easily find a way to give me a great deal of pleasure without wronging your own discretion in the least.[62]

---

[60]Newton, *Works* 1:46.
[61]Newton, *Works* 1:49.
[62]Martin, *John Newton*, 83.

Mary responded to this beggar for crumbs by giving John hope, but unfortunately none of her letters have survived. He wrote:

> I put the question in such a manner, by letter, that she could not avoid coming to some sort of explanation. Her answer (though penned with an abundance of caution) satisfied me, as I collected from it, that she was free from any other engagement, and not unwilling to wait the event of the voyage I had undertaken.[63]

After that 1748 visit with Mary, John reflected on a comedy that was playing at a London theatre. It contained these lines:

> Bold was the man who ventur'd first to sea,
> But the first vent'ring lovers bolder were.
> The path of love's a dark and dang'rous way,
> Without a landmark, or one friendly star.[64]

During his youth, there were four things that kept John from falling into irremediable depravity: remembrance of his mother's love, his father's concern, his interest in good books, and his anticipation of marrying his sweetheart. As he looked back on those dangerous years, he marveled:

> Banished to the dreadful wilds of Africa, from whence I am almost the only person (in the like circumstances) who ever returned. . . . How unlike am I now to that poor slave of the slaves who wandered almost naked, and like a hungry dog was glad to receive a morsel of food from any hand that offered it!"[65]

---

[63]Newton, *Works* 1:50.
[64]Mrs. Centlivre, "A Bold Stroke for a Wife," in Martin, *John Newton*, 85.
[65]Bull, comp., *John Newton*, 196-97.

2

# Was Blind

## Slavery in European History

Before the Europeans arrived, black Africans, as Daniel Mannix shows, "were far from being 'naked savages' living in primitive squalor." Although they lacked gunpowder, "that hallmark of an advanced culture," they had abundant qualities of a "civilized" society:

> There were kingdoms and commonwealths comparable in size with many European nations, and even the smaller tribes had definite and often complex cultures. The West Africans had invented their own forms of architecture and their own methods of weaving. Many of them possessed flocks of donkeys and great herds of cattle, sheep, and goats. They were skilled workers in wood, brass, and iron, which last they had learned to smelt long before the white men came. Many of their communities had highly involved religions, well-organized economic systems, efficient agricultural practices, and admirable codes of law.[1]

The Portuguese were the first Europeans to take advantage of new maritime technology in the fifteenth century that made voyages between Africa and other continents feasible. The caravel, equipped with square sails, plus fore and aft triangular sails, could move windward by tacking back and forth. Portuguese ventures along the coast of tropical Africa were initially motivated by a desire to compete with Muslims, whose trans-Saharan caravans had given them a monopoly on West African gold and ivory trade. But in 1452, Renaissance Pope Nicholas V authorized King Alfonso of Portugal to "reduce to perpetual slavery" the inhabitants of Guinea.[2] Bolstered by superior ships and papal encouragement, the Portuguese began to obtain and sell "black ivory" in the never-saturated plantation market, beginning with Portuguese islands off the African coast. West Africa was the preferred source for black captives because of

---

[1] Daniel Mannix, *Black Cargoes* (New York: Viking, 1962) 12.
[2] Josiah Bull, *Dum Diversas* (16 May 1452); John Maxwell, *Slavery and the Catholic Church* (London: Rose, 1975) 53.

its proximity both to Europe and to the plantations; transportation was therefore less expensive than from other areas of sub-Saharan Africa.

Slavery may have begun in ancient times as a humanitarian option to the slaughter of war captives. It was not based on skin pigmentation but on matters of culture: religion, language, and tribe. With the exploitation of mines and development of plantations in the New World, experimentation disclosed that the use of white or Indian slaves was ineffective. After settling in the Caribbean soon after Columbus's discovery, the Spanish subjected Carib Indians to forced labor but soon found that they preferred death to slavery. Also, their low resistance to European diseases, as well as the susceptibility of first generation white field hands to tropical diseases, was causing a high mortality. In 1517, Bartolome de Las Casas persuaded Charles V, emperor of the Holy Roman Empire, to halt the decimation of aborigines in the West Indies by sending a dozen Africans to mine precious metals. That same year, fellow Dominican friars recommended that more be sent. In granting their petition, the Emperor stipulated that the slaves be baptized as they embarked from Africa. Ironically, the introduction of African slavery into the New World resulted in part from a benevolent concern for native Americans.[3]

Las Casas's request was in accord with the assumption made by religious leaders, beginning more than a millennium earlier, that blackness and everlasting servitude were caused by the curse God placed on the descendants of Canaan, Noah's grandson. According to the Bible, drunken Noah declared that Ham's son, Canaan, would be "a servant of servants" because his father had looked at him when he was naked (Genesis 9:20-25). The story was probably included in the Genesis saga to provide justification for subduing the Canaanites, the indigenous people of Palestine whom the Israelites conquered. (Actually, nothing is said in the Bible about the descendants of Canaan being negroid, but facts have always been irrelevant to those seeking to rationalize racial prejudices.) According to medieval Jewish oral tradition, Noah said to Ham: "It must be Canaan, your firstborn, whom they enslave. . . . Canaan's children shall be born ugly and black. . . . Your grandchildren's hair shall be twisted into kinks and their . . . lips . . . shall swell; . . . and their male members shall be shamefully elongated."[4] When Richard Jobson, an early trader along the African coast, noticed "the enormous

---

[3]Colin Palmer, *Slaves of the White God* (Cambridge MA: Harvard University Press, 1976) 8-9.
[4]Robert Graves and Raphael Patai, *Hebrew Myths* (New York: Doubleday, 1964) 121; *The Babylonian Talmud*, Sanhedrin 108b.

size of the virile member among the Negroes," he announced that he had found "an infallible proof that they are sprung from Canaan."[5]

The English transatlantic slave trade began when buccaneer John Hawkins captured several hundred Africans from Sierra Leone, transported them to the West Indies, and exchanged them for commodities desired in Europe. He became the richest person in Plymouth after his first voyage, and in England after his second. When Queen Elizabeth first heard that he had destroyed villages, and killed or kidnapped unoffending Africans living in them, she thought it was "detestable and would call down the vengeance of Heaven." But on learning of the handsome profit from his venture, the head of the Church of England became a shareholder. Elizabeth loaned him her large and heavily armed ship *Jesus* for his fleet, and in 1565 she knighted him.[6] Commensurate with his high status, Sir John issued lofty orders that became a tradition in the British Navy: "Serve God daily, love one another, preserve your victuals, beware of fire, and keep good company." Empowered by the Queen's support, on his third voyage Hawkins seized a slave ship from the Portuguese and rechristened it *Grace of God*.[7] During the next century, the Royal African Company was chartered; it enabled the Crown to continue to share in the profits of the slave trade in exchange for protecting the enterprise. In West Africa, forts were established at Sherbro and elsewhere; their primary purpose was not to protect the British from the Africans, who were generally hospitable, but from European trade rivals. Several European powers saw Guinea as a vast hunting ground for human game.

The triangular trade route that tied Britain, Africa, and America together was the centerpiece of the state-controlled mercantile system. A triple profit was made from shipping to and from the three continents. British manufactured goods, principally guns, cloth, liquor, and trinkets, were exchanged in Africa for human merchandise. In a typical manner, a Guinea ruler informed one trader that he could provide "men, women, and children" for "powder, ball, and brandy."[8] The captives that survived the "middle passage," the second segment of the triangle, were sold for agricultural products in the New World. Sugar was especially sought after because it brought premium prices in England. Previously,

---

[5]David Davis, *The Problem of Slavery in Western Culture* (Ithaca NY: Cornell University Press, 1966) 452.

[6]Mannix, *Black Cargoes*, 22.

[7]Hugh Thomas, *The Slave Trade* (New York: Simon & Schuster, 1997) 157.

[8]Oliver Ransford, *The Slave Trade* (London: Murray, 1971) 60.

Europeans had depended mainly on honey for sweetening, but now there was a craving to use sugar in tea and for making rum.

In 1713, England received the exclusive license to supply Spanish colonies with slaves. Other reasons why the English became the main country in the world engaged in transporting Africans abroad are succinctly stated by Robin Blackburn: "The English preeminence in eighteenth-century slave trading was based on sea power, financial and maritime resources, colonial development, and manufacturing strength."[9] James Walvin tells of the economic importance of the Caribbean plantations:

> The West Indian islands became the hub of the British Empire, of immense importance to the grandeur and prosperity of England. It was the Negro slaves who made these sugar colonies the most precious colonies ever recorded in the whole annals of imperialism. . . . For the years 1714–1773, British imports . . . from Antigua were over three times those from New England.[10]

Liverpool, Newton's home port, had mushroomed from a fishing village by the Irish Sea to become the largest and most prosperous port in Europe. Slave trade had increased its shipping fourteen times from 1719 to 1792, resulting in the city having the world's finest docks for ship construction. Two Liverpool distilleries operated on imported molasses, which was converted to rum by fermentation and distillation. At the nearby Lancashire mills, cotton brought into the port was woven into textiles. Birmingham, also not far away, had foundries for producing muskets. Another reason Liverpool overtook the rival ports of London and Bristol for slave trading was that the owners of Liverpool shipping companies skimped on the size of crews and paid lower wages, enabling them to sell their black merchandise for more profit.[11]

The source of Liverpool's wealth was revealed in what could be seen around the city. "Collars for blacks and dogs" were advertised in shop windows. Fashionable ladies sometimes appeared with a slave boy wearing a turban and shiny pantaloons. When a famous actor was booed on a Liverpool stage, he responded, "I have not come here to be insulted

---

[9]Robin Blackburn, *The Making of New World Slavery* (London: Verso, 1997) 389.

[10]Eric Williams, *Capitalism and Slavery* (Chapel Hill: University of North Carolina Press, 1994) 52, 54.

[11]Mannix, *Black Cargoes*, 71.

by a set of wretches, every brick in whose infernal town is cemented with an African's blood."[12]

## To Charleston as First Mate

In order to learn a commander's responsibilities on a slave ship, John Newton, at the age of twenty-four, became the first officer of Joseph Manesty's ship, the *Brownlow*. It was one of the seventy slave ships sent out from Liverpool in 1749.[13] With respect to his moral state at that time, Newton later wrote:

> Soon after my departure from Liverpool I began to intermit . . . and was (profaneness excepted) almost as bad as before. The enemy prepared a train of temptations, and I became his easy prey; and, for about a month, he lulled me asleep in a course of evil, of which, a few months before, I could not have supposed myself any longer capable.[14]

Newton's previous life-threatening predicaments and his religious experience during the storm at sea resulted in little long-term conduct change. He no longer laced his conversation with salty expletives, but otherwise his behavior was much the same. In a diary entry on a later voyage, Newton referred "to those brutish lusts by which I was once so long and deeply enslaved." He confessed, "Within six months after making a covenant with my Lord, I again returned for a season like a dog to my vomit."[15] Newton admitted that he felt like Samson who was stripped of his strength by the foreign woman with whom he was fornicating.[16]

One of Jesus' parables tells of seed falling in four kinds of soil; the seed represents the gospel and the soils represent different types of persons who hear it (Matthew 13:4-8). Newton's receptivity to the good news at this period was like what he later described as "stony-ground hearers" who are "destitute of that faith and love which are necessary to perseverance in the face of dangers":

---

[12]Mannix, *Black Cargoes*, 74.
[13]Thomas, *The Slave Trade*, 264.
[14]Newton, *Works* 1:51.
[15]Newton, "Diary" 1:54, 87.
[16]Judges 16:19-20; Newton, *Works* 1:51.

In some it [the gospel] excites a hasty emotion in the natural affections, and produces an observable and sudden change in their conduct, resembling the effects of a real conversion to God; but the truth not being rooted in the heart, nor the soul united to Christ by a living faith, these hopeful appearances are, sooner or later, blasted, and come to nothing.[17]

On returning to the Plantanes, Newton received one great satisfaction. He said: "I was . . . courted by those who formerly despised me. The lime trees I had planted were growing tall, and promised fruit the following year; against which time I had expectations of returning with a ship of my own." But his malaria returned, prompting him to wish he had died on the *Greyhound* when he first asked for God's mercy. While delirious, he crept to a secluded part of the island and prayed earnestly that God would henceforth find him trusting and obedient. He commented on the outcome of that occasion:

The burden was removed from my conscience, and not only my peace but my health was restored. . . . From that time, I trust, I have been delivered from the power and dominion of sin. . . . His powerful grace has hitherto preserved me. . . . He will be my guide and guard to the end.[18]

Now able to "believe in a crucified Savior," Newton returned to procuring innocent slaves to incarcerate in the hold of his ship. He forgot about the compassionate slaves on the Plantanes who had shared their meager food with him when he was ill. His actions show that the kindness of those captives, who may have saved his life, had no effect on his slave-trade work. Business and religious considerations appear to have been in isolated compartments of his personality.

In a letter written to Jack Catlett, Mary's brother, after six months on the Guinea coast, Newton told of continual cruising in a canoe to purchase slaves. Often he would go ashore,

sometimes traveling through the woods, often in danger from the wild beasts and much oftener from the more wild inhabitants; scorched by the sun in the days and chilled by the dews in the night. . . . Notwithstanding what I have said in relation to the

---

[17]Newton, *Works* 2:441-42.
[18]Newton, *Works* 1:52.

difficulties I meet with here, I assure you I never was so happy
in my life as I have been since I left Liverpool.

In the same letter Newton described his pleasure in catching a sixteen-
foot "Devil fish," so called because of its horns. Its mouth, wider than
two feet, and monstrous two-hundred-pound liver provided for his satisfaction a factual validation for the story of Jonah.[19]

Newton told of other perils he experienced while collecting slaves in
Guinea. His canoe capsized several times and he was "brought to land
half dead." In addition to dangers of the surf, there were fearful long
journeys through the dense rain forest. After some crew members were
poisoned, he was wary of "the temper of the natives, who are in many
places, cruel, treacherous, and watching opportunities for mischief."[20]
Because of the hazards that resulted from taking the initiative to search
for slaves on land, the slower procedure of acquiring a full cargo by
awaiting traders who came aboard was preferred.

Following the usual practice, trading was done with whomever had
a few Africans for sale, and the *Brownlow* sailed back and forth along the
Guinea coast until the ship was full. Only a few slaves were purchased
at a time, because insurrections were less likely if the captives were
strangers to one another. Each potential purchase was carefully examined,
for only healthy specimens were marketable. Occasionally talented crafts-
men, tribal leaders, and members of royalty were enslaved, but individual skills or status were usually not known to purchasers. After haggling
was completed, the purchases may have been branded with the initials
"JM" by a red hot iron to prove that they were the property of Joseph
Manesty's company. When the quantity aboard had reached a number
sufficient to guarantee a profitable voyage, the highly perishable black
cargo was raced at full sail to one of the Caribbean "sugar islands."

A common fantasy of the terrified captives was that the crew
members were planning to use them for food and ammunition. Being
aware of the cauldrons of cannibals, they made this projection:

The whites were thought to turn their captives' flesh into salt
meat, their brains into cheese, and their blood into the red wine
Europeans drank. African bones were burned, and the gray ash
became gunpowder. The huge, smoking copper cooking kettles

---

[19]Josiah Bull, comp., *John Newton: A Biography* (London, Religious Tract
Society, 1868) 30.
[20]Newton, *Works* 1:53.

that could be seen on sailing vessels were, it was believed, where all these deadly transformations began.[21]

Olaudah Equiano, an enslaved West African who lived to have the rare experience of becoming emancipated, told of a presumed meat inspection after he was brought on board a slave ship:

> I was immediately handled and tossed up to see if I were sound by some of the crew, and I was now persuaded that I had gotten into a world of bad spirits and that they were going to kill me. . . . When I looked round the ship too and saw a large furnace of copper boiling and a multitude of black people of every description chained together, every one of their countenances expressing dejection and sorrow, I no longer doubted my fate; and quite overpowered with horror and anguish, I fell motionless on the deck and fainted. When I recovered a little I found some black people about me. . . . I asked them if we were not to be eaten by those white men with horrible looks, red faces, and loose hair.[22]

Newton's basic perspective as a slave entrepreneur was to buy able-bodied specimens at the lowest possible price and keep as many as possible healthy so they could be auctioned off to make a big profit. He once referred to a slave boy as "very dear," but that was a complaint over his high purchase price. In order to assure a profit in spite of loss in transit, slaves were stuffed into his ship so that each had little more private space than a coffin for as long as several months. An adult male slave was customarily assigned a space six feet long and sixteen inches wide. The five foot height of the center walkway in the slave confinement was divided in half to allow for thirty inch high shelves on either side. Thus, they were provided with only enough room for sleeping on their sides and not enough room to sit upright. Women and children were allowed even less room because of their smaller bodies. As the number of slaves aboard increased, the storage area from food decreased, resulting in malnutrition that increased the incidence of disease. English captains accepted the higher risk of epidemic and riot that would accompany overcrowding because of the often shortsighted hope of higher profit from the total number of survivors. The *Brownlow* carried

---

[21]Adam Hochschild, *King Leopold's Ghost* (Boston: Houghton Mifflin, 1998) 16.
[22]Paul Edwards, ed., *Equiano's Travels* (New York: Praeger, 1967) 25.

218 slaves on a ship somewhat smaller than the *Mayflower,* which arrived in New England with its capacity of 102 passengers.

Adding torment to the tight confinement were the irons in which captives were placed in same-sex pairings. This coupling made it so difficult for getting to toilet buckets in the dark that they often had to relieve themselves where they lay. Newton wrote:

> Frequently they are not thus confined as they might most conveniently stand or move, the right hand and foot of one to the left of the other, but across; that is, the hand and foot of each on the same side, whether right or left, are fettered together: so that they cannot move either hand or foot, but with great caution, and with perfect consent.[23]

Female slaves had the added indignity of being at the mercy of lecherous sailors. Such male brutality had profitable results, because mulatto pregnancies would increase a slave's value. Newton also probably raped slaves during his bachelor years, so it is possible that one who had no legitimate children during his life may have procreated some offspring who were born on either side of the Atlantic.

On Newton's first middle passage voyage, sixty-two of the slaves died in transit, amounting to a nearly thirty percent mortality from disease and suicide.[24] There were frequent outbreaks of "flux," or dysentery, a disease spread by wallowing in excrement, eating with unwashed fingers, and living in poorly ventilated and extremely hot holds. Due to this condition, the terrible odor of slave ships could often be detected miles away. Equiano remembered the infernal stench in this way:

> The air soon became unfit for respiration from a variety of loathsome smells, and brought on a sickness among the slaves, of which many died. . . . This wretched situation was again aggravated by the galling of the chains, now become insupportable, and the filth of the necessary tubs, into which the children often fell and were almost suffocated. The shrieks of the women and the groans of the dying rendered the whole a scene of horror almost inconceivable.[25]

---

[23]Newton, *Works* 4:531.
[24]Newton, *Journal,* 81.
[25]Edwards, *Equiano's Travels,* 28-29.

Newton wrote Mary: "I am shut up with almost as many unclean creatures as Noah was, and in a much smaller ark."[26] This comment not only suggests how crowded and odoriferous his ship was, but also reveals that he thought of himself as a zookeeper of African animals. Accordingly, he needed to arm himself with pistol and whip to make the potentially ferocious captives behave when their chains were loosened to allow them to come on deck to be exercised and washed.

On sighting land, the crew made preparations to make the slaves appear fit for heavy labor. They frequently arrived sickly, so drugs and ointments were given to hide wounds and diseases.[27] During this convalescent period more appetizing food was served to fatten emaciated bodies in hopes of obtaining a higher price in the slave market.

In July 1749, the *Brownlow* arrived in Antigua, where the crew presumed the middle passage had ended. But on arriving there, orders were received to deliver their cargo to Charleston. That port may have become the destination because Henry Laurens, the leading slave dealer there, had informed a Liverpool correspondent in 1748 of a heavy demand for slaves in South Carolina.[28] They were needed on plantations there mainly for rice production, which was proving to be a profitable commodity. Cotton did not become a big trade item until after the gin was invented. At the main port of slave entry in North America, the *Brownlow* captives may have been sold to Laurens. His family was among the Huguenot refugees who had come to live in the colony in search of freedom from Catholic persecution in France. He bought and resold hundreds of slaves each year and his profit was about ten percent, twice that on other imported products, enabling him to become one of the wealthiest Americans. Later he became president of the Continental Congress. At that time there were five times as many blacks as whites in South Carolina.

Newton may have had impressions of Charleston similar to that of a visitor two centuries later, but without feeling distressed that the fineness of the city and the South Carolina colony was constructed from the forced labor of slaves. James Pope-Hennessy writes:

Pacing the brick pavements and the cobblestones of Charleston, peering through wrought iron gateways at the tall town houses,

---

[26]Bernard Martin, *John Newton: A Biography* (London: Heinemann, 1950) 95.

[27]Thomas Clarkson, *History of the Rise, Progress, and Accomplishment of the Abolition of the African Slave-Trade by the British Parliament* (Wilmington NC: Porter, 1816) 200.

[28]Thomas, *The Slave Trade*, 268.

at the spacious porticoes and at the yards abloom with camellias and jessamine, with gardenias, azaleas and the coral vine, it is hard to recognize that all this civilized beauty has its roots in the sacked villages of West Africa, and in the slave dungeons of the coastal castles and forts. . . . The plantation houses of America stand on slave-dug foundations, are built of slave-baked bricks and slave-cut stones and slave-felled timber.[29]

The person who most impressed Newton during his several months in Charleston was Josiah Smith, whom he called a "powerful preacher of the gospel."[30] He was a Harvard graduate and pastor of the Independent Church of Charleston. Its members included Congregationalists from England, Presbyterians from Scotland, and Huguenots from France. It was probably through Smith that Newton first learned of the work of George Whitefield, the pioneer of the Great Awakening on both sides of the Atlantic. In 1740, after criticizing the formality of Alexander Garden, an Anglican priest, Whitefield was banned from the pulpit of St. Philip's Church in Charleston. He then attracted outdoor crowds as a spellbinding speaker, and Smith invited him to preach in his church.[31]

Newton found that some slaves were being baptized in Charleston, a practice that had elsewhere been associated with Catholics. The Portuguese baptized slaves to assist them in eventually going to heaven, but it appears that English slave traders did not consider them eligible for salvation in this world or the next. They tended to believe that enslavement was acceptable for heathen, but not for Christians. To baptize slaves would have been as sacrilegious to some Britishers at that time as to administer the sacrament to domestic animals.

But the Anglican priests in Charleston, as well as Smith, thought slave baptism was proper. They conveniently thought that becoming a Christian pertained to salvation and liberty after going to heaven and not to physical freedom on earth. Some Charlestonians agreed with George Berkeley, an influential philosopher and bishop in the Church of England, who argued that being baptized was consistent with a state of slavery. For the benefit of English planters, he wrote in 1725: "Slaves would only become better slaves by becoming Christian, since they would learn from the New Testament that they should 'obey in all things their masters

---

[29]James Pope-Hennessy, *Sins of the Fathers* (New York: Knopf, 1968) 224-25.
[30]Newton, *Works* 1:55.
[31]David Ramsay, *The History of the Independent or Congregational Church in Charleston, South Carolina* (Philadelphia: Maxwell, 1815) 14.

according to the flesh; not with eyeservice, as menpleasers; but in single-
ness of heart, fearing God' [Colossians 3:22]."[32] Since planters most feared
insurrection, some thought that Christianized slaves would more likely
be content with their lot. For slaves to have both a divine Master and a
human master would reinforce their obligation to be humble and faithful
servants.

Since Whitefield was to have a profound impact on Newton in the
coming years, his complex outlook on slavery deserves a closer look here.
In 1740, during his second tour in America, Whitefield wrote a letter
denouncing slaveholders for their "cruelty to the poor negroes." He
pointed out that he was not dealing with whether it was right to possess
slaves but with the atrocious way they were often handled. Whitefield
observed from his travels in the Southern colonies that many owners
treated their slaves worse than their pet animals. "Your dogs are caressed
and fondled at your tables," he said; "but your slaves, who are frequently
styled dogs or beasts, have not an equal privilege." He reported on eye-
witness reports that masters have "ploughed upon their backs," making
furrows with whips. Whitefield expressed his anger over seeing plantation owners living luxuriously while their slaves had neither adequate
food nor clothing. He asked, "Think you, your children are in any way
better by nature than the poor negroes?" Convinced that both races were
"naturally capable of the same improvement," he advocated that they be
instructed in Christianity.[33] Whitefield's letter was published by Benjamin
Franklin and widely circulated, causing resentment among the Southern
aristocracy.

Whitefield's journal told of many slaves coming to hear him preach
in Charleston and of many of their "awakened" owners having resolved
to teach them Christianity. To the slaves, he affirmed with the apostle
Paul that "in Jesus Christ there is neither male nor female, bond nor free;
even you may be the children of God, if you believe in Jesus" (Galatians
3:28).[34] Yet, it was in part due to pressure from Whitefield that the
Georgia colony dropped its prohibition of slavery in 1750. With offerings
taken at Charleston in 1751, Whitefield purchased a Georgia plantation
and some slaves. He said, "As for the lawfulness of keeping slaves, I
have no doubt, since I hear of some that were bought with Abraham's
money, and some that were born in his house. . . . Hot countries cannot
be cultivated without Negroes." When he died, fifty Georgia slaves were

---

[32]George Berkeley, *Works* (London: Dove, 1820) 3:214, 244.
[33]Arnold Dallimore, *George Whitefield* (London: Billing, 1970) 494-96.
[34]Dallimore, *George Whitefield*, 499-500.

listed in his will as property to be bequeathed. Whitefield tried to combine notions of spiritual equality with the plantation caste system.[35]

Whenever Newton could free himself from business comrades in Charleston, he went into the fields or woods to have private devotions. He wrote:

> I began to taste the sweets of communion with God in the exercises of prayer and praise. . . . My relish for worldly diversions was much weakened, and I was more a spectator than a sharer in their pleasures. . . . I had, for the most part, peace of conscience, and my strongest desires were toward the things of God.[36]

Newton aspired to be a "gentleman" as well as a Christian, especially since he realized that he was being trained to become a ship captain, a position with considerable social status. Anyone then who had a full formal education could read Latin and garnish his writings with quotations from Roman writers. To compensate for that deficiency, Newton devoted much of his leisure on the *Brownlow* to reviving the study of Latin he had begun as a child. He persisted in this study despite a paucity of literary tools. Having no Latin dictionary, he compared words from the Vulgate Bible with the English Bible to assist him in understanding Latin vocabulary. About his "classical enthusiasm," he had this to say: "I had Horace more assimilated than some who are masters of the Latin tongue, for my helps were so few that I generally had the passage fixed in my memory before I could fully understand its meaning."[37]

It was more than a year before Newton completed his duties as first officer of his ship and returned to Liverpool. The wages he then received enabled him to afford to marry the one he had courted for seven years. But, on confronting Mary, he was again tongue-tied. She wondered if she would live to regret becoming wedded to such an unusual person, but after deliberation she overcame her reluctance. A year later he told of this occasion in a letter to her:

> I shall never forget . . . the evening when you first gave me your hand; . . . how I sat stupid and speechless for some minutes, and, I believe, a little embarrassed you by my awkwardness. My heart

---

[35]George Whitefield, *Works* (London, 1772) 2:208, 404; 3:496.
[36]Newton, *Works* 1:55.
[37]Newton, *Works* 1:53.

was so full, it beat and trembled to that degree, that I knew not how to get a word out.[38]

In February 1750, their union was solemnized in Kent at St. Margaret's Church of England. At the beginning of their wedded life, Newton boldly prayed:

Gracious God! favour me and my dearest Mary with health, and a moderate share of the good things of this life! Grant that I may be always happy in her love, and always prove deserving of it! For the rest, the empty gewgaws and gilded trifles, which engage the thoughts of multitudes, I hope I shall be always able to look upon them with indifference.[39]

Financial embarrassment immediately threatened the couple's pursuit of that "moderate share." Finding his money exhausted, Newton recklessly went heavily into debt playing the lottery, dreaming that the fortune he would win would provide for their material needs. In vain he made a wager with God that he would give to the poor a sizeable portion of his winnings.[40]

According to her husband, Mary had a "decent religion"; she regularly received the sacrament of the Church of England but the quality of her spiritual life was minimal. By way of comparison, Newton commented that "his spiritual light was then as the first faint streaks of the early dawn; and I believe it was not yet daybreak with my dear wife."[41] He later wrote Mary: "I suppose you have your fits of fear and unbelief. I have likewise severely felt them at times. . . . Turn them to advantage by making them occasions of more frequent and earnest prayer."[42]

Not long after their marriage, Newton reported to Mary an exchange he had had with one of her friends:

"Dear Madam, wish me joy." "Of what, Sir?" "Of my marriage." "With whom, pray?" "With my dear Mary." "What Mary! Mary Catlett?" "Yes, she owned that name lately, but has now cast it off, and desires you would know her by mine." . . . "It is impossible." . . . When she had repeated this, or something like

---

[38]Newton, *Works* 4:32.
[39]Newton, *Works* 4:15.
[40]Martin, *John Newton*, 101.
[41]Bull, comp., *John Newton*, 33.
[42]Newton, *Works* 4:148.

it, two or three times, I begged her to collect herself, and give me her reasons. She did not care to speak out, but hinted an unsuitableness of tempers; that you were cheerful and sprightly, and I heavy and dull; and though I might be mad enough to match at a disparity, you were more mistress of yourself than to make such a wild experiment. . . . At length she was convinced— but still insisted it was strange, it was passing strange; but that she should love you better than ever. "With all my heart, Madam," I replied, "and so shall I likewise."[43]

## Voyages as Captain

After several months in Chatham, Mary's hometown, Newton returned to Liverpool where Manesty made him commander of the three-masted *Duke of Argyle.* At the beginning of his sailing log, Newton selected from the Latin Bible these verses: "They that go down to the sea in ships, that do business in great waters; these see the works of the Lord, and his wonders in the deep" (Psalm 107:23-24). Other verses from that Psalm also had special meaning for him because he associated them with his own past bondage—not with the persons he was sailing to capture. The psalmist thanked God for releasing those "in the shadow of death, being bound in affliction and iron" (Psalm 107:10).

During his years as a captain, Newton corresponded occasionally with David Jennings, to whose Congregational church he belonged as a child. Jennings had remained with that same London congregation and was recognized as a scholarly minister. Communicating with him provided Newton a way of reestablishing himself with the religion of his mother. As he set out on his voyage to Africa, he wrote:

When I consider that in the most inhospitable climate and the most distressed circumstances I shall be surrounded with a Providence always able, always ready, to supply my every deficiency and to further all my designs, if really conducive to my true interest, . . . I then grow composed and ready to undertake whatever is necessary with cheerfulness.[44]

As captain, Newton spent most of his time aboard his ship during the several months along the Guinea coast. Unlike his previous voyage when,

---

[43]Newton, *Works* 4:45-46.
[44]Newton, *Journal*, 4.

as first mate, he was frequently off on a boat in search of slaves, he was now in less danger from disease and attack from the predatory men, beasts, and insects on land. While off the coast Newton's days were busy with sailing and making purchases, but during the long months at sea he found an abundance of time for private pursuits. He delegated most of the work to the crew who were alert to rebellious slaves as well as energetic in operating the ship. On the high seas Newton thanked God that he had "an easy and creditable way of life."[45]

The crew was largely illiterate and Newton conversed with virtually none of them about his personal concerns. Maritine policy was for a captain to shun familiarity with subordinates lest his command be weakened. Newton's leisure was largely filled with private intellectual pursuits. To tell of the happiness of being alone with God, he transposed a love poem of Propertius. He wrote essays in "elegant Latin" and fancied that he might become a Ciceronian himself.[46] Newton's fascination with Latin authors was probably due in part to their characteristic appeal to fate and fortune as explanations for happenings. His predestinarian theology at this period, which tended to deprive humans of real choices, had overtones of the pagan Roman philosophy. In addition to ancient Roman literature, he studied essays of Renaissance scholar Erasmus and other "modern classics."

On the subject of mathematics, Newton said his "head was literally full of schemes" even though he had become "weary of cold contemplative truths which can neither warm nor amend the heart." He assessed the strength and weakness of numerical computations in this way:

> I am pleased with the mathematics, because there is truth and certainty in them, which are seldom found in other branches of learning. Yet even in these, I am discouraged; for the more I advance, the more clearly I perceive that the greatest human knowledge amounts but to a more pompous proof of our ignorance, by showing us how little we know of anything. . . . Possibly, before I have been an hour within the veil [heavenly revelation], I shall know more, intuitively, than my namesake, Sir Isaac, had ever a glimpse of.[47]

---

[45]Newton, *Journal*, xii.
[46]Newton, *Works* 1:56-57.
[47]Newton, *Works* 4:79.

Newton wrote letters to Mary two or three times a week, even though he realized that it could be months before a ship could be found for posting them to England.[48] Those letters, filling two hundred sheets for all his voyages, were usually not written in response to letters received because of the lengthy time span between packets of letters. Also, since Mary lacked his facility at literary expression, her brief letters provided little grist for his intellectual mill. Some of his letters tended to be unduly long, and he acknowledged that shortcoming to her: "The great beauty of an epistolary style is conciseness; I seem rather to study circumlocution when writing to you, that I may make some amends in quantity for what I fall short in the quality of my letters, if compared with yours."[49]

During the year after his wedding, Newton wrote: "Whether I write in a grave or a jocular strain, the subject is still love, love; which is as inseparable from my idea of you, as heat from that of fire."[50] Being isolated from friends while aboard ship, he expressed his forlorn condition:

> I have none with me now but mere sailors, to whom I should degrade your name if I mentioned it, and shall therefore keep my pleasures and my pains to myself. Yet now and then, when I am sure I am not overheard, I breathe out your name, "My dearest Mary," and find music in the sound.[51]

The Newtons agreed to gaze at the North Star at a certain time on evenings when separated on the globe, using the stimulus of that common experience to bring them psychologically closer to one another. On those occasions Newton's behavior may have resembled what he recalled happening amid the solitude of a grove near Mary's home:

> I considered in what manner I might best deserve and return your love. There is not a tree in the whole walk, but, if it could speak . . . might bear testimony to my regard for you. For I believe you know that it is my frequent custom to vent my thoughts aloud, when I am sure that no one is within hearing. I have had many a tender soliloquy in that grove concerning you,

---

[48]Newton, *Works* 1:57.
[49]Newton, *Works* 4:39.
[50]Newton, *Works* 4:31.
[51]Newton, *Works* 4:45.

and, in the height of my enthusiasm, have often repeated your
dear name, merely to hear it returned by the echo.[52]

Newton hoped that their marriage might be an exception to what
Latin writer Pliny and subsequent writers have described as the typical
course, namely, that from the wedding day onward a woman lays aside
her reserve and grows overbearing while her husband becomes sour.[53]
Newton lifted lines from *Paradise Lost* to convey his longing that Mary
would converse with him like Eve did with Adam:

Her husband . . . she preferred
Before the Angel, and of him to ask
Chose rather: he, she knew, would intermix
Grateful digressions, and solve high dispute
With conjugal caresses, from his lip
Not words alone pleased her.[54]

Newton probed the relationship between love of spouse and love of
God: "Nothing (necessary business excepted) seems deserving my attention but religion and love; the one my constant support, the other my
constant solace." He found that due to those "two principles . . . the
whole creation blooms with beauty."[55] He claimed that opportunities for
spousal reflection on the slave ship did more to improve his and Mary's
religion than if he had stayed with her in England.[56]

In some letters Newton expressed an anxiety that would remain with
him throughout his married life, that he and Mary adored each other
excessively:

Though I value your affection beyond crowns and empires,
I tremble at the thought of being over regarded, or that you
should wholly rest your peace upon such a wretched, feeble prop
as I am. A love with all our heart, and mind, and soul, and
strength, (such, I fear, ours has too much been to each other), can
be only due to our Maker and great Benefactor. . . .

Though you are dearer to me than the aggregate of all other
earthly comforts, I wish to limit my passions within those bounds

---

[52]Newton, *Works* 4:37.
[53]Newton, *Works* 4:100.
[54]John Milton, *Paradise Lost* 8:52-57; Martin, *John Newton*, 139.
[55]Newton, *Works* 4:25.
[56]Newton, *Works* 4:8.

which God has appointed. Our love to each other ought to lead us to love him supremely who is the author and source of all the good we possess or hope for. It is to him we owe that happiness in the marriage state which so many seek in vain; some of whom set out with such hopes and prospects, that their disappointments can be deduced from no other cause, than their having placed that high regard on a creature, which is due only to the Creator.[57]

One letter to Mary contains Newton's reflection on passion as viewed by the Stoics and Epicureans. He thought Christians should incorporate "the truth and morality of every sect of philosophy" while recognizing the limitations of each. The Stoics, he pointed out, "attempted to eradicate the passions, and placed happiness in a calmness." In criticism of them, Newton stated that "we have not a single *natural* inclination in our frame but what he [the Creator] designed should, under a proper restriction be gratified." Newton thought the Stoics went beyond their proper endeavour to guard against domination by passions when they diminished "tenderness" and other excellent sentiments. By contrast, Christians can say that pleasure is our chief happiness, by using the word with a propriety unknown to the Epicureans. We seek for pleasure, but it must be of the noblest kind, and most lasting duration. Upon this maxim we cheerfully renounce every present pleasure which, in its consequence, would occasion a pain greater, or more lasting, than the pleasure proposed; and we can welcome troubles, when we clearly perceive they are but light and momentary.[58]

Newton was saddened that many seek happiness "in luxury, wealth, or ambition, which nothing but mutual love can afford."[59] He also thought that being *happy* should be distinguished from being *merry*:

I now sit down to wish you a happy Christmas; a merry one is a frequent phrase, but that falls far short of my desire. For I have often found mirth and happiness to be two very different things; and that either of them, when prevalent in a great degree, is inconsistent with the other. My heart is warm with the recollection of many endeared hours passed with you, when my happiness has been, for the time, complete, and yet I have not then felt the least inclination to be merry. . . . It grieves me to

[57]Newton, *Works* 4:69; 4:95.
[58]Newton, *Works* 4:90-91.
[59]Newton, *Works* 4:35.

think that this is usually a season of festivity and dissipation. Surely they who think proper to notice it at all, should show their attention in a different manner. If we are really Christians, and do indeed believe the tenour of the Scriptures, with what serious thankfulness, and joyful composure, ought we to commemorate the coming of a Saviour into the world?[60]

Edward FitzGerald, the noted literary critic and translator of the *Rubaiyat of Omar Khayyam*, was charmed by some letters written by a fellow countryman who had never received even a secondary school education. "I think that Newton was a man of great power," FitzGerald commented. "His journal to his wife, written at sea, contains some of the most beautiful things I ever read; fine feeling in very fine English."[61]

Here are some other examples of Newton's beautiful sentiments that FitzGerald may have had in mind:

How different is today from yesterday! The sea hardly seems to be the same element. The weather is quite fair, the wind moderate, but still favourable, and the water smooth. When the country is loaded with snow, and the trees without a leaf, how pleasing is the alteration produced by the returning spring! The ground, by degrees, is covered with flowers, the woods arrayed in green, and music is heard from every thicket. Seamen often experience as great a change in a few hours. . . . A little bad weather, now and then, makes the return of fair more pleasant. I seem today to breathe a new air, and with a new life.[62]

Pining to be with her husband, Mary wrote: "Hours seem more tedious . . . than days and weeks did formerly."[63] Newton explained why he preferred that she had not accompanied him:

You are very kind to wish yourself at sea with me; but dearly as I value your company, I could not consent to pay such a price for it. I can easily submit to the inconveniences of a seafaring life while you are safe on shore; but they would distress me greatly if you were affected by them. I am like a prudent merchant who,

---

[60]Newton, *Works* 4:69-70.
[61]Alfred Terhune, *The Letters of Edward FitzGerald* (Princeton NJ: Princeton University Press, 1980) 1:76.
[62]Newton, *Works* 4:54.
[63]Newton, *Works* 4:24.

not willing to risk his whole fortune in one adventure, leaves the better and larger part of his riches at home; and then, if any thing happens, he can comfort himself with the thoughts of a reserve.[64]

Newton's range of writing to Mary included literary comments and creations:

> I am a great admirer of Aesop's Fables. They could hardly have been more adapted to the customs and humours of our times, had they been written in London. His apes, lions, foxes, geese, magpies, and monkeys, may be met in our streets every day. . . . I will confess that I myself have frequently appeared in some of these characters. . . .
>
> You have often heard of an ostrich, and perhaps seen one. This bird is common in the northern parts of Africa. . . . He has a peculiarity which, if my friend Aesop had known, he would, I think, have given him a place in his fables. . . . When an ostrich is pursued, he usually gets clear by running, if the place is open and plain; (for they are swifter than a horse;) but if he be near an enclosure or wood, he sticks his head into the first bush he can reach, and when he can no longer see his enemy, he thinks himself safe, and stands quiet till he is caught. We may smile at this folly in a bird, but how often is it an emblem of our own! When the thing we fear is impending, and before our eyes, we are alarmed; but soon drop our apprehensions . . . when the danger is over, as we suppose; that is, when we cannot see it.[65]

Newton's correspondence usually told little of his role as commander of his crew, and even less about his cargo. But his boast in one letter to Mary suggests that sailors responded to him like house slaves on a plantation:

> My condition when abroad, and even in Guinea, might be envied by multitudes who stay at home. I am as absolute in my small dominions (life and death excepted) as any potentate in Europe. If I say to one, come, he comes; if to another, go, he flies. If I order one person to do something, perhaps three or four will be ambitious of a share in the service. Not a man in the ship

---

[64]Newton, *Works* 4:51.
[65]Newton, *Works* 4:51; 4:55.

must eat his dinner till I please to give him leave—nay, nobody
dares say it is twelve or eight o'clock in my hearing, till I think
proper to say so first. There is a mighty bustle of attendance
when I leave the ship, and a strict watch kept while I am absent,
lest I should return unawares, and not be received in due form.
And should I stay out till midnight, nobody must presume to
shut their eyes till they have had the honour of seeing me again.
I would have you judge, from my manner of relating these cere-
monials, that I do not value them highly for their own sake; but
they are old established customs, and necessary to be kept up, for
without a strict discipline the common sailors would be unman-
ageable. But in the midst of my parade I do not forget what my
situation was on board the *Harwich* and at the Plantanes.[66]

On this voyage and each of the subsequent ones, Newton returned
for business reasons to where Clow lived on a Plantane isle. While
admitting that he still detested the unscrupulous tyrant he formerly
served, he nevertheless found it convenient to purchase slaves from
him.[67] Remembering how destitute he was on his first sojourn there,
Newton was pleased to overhear this when he stepped ashore: "Two
black females were passing—the first who noticed me observed to her
companion, that *there* was Newton, and, what do you think?—he has got
shoes! Ay, said the other, and stockings too! They had never seen me
before with either."[68]

Inspired by a biblical injunction, Newton then invited Clow and P.I.
on board and lavished hospitality upon them. A Hebrew wisdom writer
had advised: "If thine enemy be hungry, give him bread to eat; . . . for
thou shalt heap coals of fire upon his head, and the Lord shall reward
thee" (Proverbs 25:21-22). Newton considered his action to be a way "of
taking the noblest kind of revenge upon persons who once despised and
used me ill." Of the outcome, he said regarding P.I.: "If she has any
shame in her, I believe I made her sorry for her former ill treatment of
me."[69] In a separate note, Newton gleefully wrote of his success:

I sent my long boat ashore for her. They soon brought her on
board. I desired the men to fire guns over her head in honour of
her. . . . She seemed to feel it like heaping coals of fire on her

---

[66]Newton, *Works* 4:54-55.
[67]Newton, *Journal*, 42, 69, 91.
[68]Newton, *Letters*, 181.
[69]Newton, *Works* 4:29.

head. I made her some presents, and sent her ashore. She seemed to feel most comfortable when she had her back to my ship.[70]

When John Reader visited Sierra Leone recently, he found some tangible evidence of activity there centuries earlier:

The slave pen on Plantain Island from which John Newton collected his merchandise occupies a small rocky bluff on the island's northery tip. . . . These days the bluff is used as a communal latrine. . . . The bluff reeks—the pen especially so— and the visitor's gasp for air is a pungent personal encounter with the depravity of the slave trade. The pen is a square of stone walls, ten metres along each side and over two metres high, mortared and plastered: stout solid walls, with sharp fragments of eighteenth-century bottle-glass still firmly embedded along the top.[71]

As shipmaster, Newton had the right to conduct himself as slave masters commonly did on plantations, and rape any of his possessions whenever the urge arose. To brace himself from the temptation to exploit slave girls on shipboard or to solicit prostitutes on shore, Newton reverted to his earlier pattern of abstaining from meat and alcohol, believing that such indulgences "add fuel to our lusts."[72] This fasting enabled him, he claimed, to achieve "mastery over the fleshly appetites."[73] He informed Mary that other sea captains on the Guinea coast teased him for being "a slave to one woman" and for not having adulterous affairs. He retorted that his marital commitment was better than being "slaves to a hundred," as some of them were.[74] Newton boasted to Mary of the change in what gave him satisfaction: "They who pity me because I am not fond of what *they* call pleasure, know not the motives which render me superior to it. I was once no less eager after their pleasures than they are now. But you have so refined my taste since, that nothing short of yourself can thoroughly please me."[75] He told of one sailor who had "brutelike" sex with pregnant "No. 83" on the deck

[70]Newton, *Letters*, 191.
[71]John Reader, *Africa* (New York: Knopf, 1997) 390.
[72]Newton, "Diary" 1:31.
[73]Bull, comp., *John Newton*, 42.
[74]Newton, *Works* 4:35.
[75]Newton, *Works* 4:28.

in general view; Newton expressed his determination to keep such affairs out of sight in the future.[76]

A Captain Drake described the middle passage in this way: "Once off the coast the ship became half bedlam and half brothel."[77] On the other side of the Atlantic there were similar opportunities for sexual exploitation. In 1756, an officer in the British naval fleet wrote about port activity in the West Indies: "I have known 350 negro women sup and sleep on board on a Sunday evening, and return at daybreak to their different plantations."[78]

To depersonalize purchases, Newton recognized no slaves by their African name or by an assigned name. Loss of name went with the loss of liberty, as this typical entry in his ship journal shows: "The man that was on board yesterday promised to sell me two more for arms and powder. Buried a man slave (No. 101) of a fever."[79] Such slave burials were an unceremonious dumping of corpses into the ocean.

Newton helped complete his cargo for the *Duke of Argyle* by purchasing eighteen slaves from "rascals" who had obtained them by capturing a French slave ship and murdering all the crew. Over the course of two months at sea, nineteen slaves identified by numbers were reported as having died of flux.[80] Even though each African had been examined when purchased and had been declared healthy by the ship's physician, many succumbed to disease or died from captivity trauma.

One of Newton's entries shows that his ship was also crowded with some four-legged creatures:

> At work all spare times mending the sails, yet cannot repair them half so fast as the rats destroy. We have so many on board that they are ready to devour every thing, and actually bite the people when they catch them asleep, and have even begun to nibble at the cables.[81]

As Newton set out from Africa with his full cargo, he thought about all he had endured in slave trading. He expressed relief that "by the goodness of God" he had survived "innumerable dangers and difficulties,

[76]Newton, *Journal*, 75.
[77]Ransford, *The Slave Trade*, 90.
[78]Martin, *John Newton*, 86.
[79]Newton, *Journal*, 40.
[80]Newton, *Journal*, 47-57.
[81]Newton, *Journal*, 52.

which, without a superior protection, no man could escape."[82] Newton's main worry was over the possibility of a slave insurrection, but that danger diminished when his ship was no longer anchored where the African shore was in sight. Yet, while on the middle passage, "by the favour of Providence, [he] discovered a conspiracy among the men slaves to rise upon us." One African, who was on deck because of sickness, found a sailor's marlinespike and passed it down a grating to his fellows. By using that instrument, twenty broke out of their irons overnight, but the crew aborted an uprising. Two days later Newton noted: "They still look very gloomy and sullen and have doubtless mischief in their heads, if they could find opportunity to vent it. But I hope (by the divine assistance) we are fully able to overawe them now."[83]

When the ship arrived at its destination, Newton may have disposed of his slaves by the "scramble" method that Equiano described:

> We were sold after their usual manner, which is this: on a signal given (as the beat of a drum) the buyers rush at once into the yard where the slaves are confined, and make choice of that parcel they like best. The noise and clamour with which this is attended and the eagerness visible in the countenances of the buyers serve not a little to increase the apprehensions of the terrified Africans, who may well be supposed to consider them as the ministers of that destruction to which they think themselves devoted. In this manner, without scruple, are relations and friends separated, most of them never to see each other again.[84]

The mail Newton received in the West Indies informed him that his father had died while bathing at the Canadian fort he commanded. He wrote Mary: "Had not that news been accompanied by the confirmation of your health and affection, I should have felt it more heavily, for I loved and revered him. But enough of this: my tears drop upon the paper."[85]

Only about five percent of the slaves brought to the New World by English ships were taken to ports in North America, so it is understandable that all the deliveries made by Captain Newton were to the Caribbean. The prevailing labor policy on plantations there made the demand for slaves continual. West Indies planters generally recognized

---

[82]Newton, *Journal*, 54.
[83]Newton, *Journal*, 55.
[84]Edwards, *Equiano's Travels*, 31-32.
[85]Newton, *Works* 4:40.

that it was more economical to buy than to breed units of labor, so the death rate greatly exceeded the birth rate. Allowing male and female slaves relaxation time for propagating and nurturing children was not as efficient as working them to death and bearing the replacement cost. In Jamaica, for example, the net import of slaves from 1702 to 1775 was 360,622 but the net increase was 158,614. A new slave could add 600 pounds to sugar production in one year, and the worth of that much sugar would pay for a slave's initial cost. Newton told of a "gentleman" at Antigua, where his ship was consigned in 1751, who calculated that it was "much the cheaper" to strain slaves' strength to the utmost so that none would live to a useless old age. The informant estimated that on some plantations "it was seldom known that a slave lived above nine years" after purchase.[86] The ghastly mortality rate resulted from the practice of herding slaves like two-legged sexless mules and exhausting them on plantation work gangs.

Mannix explains the strict balance-sheet operation of the islands to which Newton made his deliveries:

> Slaves in the West Indies were treated more harshly than those in the English colonies on the mainland. One reason was that sugar—much more than such mainland slave crops as tobacco, rice, and cotton—was grown and prepared for market by factory methods. There was little room for human regard between master and slaves; often the West Indian master was an absentee land-lord or a joint stock company. . . . Defenders of slavery often argued that, as slaves were worth money, the planter's interest lay in keeping them well and happy; he could not afford to be brutal. The fact seems to be that brutality was often profitable. Henry Coor, who visited Jamaica in 1774, was told by an over-seer, "I have made my employers 20, 30, and 40 more hogsheads per year than my predecessors and tho I have killed 30 or 40 negroes per year more, yet the produce has been more than adequate to the loss."[87]

Unlike owners in Charleston, Caribbean plantation owners showed little interest in treating slaves as religious beings. To baptize them and allow them to worship on Sunday, would curtail the work week to six days. Also, any gathering of slaves in groups would provide opportuni-

---

[86]Newton, *Works* 4:541.
[87]Mannix, *Black Cargoes*, 52.

ties for uprisings to be organized. Moreover, when Christians viewed slaves as sharing the same religion, a bonding sometimes resulted that tended to weaken the slave institution. With conversion came education, which sometimes resulted in more docility, but often in more zeal for emancipation. Widely accepted was the argument of Francis Brokesby, an early West Indies planter, "that negroes are creatures destitute of souls, to be ranked among brute beasts, and treated accordingly (as generally they are) and whom religion (apt only to make subjects mutinous) doth in no way concern."[88]

To what extent did Newton include slaves among the human species? He appeared to think they were not entitled to any possessions—family, freedom, property, or even souls. He treated slaves like valuable livestock, placing them on a short tether so they could be preserved to be auctioned off for a substantial profit. Aristotle's classic definition of a slave as "an animated tool" was in accord with Newton's outlook, for he presumed that a slave was a mobile piece of property whose exclusive role was to increase economic production. They were appropriately called "chattel," a term that came from roots meaning "cattle" and "capital."

Since Newton did not accept that Africans were human, it is understandable that he had no missionary zeal toward them. What French philosopher Montesquieu published in 1748 would probably not have been recognized by Newton as irony:

> The Europeans, having extinguished the Americans, were obliged to make slaves of the Africans, for clearing such vast tracts of land. Sugar would be too dear if the plants which produce it were cultivated by any other than slaves. . . . It is hardly to be believed that God, who is a wise Being, should place a soul, especially a good soul, in such a black ugly body. . . . The negroes prefer a glass necklace to that gold which polite nations so highly value. Can there be a greater proof of their wanting common sense? It is impossible for us to suppose these creatures to be men, because, allowing them to be men, a suspicion would follow that we ourselves are not Christians.[89]

As the *Duke of Argyle* headed back to England with a cargo of sugar, it followed the Gulf Stream during the hurricane season. Newton

---

[88]Peter Fryer, *Staying Power: The History of Black People in Britain* (London, 1984) 148-50.

[89]Montesquieu, Charles de Secondat, baron de, *The Spirit of Laws*, 2 vols., trans. Thomas Nugent (London: J. Jourse and P. Vaillant, 1750) 15, 5.

encountered a raging storm in the North Atlantic that resembled the one that had traumatized him several years earlier. He provided Mary with this description:

> Imagine to yourself an immense body of water behind you, higher than a house and a chasm of equal depth just before you. . . . In the twinkling of an eye the ship descends into the pit which is gasping to receive her, and with equal swiftness ascends to the top of the other side, before the mountain that is behind can overtake her. And this is repeated as often as you can deliberately count four."[90]

In high spirits over the anticipation of returning to Mary after their fourteen month separation, Newton wrote:

> The wind blows very hard. . . . I have shortened the distance between us about one hundred and eighty miles within the last twenty-four hours. . . . Every puff pushes me nearer to you. . . . I write from my feelings. My heart dictates every line. And though my head often interposes, and observes that this expression is hardly grammar, the next not well turned, the third unnecessary, and so on; yet heart persists in his own way, and whatever occurs to him goes down upon the paper, in defiance of head's wise remonstrances. The contention arises sometimes to such a height, that head tells heart, he raves and is an enthusiast. And heart calls head a conceited pedant, whose narrow views are confined to a little nicety and exactness in trifles, because he is a stranger to the emotions of love.[91]

During the several-month break before being given the command of a new ship in Manesty's fleet, Newton devoted most of his attention to Mary. Afterwards he apologized for not renewing his friendship with her brother with this explanation: "When I am with her, I am a little negligent of everybody else. Just as (if you will allow such a blazing comparison) the presence of the sun makes us bear the loss of the stars without regret."[92]

While on shore leave, Newton became acquainted with a variety of Christian literature. He read closely Philip Doddridge's *Life of Colonel*

---

[90]Newton, *Works* 4:53.

[91]Martin, *John Newton*, 120.

[92]Bull, comp., *John Newton*, 45.

*James Gardiner.* Newton wrote that Gardiner's life story greatly impressed him because of its parallels to his own: both had influential Christian mothers, became apostates and moral degenerates, encountered near-death situations, were converted, and were devoted to a Whitefield-type Protestantism.[93]

As skipper of the *African*, Newton embarked from her berth on the Mersey River at Liverpool. Separate from his ship journal, he started in 1751 a diary in which he would make entries for the rest of his life. At its beginning he set down some resolutions, the first of which was "to peruse the scriptures . . . with a diligence and attention suitable to the dignity of the subject, being firmly persuaded that there are many excellences in that divine book which can never be discovered by a superficial eye, or an unprepared heart." Another resolution was this: "Whenever I hear my Maker or my Saviour blasphemed, . . . to speak boldly for their honour; . . . yet being careful to express myself without personal ill will or comparative contempt."[94] Pertaining to talking with others, he set down this rule:

> Taking care that my conversation has at no time anything in it contrary to truth, to purity, or to the peace and good name of my neighbour, and ever endeavouring to introduce some useful re-mark or admonition, yet habituating myself to a constant cheer-fulness of behaviour, that I may not bring an evil report upon religion, or discourage those around me from the pursuit of piety, but rather let them see that a good conscience is a continu-al feast, and the ways of wisdom are ways of pleasantness.[95]

Back on the Guinea coast searching for slaves, Newton reflected on the human qualities he believed were lacking in the Africans he was encountering. He expressed to his wife his pride "that we were born in an age and land of light and liberty, and not among the . . . multitudes who are trained up, from their cradles, to substitute superstition for religion."[96] Again, he wrote Mary:

> In this unhappy country, I am in the midst of scenes, not only inferior, but opposite to those which are inseparable from your company. . . . The three greatest blessings of which human

---

[93]Newton, "Diary" 1:21.
[94]Newton, "Diary" 1:4-5.
[95]Bull, comp., *John Newton*, 41.
[96]Newton, *Works* 4:118.

nature is capable are undoubtedly religion, liberty, and love. In each of these, how highly has God distinguished me! But here are whole nations around me . . . [who] have no words among them expressive of these engaging ideas: from whence I infer that the ideas themselves have no place in their minds. . . . These poor creatures are not only strangers to the advantages which I enjoy, but are plunged in all the contrary evils. . . . They are deceived and harrassed by necromancy, magic, and all the train of superstitions that fear, combined with ignorance, can produce in the human mind. The only liberty of which they have any notion, is an exemption from being sold; and even from this, very few are perfectly secure; . . . for it often happens, that the man who sells another on board a ship, is himself bought and sold, in the same manner, and perhaps in the same vessel, before the week is ended. As for love, . . . when I have spoken of its effects I have never been believed. To tell them of the inexpressible and peculiar attraction between kindred minds: the pains of absence, the pleasures of a re-meeting . . . which I owe to you, would be labour lost; like describing the rainbow to a man born blind. . . . Their passions are strong; but few, indeed, have any notion of what I mean by tenderness.[97]

Newton was not only the sole ship commander but also his employer's ultimate slave merchant. He determined the limits on payment and sent his officers out to barter. When his ship was off the Sierra Leone coast, Newton knew he had come at a good time because "the whole country is a flame of war."[98] Such was to his advantage because the likely abundance of war prisoners for sale would provide cheaper slaves. The warring to which he referred was probably the jihad of the militant Ibrahim Sori (the Maud), who became the Fulani ruler in 1751. Islam had penetrated the tribes of Fulani herdsmen in the northern Guinea grasslands, and they were in the forefront of slave trading.[99]

Prisoners of war were the primary source of slaves, and raids were frequently carried out merely to capture them. An English ship officer testified with regard to Sierra Leone: "Whatever rivers I have traded in, I have usually passed burnt and deserted villages and learnt from the

---

[97]Newton, *Works* 4:71-72.

[98]Newton, *Journal*, 25.

[99]Walter Rodney, *A History of the Upper Guinea Coast 1545–1800* (Oxford: Clarendon, 1970) 233-38.

natives in the boat with me that war had been there and the natives taken and carried to the ships."[100] Aggressiveness had been greatly compounded by the guns and ammunition brought by the Europeans. From his experience in Africa in the slave-trading era, a Major Denham told of two instances where many more were killed in raids than were carried away into slavery.[101]

Some Africans had become slaves within their tribes before being sold for export. This was punishment they received for crimes such as theft, murder, adultery, and nonpayment of debts. Also, starving parents might sell a child to relieve their poverty.

Kidnapping was another way by which slaves were procured, but usually this was not done directly by Europeans.[102] Equiano gave this description of his capture:

> One day, when all our people were gone out to their works as usual and only I and my dear sister were left to mind the house, two men and a woman got over our walls, and in a moment seized us both, and without giving us time to cry out or make resistance they stopped our mouths and ran off with us to the nearest wood. . . . For a long time we had kept to the woods, but at last we came into a road which I believed I knew. . . . I discovered some people at a distance, on which I began to cry out for their assistance; but my cries had no other effect than to make them tie me faster and stop my mouth, and then they put me into a large sack. . . . The next day proved a day of greater sorrow than I had yet experienced, for my sister and I were separated while we lay clasped in each other's arms. It was in vain that we besought them not to part us; she was torn from me, and immediately carried away.[103]

For prudential reasons, Newton avoided direct seizure, called "panyaring," in which some slave ship captains engaged. It was the practice of luring Africans on board for trading and then enslaving them. Ironically, a native bringing a boatload of slaves to a ship might find himself also becoming a victim. On one such occasion, a captain invited an African trader aboard and gave him as much rum as he could

---

[100]Mannix, *Black Cargoes*, 96.

[101]Thomas Buxton, *The African Slave Trade and Its Remedy* (London: Cass, 1967) 99.

[102]Thomas, *The Slave Trade*, 374.

[103]Edwards, *Equiano's Travels*, 16.

consume. The next day he awoke to find he had been branded and put in irons with the other slaves.[104] Newton recognized that panyaring would frighten away other Africans who might want to make future deliveries and cause retaliation on the next crew from the same European port. Invidiously comparing himself with other slave traders, he thought that "a guilty conscience haunts them all" because they are cheaters in their dealings.[105] Since Newton honored his business agreements with sellers, he thought of himself as righteous. His journal shows no awareness that his conscience bothered him about his work.

On one occasion Newton exchanged seven kettles and twenty-one pounds of glass beads for seven slaves, but the most desired barter item was the weapon that European slave traders had introduced and made essential. African rulers found guns necessary for security, realizing that spears and knives could not match them. A man slave was usually worth one or two muskets, plus a supply of gunpowder, but the barter rate fluctuated considerably. The guns used in trading were made so cheaply that those firing them were sometimes in as much danger as the ones being fired upon. One woman was obtained for twenty-four handkerchiefs, one gun, one jug of rum, and one roll of tobacco.

Slave traders had a sinister purpose in proliferating guns and distributing rum. After a tribe received a supply of arms and intoxicants, they became eager—especially when drunk—to try their guns out against a neighboring tribe with whom they may have traditionally been at peace.[106] If the aggressor was successful in taking captives, they would be exchanged for more guns, powder, and spirits. If the defending tribe was victorious, it also would obtain prisoners to pay for desired European goods. Regardless of who prevailed on the battlefield, the Europeans who manipulated the hostilities were the big economic winners. This exploitive vicious circle enabled the technologically more advanced British to keep the underdeveloped Africans dependent. Shipments of munitions to whomever might want to fight in Guinea also stimulated industry in England.

Other than God's support, Newton was unsure of the allegiance of any other persons aboard; he was fearful that rebellious crew members might join with liberty-seeking slaves. Vessels owned by European companies occasionally became pirate ships after crews mutinied successfully. While off the African coast, several sailors conspired to seize

---

[104]Williams, *Capitalism and Slavery*, 79.
[105]Newton, *Journal*, 44.
[106]Clarkson, *History of the . . . African Slave-Trade*, 284.

the *African*, but Newton learned of it in the nick of time.[107] When the threat was over, he entered into his diary that he had been unaware that trouble was brewing among fellow Englishmen. While ever aware of "the mutinous disposition of the slaves," he admitted: "Little did I imagine that I have more dangerous and cruel enemies" among the crew. Whereas he usually called slaves "creatures," rebellious crew members were treated as "persons" who needed discipline. He boasted that he restored order with them without "ill language or any kind of abuse," remembering that he also had "a Master in Heaven and that there is no respect of persons with him." "I will treat them with humanity while under my power," he resolved, "and not render their confinement unnecessarily grievous."[108]

Newton continually kept a wary eye on his slaves who were "frequently plotting insurrections."[109] When he learned from some boy slaves of an intended uprising, he put the four ringleaders in neck yokes and inflicted thumbscrew torture on them.[110] When the pressure of the latter is sufficient, blood bursts forth. At another time, after finding some shackles broken, he restored security in this manner:

> By the favour of Divine Providence made a timely discovery today that the slaves were forming a plot for an insurrection. . . . Found some knives, stones, shot, etc., and a cold chisel. . . . Put the boys in irons and slightly in the thumbscrews to urge them to a full confession.[111]

Newton's ship log tells of a slave who committed suicide by jumping overboard.[112] Such would have happened more often had it been easier to accomplish. To avoid the loss of valuable cargo, the chains of slaves were secured on deck and nets were sometimes placed around the outer edge of a deck to restrain slaves from thrusting themselves into the ocean and drowning. Since refusing food was the most common means of suicide, the crew used a metal apparatus that screwed the jaw open, enabling gruel to be poured through a funnel into the victim.

James Thomson, the celebrated eighteenth-century Scottish poet, told of sharks that followed slave ships to feed on dead slaves:

[107]Newton, *Journal*, 69.
[108]Newton, "Diary" 1:50.
[109]Newton, *Works* 1:60.
[110]Newton, *Journal*, 77.
[111]Newton, *Journal*, 71.
[112]Newton, *Journal*, 75.

Lured by the scent
Of steaming crowds, of rank disease, and death,
Behold, he, rushing, cuts the briny flood,
Swift as the gale can bear the ship along;
And, from the partners of that cruel trade,
Which spoils unhappy Guinea of her sons,
Demands his share of prey.[113]

During the two months along the middle passage, Newton noted in his diary that the previously rebellious slaves "have behaved more like children in one family than slaves in chains and irons, and are really upon all accounts more observant, obliging, and considerate than our white people."[114] He thought of God as a heavenly guard who was on the side of slave merchants, helping them to keep their slaves subdued. In this regard, he quoted Psalm 127:1b: "Except the Lord keep the city, the watchman waketh but in vain."[115]

A monastic rigor is revealed in Newton's daily schedule: "I allotted eight hours for sleep and meals, eight hours for exercise and devotion, and eight hours to my books."[116] Did he combine his shipboard work with his exercise? Page after page of his diary could have as easily been written by a hermit, for he provides little indication of his physical situation or environs. The beginning of each day was consumed in Bible reading and prayer, and later in the day he tried to "find another opportunity of solemn prayer and devotion."[117] His observance of the Lord's day conformed to the time of day when the Jewish Sabbath commenced, but it began at dusk on Saturday when the Jewish Sabbath ended.[118]

Newton told about conducting Anglican worship services on the *African*: "Nothing but an indispensable necessity has prevented me from requiring from all on board a solemn observation of the Sabbath day. . . . Few moments of my life afford me a more real pleasure than when I am thus attempting the part of a minister to about twenty-five people."[119] After the ship's bell rang at eleven o'clock, he read to his sailors from the *Book of Common Prayer*. Finding that the formal Anglican liturgy needed

---

[113]James Thomson, *The Seasons*, "Summer," lines 1015-21.
[114]Newton, "Diary" 1:91.
[115]Newton, *Journal*, 80.
[116]Newton, *Works* 1:61.
[117]Newton, *Journal*, 64-65.
[118]Newton, "Diary" 1:7.
[119]Newton, *Journal*, 84.

adaptation for his "congregation," Newton composed a short prayer and substituted it for part of the assigned ritual. In the afternoon Newton again assembled the crew for worship. He ended Sundays as he began with a period of private prayer in which he petitioned that others would be called out of the "apostasy and licentiousness" into which he had once sunk. This was one of his prayers: "[I am grateful that] I was born in an age and country favoured with the light of the Gospel when there are millions of my species who have neither the means of grace nor the hope of glory."[120]

Newton became ill on arriving at St. Christopher's Island in the Caribbean because no letters from Mary were awaiting him. Concluding that she must have died, he thought for several weeks that he might be dying of a broken heart. His mental anguish caused a loss of appetite and an inability to sleep. He then found that the anticipated letters had been mistakenly forwarded to Antigua; his health was restored when a packet with a number of her letters arrived.[121]

After exchanging his cargo in the West Indies for seventy-four hogsheads of sugar and twenty-five bags of cotton, Newton headed homeward. As might be expected, during the last months of the voyage he focused upon the pleasure of connubial reunion. In a Pauline letter that renounced celibacy, he found an appealing outlook on physical things:

> Nor is religion a restraint upon any real or rational pleasure. For, as the apostle emphatically expresses it, God gives us *all* things *richly*, to *enjoy* (1 Timothy 6:17); not grudgingly, but freely and richly; not to raise desires which may not be gratified; what he gives, is with the design that it may be enjoyed. It is true, there is a modus a moderation enjoined; but this, likewise, is for our benefit, that we may not spoil the relish of our comforts, nor indispose ourselves for the reception of his further and better gifts.[122]

At the end of Newton's second voyage as commander he received a bonus of 257 pounds in addition to his monthly salary of five pounds sterling.[123] Even though the bonus was greater than his entire salary during his time on the *African*, it was comparatively low because Manesty's profit on the voyage was less than expected. The sailors

---

[120]Newton, *Works* 4:117.
[121]Newton, *Works* 1:62.
[122]Newton, *Works* 4:88.
[123]Newton, *Journal*, 87.

received little pay or bonuses for their dangerous work. Newton wrote Jennings on returning to England:

> I have now by God's helping finished a long, troublesome, and precarious voyage, with entire satisfaction to myself, my friends and my employers. . . . I am more than content, in some degree thankful for my lot, which with all its inconveniences I know preferable to many millions of my fellow creatures.[124]

On his next and last voyage, Newton was again master of the *African.* For companionship, he took with him a seaman he had come to know on the *Harwich.* Newton believed his earlier bad influence had infected this friend with "libertine principles" so he now hoped that he could, by word and example during this voyage, persuade him "to relinquish his infidel schemes." But he only succeeded in completely alienating his former buddy, who then died of fever on the African coast.[125]

Henry Tucker, a mulatto, was the person with whom Newton most often did business on the African coast. The mulattoes there were descendants from Britons who established themselves in Sierra Leone in the seventeenth century. Irishman Nicholas Owen, a fellow slave trader, claimed that Tucker was wealthier than a king and that the community surrounding him was composed of six wives, numerous children, and slaves. He provided chiefs with European goods on credit, and when they did not pay he attacked them and took slaves. Owen described Tucker as one considered to be fair by the Europeans but unfair and feared by the Africans.[126] Newton used the services of "my friend Harry" as an intermediary to obtain slaves on every voyage to Guinea, and claimed that he was never deceptive. Newton gave Tucker's favorite wife a dress that Mary had sent, which she then modeled for them. Newton reassured his spouse that the African provided her no competition, saying that he preferred Mary's picture to Mrs. Tucker's reality.[127] Tucker also operated a plantation on which food, such as yams and rice, was grown for sale to slave ships.

Newton's significant accomplishment on his last voyage was to have no loss of life from either sailors or slaves. The average death rate of slaves on the middle passage in English ships in the eighteenth century was about fifteen percent. This mortality rate could have been cut

---

[124]Newton, *Journal*, 84.
[125]Newton, *Works* 1:63.
[126]Nicholas Owen, *Journal of a Slave-Dealer* (London: Routledge, 1930) 76.
[127]Newton, *Works* 4:97.

drastically if Africans had been offered as much space as Europeans were usually given on transatlantic voyages. But this would have required a cut of about half of the slaves per ship, which would have turned a profit into a loss for the entire cargo.[128]

Newton would probably not have achieved his rare safety record if he had accomplished what his employer desired. His log shows that there was fierce competition for slaves due to overharvesting on the Guinea coast. The acute shortage was caused by increased demand and tribal decimation. Also, Newton's fewer slaves on this voyage may have resulted from Europeans having been lax in fomenting raids between tribes. Because men slaves were often too expensive, he occasionally ended up purchasing children, often separated from their parents, and young women. There was no market for older "long-breasted" women, so none were acquired. The *African* carried less than half of the expected load of 220 slaves, so there was adequate space for the eighty-seven aboard.[129] With the increased worth of a slave, tossing overboard someone who was presumed to have a contagious disease was not done. Self-interest caused ship officers to exercise some care for their slaves. One captain explained, "If any of the slaves die, the surgeon loses his head money, and the captain his commission."[130] By contrast, there was no monetary incentive for keeping crew members healthy, so their mortality rate was sometimes higher than that of the slaves.

Newton summarized the way his religion was strengthened during his years as slave captain, both when on ship and on shore:

> I know not any calling that affords . . . greater advantages to an awakened mind, for promoting the life of God in the soul; especially to a person who has the command of a ship, and thereby has it in his power to restrain gross irregularities in others, and to dispose of his own time, and still more so in African voyages, as these ships carry a double proportion of men and officers to most others. . . . To be at sea in these circumstances, withdrawn out of the reach of innumerable temptations, with

---

[128]If a ship carrying 125 slaves generally resulted in a ten percent loss, and carrying 250 resulted in a twenty-five percent loss, and if the selling price was triple the purchase price, it would be more profitable to take the larger number even though it was likely that fifty more would die during the middle passage.

[129]Newton, *Journal*, 95.

[130]Roger Anstey, *The Atlantic Slave Trade and British Abolition 1760–1810* (London: Macmillan, 1975) 34.

opportunity and a turn of mind disposed to observe the wonders
of God in the great deep, with the two noblest objects of sight,
the expanded heavens and the expanded oceans, continually in
view; . . . these are helps to quicken and confirm the life of faith.
. . . I never knew sweeter or more frequent hours of divine
communion than in my two last voyages to Guinea, when I was
almost secluded from society on shipboard, or when on shore
amongst the natives. I have wandered through the woods,
reflecting on the singular goodness of the Lord to me, in a place
where, perhaps, there was not a person that knew him for some
thousands of miles round me.[131]

Newton's devotional life on ship was accompanied by abstaining
from "theatres, assemblies, balls, and the various scenes of dissipation"
when in port. His moral sensitivity was similar to that of King George III
who issued a condemnation of swearing, drunkenness, Sabbath-breaking,
obscene literature, and immoral amusements, while finding slavery
acceptable.[132] Newton's values were also akin to those of his fellow slave
merchant Owen who admired a Yankee slave ship captain because he not
only eschewed profanity but was honest, industrious, and sober.[133]

As Newton was returning to Liverpool on his final voyage he showed
that he could identify his past with only ancient slaves in Africa. To Mary
he expressed this thanksgiving to God: "He brought me . . . out of the
land of Egypt, out of the house of bondage; from slavery and famine on
the coast of Africa, into my present easy situation."[134] His diary contains
dozens of pages largely filled with his confessions of personal wrong-
doings, but one searches in vain for any awareness of sin in relation to
his slaving business. If one did not know what his ship's mission was,
one might presume that he had been on an extended spiritual cruise for
meditating about his Savior. By way of declaring that his work was a
religious enterprise, Newton began his ship's log for each voyage with
the invocation, *Laus Deo* (by God's permission), and concluded it with
*Soli Deo Gloria* (solely to God's glory). (The latter inscription was then a

[131]Newton, *Works* 1:59-60.
[132]Will Durant and Ariel Durant, *The Age of Napoleon: A History of Civilization
from 1789 to 1815*, part 11 of *The Story of Civilization* (New York: Simon and
Schuster, 1975) 367.
[133]Owen, *Journal of a Slave-Dealer*, 67.
[134]*Works* 4:114.

practice of religiously oriented artists; Bach, for example, placed it at the end of each of his musical compositions.)

Stephen Vincent Benét may have had Newton in mind when he composed *John Brown's Body*. That narrative poem begins with a description of a slave-ship captain who spent much of his time studying the Bible and avoiding the stench below deck. His crew composed a shanty containing this line about their skipper: "He traded in niggers and loved his Savior." Liking the song, the captain chimed in: "The pay's good pay, but it's the Lord's work, too."[135]

After examining Newton along with some other cultivated and religious Atlantic slave traders, Pope-Hennessy asks how they should be evaluated:

> Do we dismiss them as hypocrites? Do we employ that fashion-able label, schizoid, to describe their personalities? Do we take refuge with the old cliche "the brutality of the age"? Yet that age is known to history as the Age of Sensibility, and Newton's love letters to his wife are sensitive and affectionate. We must prob-ably conclude that Newton, in his youth and early middle age, belonged to that vast and dangerous multitude of human beings who take the established order of things for granted. . . . A recognized and even a respected way of making money, the slave trade seemed to Newton and his colleagues of every nationality a legitimate and indeed a seemly form of commerce. The dangers it involved even gave it on occasion an heroic slant.[136]

There are numerous recorded examples of Newton's business ability, literary acumen, and romantic charm during his seafaring years. But spiritual devotion, restless mental energy, and wide travels did not dispel his moral blindness in treating Africans like beasts of burden. Over the years when Newton was captain, English ships carried more than 100,000 slaves to the New World, surpassing the combined total of all other ships. He participated in the largest intercontinental movement of humans in history, when more Africans than Europeans were being transported to the New World. Marcus Loane points out that Captain Newton "felt no sense of scruple at this wretched traffic in human life;

---

[135]Stephen Vincent Benét, *John Brown's Body* (New York: Doubleday, 1929) 15.
[136]Pope-Hennessy, *Sins of the Fathers*, 272.

he was the child of an age which saw no scandal in that hateful market of murder and man stealing."[137]

Newton would later confess that custom and profitable business had blinded his eyes to the inhumane slave business.

---

[137]Marcus Loane, *Oxford and the Evangelical Succession* (London: Lutterworth, 1950) 98.

# 3

# Now Am Found

## The Evangelical Liverpudlian

Several months after his fourth Liverpool harbor entry, Newton prepared a new ship he named the *Bee* for sailing to Guinea, but he fell ill a few days before the scheduled time for departure. He described it as "a violent fit, which threatened immediate death, and left me no signs of life, but breathing for about an hour."[1] Because of that stroke, the *Bee* departed without Newton, and he never sailed again. The ship wrecked on the African coast after the captain and the crew were assassinated by slaves who had broken loose.

Newton's illness had more long-term medical effect on his wife than himself. "I soon grew better," he said; "but the sudden stroke made such an impression upon my dear wife that it cost her more than a twelve-month's severe illness."[2] During her slow recovery they went to live with her family in Chatham, and with friends in London.

While in Kent, Newton hiked in remote woods while engaging in devotional exercises. He said: "A beautiful, diversified prospect gladdens my heart. When I am withdrawn from the noise and petty works of men, I consider myself as in the great temple which the Lord has built for his own honour."[3] As he found serenity through retreating to the verdant woods, he may have recalled these words of Lord Shaftesbury: "Thou impowering Deity, supreme Creator! Thee I invoke, and thee alone adore. To thee this solitude, this place, these rural meditations are sacred."[4] Understandably, Wordsworth and other romantic poets would later appreciate reading Newton's autobiography.

Newton took advantage of his time in London to follow up on the recommendations of a friend acquired on his last voyage to the West Indies, Captain Alexander Clunie. They had visited together every

---

[1] Newton, *Works* 4:123.

[2] Newton, *Works* 4:124.

[3] Newton, *Works* 1:67.

[4] Shaftesbury, Anthony Ashley Cooper, Earl of, *Characteristics of Men, Manners, Opinions, Times*, 2 vols., ed. J. M. Robertson (New York: Bobbs-Merrill, 1964) 2:98.

evening during their month in the same port. Clunie provided "Christian conversation," something Newton had lacked for years on his voyages. Intrigued by Clunie's "experience with things of God," Newton said:

> My conceptions became clearer and more evangelical; and I was delivered from a fear which had long troubled me; the fear of relapsing into my former apostasy. But now I began to under-stand the security of the covenant of grace, and to expect to be preserved, not by my own power and holiness, but by the mighty power and promise of God, through faith in an un-changeable Saviour. He likewise gave me a general view of the state of religion, with the errors and controversies of the times, (things to which I had been entirely a stranger) and finally directed me where to apply in London for further instruction.[5]

What did Newton mean when he began at this time to call himself "evangelical"? That word, the transliteration of a term in the Greek New Testament, is the adjectival form of εὐαγγέλιον (*euaggelion*), rendered in earlier English versions as "gospel" or "glad tidings" and translated in some modern English versions as "good news." In the broadest sense, all Christians accept the gospel message and could be called "evangelical." But from Newton's era onward the word has had a specialized meaning, referring to a movement in Anglo-American Protestantism associated with fervent personal devotion to Christ and an eager desire to persuade others to have a similar faith.

Evangelicals stressed the need for an identifiable conversion experi-ence at the start of one's Christian life, and lessened the traditional emphasis on baptism as marking that beginning. Holy communion, the other Protestant sacrament, also became secondary to repenting, praying, singing, and testifying. Newton commented on those who gathered at "the Lord's table" but lacked a sincere desire to repent of their evil ways: "Many rush upon this sacrament as though it were a mere ceremony, . . . or a sponge to wipe off their past offences, that they may begin a new score."[6] In the Church of England, congregations that did not have an exalted view of sacraments as a means of grace came to be known as the Low Church.

---

[5]Newton, *Works* 1:65.
[6]Newton, *Works* 4:112.

In London, Newton drank from what he called "the fountainhead" of spiritual refreshment.[7] The pastor of his childhood church was still Davis Jennings, so he returned there to worship. He also attended the largest Congregational church in London, one to which many seafaring people belonged, and heard Samuel Brewer preach. Brewer was Clunie's minister and had received some of his theological education from Jennings. Newton also heard Anglican William Romaine preach and was pleased to find someone in the established church with an evangelical message.[8] Whereas Newton's religion on shipboard had been noted by a solitariness, now spiritual loneliness was being replaced by an abundant camaraderie. Being with those fellow evangelicals caused him to feel that he been found by God's beloved community.

Having become intrigued with the emerging Methodist movement within the Church of England, Newton read John Wesley's journal and George Whitefield's letters. In his diary, Newton told of becoming personally acquainted with Whitefield in June 1755, after Whitefield had returned from one of his many trips to America. Newton heard Whitefield preach and spoke with him briefly. The next Sunday, Newton attended a three-hour worship service conducted by Whitefield in the London Tabernacle, and recorded this description: "It seemed as though that composure, that elevation, and that assurance of faith which shone in his frame and discourses were in some measure diffused over the whole assembly. He made many little intervals for singing hymns—I believe nearly twenty times in all." That evening Newton returned to hear Whitefield preach and found that hundreds had to be turned away from the Tabernacle, although it had a capacity of five thousand. Two days later Newton arose at daybreak to hear Whitefield, and afterward wrote: "My heart was greatly impressed, and I had little relish either for company or food all day." Newton felt like he had received a "foretaste of heaven" from Whitefield's revival meetings.[9] He commented that Whitefield "was the original of popular preaching, and all our popular ministers are only his copies."[10]

Whitefield was the forerunner of mass evangelists in subsequent centuries. He could attract as many as thirty thousand commoners to hear him preach in the public squares of London. It was said he could cause

[7]Newton, *Works* 1:67.
[8]Newton, "Diary" 1:179.
[9]Newton, "Diary" 1:225-26.
[10]Bruce Hindmarsh, *John Newton and the English Evangelical Tradition* (New York: Oxford University Press, 1996) 74.

listeners to swoon just by the way he pronounced "Mesopotamia." At his rallies, huge collections were taken for charitable causes. Being with Whitefield made Newton feel part of the Great Awakening that was sweeping Anglo-American culture. He might have heard Whitefield give this ecumenical analogy to the London water supply:

> I have often thought since I went to see the waterworks, that it was an emblem of Christ; there is a great reservoir of water from which this great city is supplied; but how is it supplied from that reservoir? why by hundreds and hundreds of pipes: but where does this water go, does it go only to the dissenters or to the church people, only to this or that people? no, the pipes convey the water to all; and I remember when I saw it, it put me in mind of the great reservoir of grace, that living water that is in Christ Jesus, and the pipes are the ordinances by which his grace is conveyed to all believing souls. God grant we may be of that happy number.[11]

Newton would have willingly taken command of another slave ship if Manesty had needed his services and had found his health acceptable. The former employer had no opening, but secured for him an excellent and hard-to-obtain royal appointment as customs supervisor (called "tide surveyor"). Since Mary was still too ill to travel with him to his new Liverpool position, Newton wrote before taking a coach from London:

> I am going to leave her at the time I would most earnestly choose to be with her, to leave her at an uncertainty of ever seeing [her] again, to take possession of an office which without her will be a burden. This is the language of sense, but faith talks in a different strain, only my ears are deaf to hear, and my heart heavy to understand.[12]

In the eighteenth century, Liverpool had grown from a small town to a booming city. When Newton began to work there it was the home port for about a hundred slave ships. It was a matter of pride to live in the leading European slave port that generally brought back a high return on capital investment. "This was the golden harvest which accounts for all," wrote James Pope-Hennessy, "for the fetid, feverish weeks upon the African coast, for the vile and dangerous Atlantic crossing, . . . for the

---

[11]George Whitefield, *Eighteen Sermons* (Boston, 1820) 16.
[12]Newton, "Diary" 1:254.

callous division of Negro families condemned to a servitude which offered no future."[13] Eric Williams commented on the city:

> Dock duties increased two and a half times between 1752 and 1771. . . . It was a common saying that several of the principal streets of Liverpool had been marked out by the chains. . . . The red brick Customs House was blazoned with Negro heads.[14]

Newton had no regrets over taking a position on shore because it ended the long separations he and his wife had endured during their five years of marriage. He described for Mary his new situation: "I have a good office, with fire and candle, fifty or sixty people under my direction, with a handsome six-oared boat and a coxswain to row me about in form."[15] Being a ship inspector was a lucrative position inasmuch as he received one-half the value of confiscated contraband. Also, bribes were easily obtained if he permitted goods to be smuggled into the port. As with his work as captain, Newton soon organized his staff so that subordinates did most of the work and he had much leisure time to pursue his religious interests.

A month after Newton began his new work, Whitefield came to Liverpool for a preaching mission. Newton heard him preach nine times in one week and observed that he was appreciated by "many of the poorer sort" but not by most of "the fashionable folks."[16] He confided to Mary that Whitefield "warms my heart" and "strengthens my faith."[17] Newton had long conversations with Whitefield and invited him to supper at his boarding house.[18] Whitefield was generally disappointed with the response from the Liverpudlians even though he attracted some four thousand to an outdoor square.

In 1755, shortly after Newton was in Liverpool, Europe was aghast by the earthquake in Lisbon that killed 60,000 and destroyed most of the city. "O may this sinful nation take warning," Newton cried, fearing that Liverpool might also be hit as an expression of divine judgment.[19]

---

[13]James Pope-Hennessy, *Sins of the Fathers* (New York: Knopf, 1968) 145-46.

[14]Eric Williams, *Capitalism and Slavery* (Chapel Hill: University of North Carolina Press, 1994) 62-63.

[15]Newton, *Works* 4:129.

[16]Newton, *Works* 4:135.

[17]Newton, *Works* 4:134.

[18]Newton, "Diary" 1:273.

[19]Newton, "Diary" 1:300.

Noticing that Newton had become Whitefield's constant companion and disciple, some in Liverpool called him "young Whitefield" and "a Methodist," associations that he did not disdain.[20] "There seems a great deal of earnest piety amongst these poor despised people," he said; "and though I think them wrong in some things, I believe their foundation is good."[21] Newton pointed out that "Christian" was also an "extremely odious" name to ancient pagan Roman writers. "The word *Methodist* has a degree of the like effect in our day," he observed; "the very sound of the word is sufficient to fill the minds of many with prejudices against the truth."[22] He also noted:

> The term of a Methodist preacher does not frighten me from attending upon them, for though I will not give them the preference to other able ministers of the gospel whom I love and honour, yet if I mistake not these have been more owned and blessed to me, for the little time I have known them than any. Happy shall I be if I am accounted worthy to stand near the meanest of these despised persecuted people at the great day.[23]

As usual, Newton wrote Mary frequently while they were separated. His letters tended to be more homilies to raise her depressed spirit than a communication of his personal situation in Liverpool. He exhorted: "True religion has nothing in it of the unsociable or gloomy; but is, on the contrary, the source of peace, cheerfulness and good humor."[24] On that positive theme, he elaborated:

> The Lord is not a hard master; he gives us all things richly to enjoy. . . . [Some] think to please him by self-invented austerities and mortifications, and suppose they shall be acceptable to him, in proportion as they make themselves miserable. . . . He has placed us in a world in which everything is beautiful in its season. . . . It has pleased God, of his goodness, to make us susceptive of social affections, which sweeten our intercourse with each other, and combine duty with pleasure. . . . Love sweetens

---

[20]Newton, *Works* 4:136-37.

[21]Josiah Bull, compiler, *John Newton of Olney and St. Mary Woolnoth: An Autobiography and Narrative*, compiled chiefly from his diary and other unpublished documents (London: Religious Tract Society, 1868) 86.

[22]Newton, *Works* 2:249.

[23]Newton, "Diary" 1:237.

[24]Newton, *Works* 4:139.

labour, and blunts the sting of sorrow. The gospel is not designed to make us stoics: it allows full room for those social
feelings which are so necessary and beneficial in our present
state, though it teaches and enjoins their due regulations.[25]

Several days later, he again counseled Mary: "If you are really afraid
of being a hypocrite, it is a good sign that you are not one. For the hypocrite is secure and confident, and has no suspicion of a mistake."[26] At that
time she responded, and it is one of the few extant messages from her:

> I delight, admire, and love to hang upon every sentence, and
> every action of my dearest John; and yet how wanting, and how
> cold, am I to the gracious Author of all our mercies, to whom we
> owe each other, our happy affection, and all the satisfaction that
> flows from it![27]

A friend wrote Newton: "I have several times had the pleasure of
conversing with Mrs. Newton. God has been pleased to give her a great
measure of your spirit. . . . She told me that the healing of the great
Physician had done her more good than all her other medicines."[28] After
Newton had worked in Liverpool for two months, Mary came to live
there; he was grateful that her health had recovered beyond his expectation.

Newton found that money was like sea water: the more he consumed
the thirstier he became. While admitting he had an abundant salary for
his needs, he noted in his diary: "Began to reap some of the profits of my
new office, and to my grief and surprise found too much of the love of
money which is the root of all evil springing up in my heart."[29] Like
Jacob the patriarch, he attempted to enter into a scheme with God by
vowing to return for the Lord's work a fraction of the material success
that he might obtain. Assuming that God, not luck, controlled gambling,
he wrote in his diary:

> I have determined this day to have a ticket in the ensuing lottery;
> not I hope with a desire to amassing money merely. . . . I know
> when the lot is cast into the lap, the disposal is in the Lord's

---

[25]Newton, *Works* 4:498-501.
[26]Newton, *Works* 4:141.
[27]Newton, *Works* 4:138.
[28]Newton, *Works* 4:137.
[29]Newton, "Diary" 1:261.

hand, and I hope and pray that it may not succeed to me unless I shall be enabled to be useful proportionably. . . . If I gain a prize . . . I will dedicate a fourth part . . . to works of mercy, charity, and for promoting his glory.[30]

After losing, he soberly admitted he "forgot to apply the principle that the end does not justify means that are in themselves at least questionable."[31]

Newton wrote Whitefield to request that Methodist evangelists be sent to Liverpool:

> It is with pleasure I hear of a work of revival going on in so many different parts of the kingdom; and, as an inhabitant of this town, I am grieved to think that we should be as yet excluded from a share in it. . . . I wish you would represent some part of what I have written to Mr. Wesley, to set before him the importance of this great town, and urge him to send such preachers here as have skill to divide the word of truth in a lively, affecting manner, and may dwell upon the great essentials of the gospel.[32]

A year later, in April 1757, John Wesley himself came to preach in Liverpool, affording Newton his first opportunity to converse with him. When Wesley returned to Liverpool in 1760, Newton "availed himself of every opportunity of hearing and holding intercourse with him."[33] The following year Newton again heard Wesley preach in Liverpool and dined with him.[34] Comparing the man as he had come to know him, with his bad reputation among members of the established church, he wrote: "I shall no more venture to censure and judge without hearing or dare confine the Spirit of the Lord to those only who tally in all things with my sentiments."[35] Newton no doubt appreciated Wesley's testimony of his evangelical conversion in 1738, when he felt his heart "strangely warmed" as he began to trust solely in Christ for salvation.[36]

---

[30]Newton, "Diary" 1:359.

[31]Bull, comp., *John Newton*, 88.

[32]Newton, *Works* 1:83–84.

[33]Bull, comp., *John Newton*, 105.

[34]Bull, comp., *John Newton*, 110.

[35]Martin, *John Newton*, 176.

[36]Nehemiah Curnock and John Telford, eds. *The Journal of the Rev. John Wesley, Enlarged from Original Mss., with Notes from Unpublished Diaries, Annotations, Maps, and Illustrations* (London: Epworth, 1938) 1:476.

Reading what Wesley wrote about unethical business practices awakened Newton's conscience to one of his own.[37] On becoming a customs officer he swore that he would not take bribes, using the affirmation "so help me God." But Newton admitted: "I am led to question my conformity to the oath I took on entering into office, by which I renounced all taking of fees or gratuities, which, however, according to custom I have done."[38] As a port officer, he realized he had deprived his government of revenue by taking kickbacks from unlawful traders. He said: "The vending smuggled goods, or the buying them, if known to be so, is . . . injurious to the fair trader, who, conscientiously paying the prescribed duties, cannot afford to sell so cheap as the smuggler, and therefore must expect the fewer customers." Newton changed his conduct, acknowledging that the New Testament directs Christians to pay just taxes and to apply the Golden Rule by putting oneself into the situation of the honest merchant.[39]

While living in Liverpool, Newton came to like the Baptist congregation there so much that he considered becoming a member. They tried to convince him that baptism was not the replacement in Christianity for infant circumcision in Judaism, as John Calvin had taught. Since Baptists believed that adult immersion was the only permissible New Testament mode of baptism, Newton would have had to submit to it to become a Baptist. Weighing the arguments for and against infant baptism, he was put off by the "air of infallibility" expressed by its apologists and concluded that on the disputed matter a Christian should have liberty to choose.[40] Later, in a letter, Newton said: "Whether water-baptism should be administered by a spoonful or tub-full, or in a river, . . . are to me points of no great importance."[41] He made this diary entry about rebaptism:

> Though I still think my infant sprinkling to be a really valid baptism, so far as to render any repetition unnecessary, I dare not pronounce absolutely upon a point wherein so many great and good men have been and are divided. With respect to persons, I look upon neither circumcision nor uncircumcision to be anything. . . . Though I am apt sometimes to think highly of

---

[37]Newton, *Letters*, 159.
[38]Bull, comp., *John Newton*, 93.
[39]Newton, *Works* 1:247.
[40]Newton, *Works* 3:424-25.
[41]Newton, *Works* 4:351.

my catholicism, I cannot but confess to much bigotry and spiritual pride remaining in me.[42]

Newton's customs work was curtailed when the Seven Year War began with France and Spain in 1756. On its eve, he wrote in his diary: "It is melancholy to see such carelessness throughout the nation; instead of receiving war with humiliation as a chastisement from God; most people seem to wish for it and (here especially) to prefer it to a well-grounded peace, quite unapprehensive what the event may be."[43] Liverpool became more aware of war's deprivations than most of England because the French effectively blockaded the harbor and captured many of its ships.

The lessening of port activity at Liverpool provided Newton with more time to prepare himself for another career. Beginning in 1757, he taught himself biblical languages and theology in order to qualify for ordination in the Church of England. He learned to read the Greek New Testament and the Septuagint (the Greek translation of the Hebrew Bible), but not classical Greek. He decided to compose a Greek lexicon for New Testament study and devoted many pages to words beginning with the letter alpha, but then turned his attention elsewhere.[44] Also, he studied Hebrew, and within a year claimed: "I can read the historical books and Psalms with tolerable ease; but in the prophetical and difficult parts I am frequently obliged to have recourse to lexicons."[45]

By way of depreciating the significance of his linguistic perspicacity, Newton said: "A man may be able to call a broom by twenty names, in Latin, Spanish, Dutch, Greek, etc., but my maid, who knows the way to use it, but knows it only by one name, is not far behind him."[46] Yet, skill with biblical languages gave Newton a depth of interpretation that he would have otherwise lacked. For example, he noticed a Greek word Paul used and that the King James Version translates "being affectionately desirous (of you)" (1 Thessalonians 2:8). Newton explained the original Greek word in this manner: "It denotes a desire connected with the finest and most tender feelings of the heart; not like the degrading, selfish

---

[42]Bull, comp., *John Newton*, 89.
[43]Newton, "Diary" 1:290.
[44]Bull, comp., *John Newton*, 109.
[45]Newton, *Works* 1:69-70.
[46]Newton, *Letters*, 167.

desire of the miser for gold; but such an emotion . . . as that with which the nurse, the mother while a nurse, contemplates her own child."[47]

Newton's ability, interest, and discipline to teach himself difficult subjects had enabled him to learn the philosophy of Shaftesbury and the geometry of Euclid as a youth, the Latin classics and a reading knowledge of French while a captain, as well as biblical languages and abstruse theology while in Liverpool. Newton's theological study included Augustine of Hippo's *Confessions*, on which he commented: "In that book I think there is a lively description of the workings of the heart, and of the Lord's methods in drawing him to himself. It has given me satisfaction to meet with experiences very much like my own, in a book written so long ago."[48] Indeed the beginning of Augustine's spiritual autobiography contains a prayer that would seem to express well the theme of Newton's life: "Thou, O God, made us for Thyself, and our heart is restless until it reposes in Thee" (*Confessions* 1.1). Augustine told of his mother Monica influencing his Christian career, paralleling what Newton said while studying for ordination: "This was my dear mother's hope concerning me."[49] Newton may also have discerned parallel lives when he read about Augustine's struggle to discipline his sexual desires.[50] Writing about his personal odyssey in a confessional and theological mode similar to that of Augustine, Newton's diary of nearly a thousand pages is filled with self-examination and prayers.

Newton also studied the writings of Calvin, the sixteenth-century leader of the Protestant Reformation. The Calvinistic faith he had received from his mother was now rejuvinated. But Newton did not follow Calvin in believing that God had predestined some to eternal life and others to everlasting damnation. Like Wesley, he thought it a waste of time to urge people to repent if they had no control over their will. After a thorough examination of Newton's doctrine on the subject, Bruce Hindmarsh concludes: "However much Newton sought to exalt the sovereignty of God in salvation, he remained equally concerned boldly to address the will of individual men and women."[51] Newton believed that divine initiating grace did not preclude free choice, so he was neither in the camp of the strict Calvinists or of the freewill Arminians. Newton resonated with some of Jonathan Edwards's theology, but he thought the New En-

---

[47]Newton, *Works* 3:545.
[48]Newton, *Works* 3:444.
[49]Newton, *Works* 1:70.
[50]Augustine, *Confessions* 8.28.
[51]Hindmarsh, *John Newton and the English Evangelical Tradition*, 159.

glander's *Inquiry into Freedom of Will* "rather establishes fatalism and necessity than Calvinism in the sober sense."[52] As a way of removing himself from speculative theology about predestination, Newton identified himself with the unassuming woman who said, "I have long settled that point; for if God had not chosen me before I was born, I am sure he would have seen nothing in me to have chosen me for afterwards."[53]

Newton's literary interests were similar to those of Calvin. Both had been thorough students of the Latin classics before becoming infatuated with the sources of Protestantism. Both retained a breadth of literary interests after becoming theologians. "Admirable light of truth" shines in the classical secular writers, Calvin maintained.[54] Newton's curiosity was not exclusively on religious texts: for example, he attended a scientific lecture illustrated by a microscope. After reading Voltaire's *Histoire de Charles XII*, he remarked: "Many useful lessons may be drawn, especially the grand lesson of the vanity of the world. . . . What a mixture of grandness and meanness there is in the human mind."[55] Newton believed that Englishmen such as Francis Bacon, Isaac Newton, John Locke, and John Milton were "no less remarkable for their philosophy and literature, than for their defense of the essentials of the Christian religion."[56] Daniel Defoe's book on *Religious Courtship* so engrossed Newton's attention that he thought he might also write on the topic.[57] Reflecting on his own courtship, he stated: "I have seen and observed so much and have so plain a knowledge of what I myself failed in, that perhaps there are few people better qualified than myself, . . . but I am not master enough of style to venture at it."[58]

In 1758, at a "dissenting meetinghouse" in Leeds, Newton ventured into preaching. His hearers suffered with him through the first attempt. He selected this text: "I foresaw the Lord always before my face, for he is on my right hand, that I should not be moved; therefore did my heart rejoice, and my tongue was glad" (Acts 2:25-26). But after a few minutes he became confused and the regular minister had to take over the

---

[52]Bull, comp. , *John Newton*, 327.
[53]Bull, comp., *John Newton*, 371.
[54]John Calvin, *Institutes of the Christian Religion* (1559) 2.2.15.
[55]Newton, "Diary" 1:217.
[56]Martin, *John Newton*, 102.
[57]Newton, "Diary" 1:265.
[58]Martin, *John Newton*, 149.

service.[59] He later explained the incident in two letters to William Barlass, a Scottish theological student:

> I attempted it wholly *extempore*. . . . I set off tolerably well, though with no small fear and trembling. . . . Before I had spoken ten minutes, I was stopped like Hannibal upon the Alps. My ideas forsook me; darkness and confusion filled up their place. I stood on a precipice and could not advance a step forward. I stared at the people, and they at me, but not a word more could I speak, but was forced to come down, and leave the people, some smiling, and some weeping. My pride and self-sufficiency were sorely mortified. . . . The next time I was asked to preach, I did not feel much trepidation. I had my discourse in my pocket, and did not doubt but I was able to read it. And I read it sure enough. But being nearsighted, and rather ashamed to hold up my notes to view, I held my head close down to the [pulpit] cushion; and when I began I durst not take my eyes off for a moment, being impressed with a fear that I should not readily fix it again upon the right part of the page. Thus I hardly saw anybody in the place during the whole time, and I looked much more like a dull school boy poring over his lesson than a preacher of the gospel. I was not much less disconcerted this time than the former. I had tried the two extremes to little purpose, and there seemed to me to be no medium between them.[60]

For several months Newton supplied a Congregational pulpit at Warwick while on leave of absence from his Liverpool employment. On arriving there, he allayed his anxiety by identifying with the divine assurance Paul once received: "Be not afraid, but speak. . . . for I have much people in the city" (Acts 18:9-10). Even so, he did not have a satisfying work there, and said, "I soon afterwards was disappointed in finding that Paul was not John, and that Corinth was not Warwick!"[61]

Newton began a notebook in 1758 on "Miscellaneous Thoughts" in which he recorded his reflections on becoming a clergyman. He was

---

[59]John Waddington, *Congregational History 1700–1800* (London: Longmans, 1876) 520.

[60]William Barlass, *Sermons and Correspondence* (New York: Eastburn, 1818) 545, 579.

[61]Richard Cecil, "Memoirs of John Newton," in *The Works of the Rev. John Newton*, 2 vols., ed. Richard Cecil (Philadelphia: Hunt, 1831) 1:62.

continually concerned as to how someone with his past might be qualified for such a profession. Also, he engaged in other introspection:

> I do not think either sourness or gloominess become a preacher.
> . . . True gravity is far from these and is a temperament of
> behaviour arising from a fixed persuasion of the presence of God,
> the value of souls, the shortness of time, the influence of
> example, the love of mankind and the vastness and reality of
> eternal things, all impressed upon the mind together.[62]

After going through an intensive self-directed program of professional education, in 1759 Newton considered himself qualified to become an Anglican priest. With hopes of being accepted in that role, Newton visited the office of the archbishop of Canterbury, Thomas Secker. He "received the softest refusal imaginable,"[63] perhaps because Secker disliked those with Methodist sympathies. As he returned to Liverpool, he wrote his wife: "I left London on Saturday about ten, but soon found I had a very indifferent horse. I have been obliged to travel his pace, for he positively refuses to travel mine; and though I tell him how impatient I am to see my dear Mary, he will not move one foot the faster."[64] Two months later, the archbishop of York, John Gilbert, also refused him ordination.[65] He thought Newton showed poor judgment in wanting to exchange a position in Liverpool for one paying only one quarter as much.

On learning that Newton had been turned down for ordination by leaders of the Church of England, Wesley—although an Oxford graduate himself—made this entry in his journal:

> I had a good deal of conversation with Mr. Newton. His case is
> very peculiar. Our Church requires that clergymen should be
> men of learning, and, to this end, have a university education.
> But how many have a university education and yet no learning
> at all! Yet these men are ordained! Meantime, one of eminent
> learning, as well as unblameable behaviour, cannot be ordained
> *because he was not at the University!* What a mere farce is this! Who

---

[62]Martin, *John Newton*, 180.
[63]Newton, *Works* 4:146.
[64]Newton, *Works* 4:149.
[65]Bull, comp., *John Newton*, 100.

would believe that any Christian bishop would stoop to so poor an evasion?[66]

Wesley encouraged Newton to become a Methodist, which then was distinguished by laymen-led revivals for commoners in the out-of-doors. At that time Wesley and Whitefield did not think of their movement as a denomination separate from the Church of England. Methodists were especially effective in new industrial and mining towns neglected by the established church. To Wesley's invitation that Newton become an itinerant preacher, he responded 1760: "Though I love the Methodists, and vindicate them from unjust persons upon all occasions, and suffer the reproach of the world for being one myself, yet it seems not practicable for me to join them farther than I do."[67] Newton wanted to be a settled pastor; he did not care to travel continually down highways and byways to wherever a crowd could be gathered. Moreover, he and Mary disliked having to confront more of the spouse-separation stress that they endured during his seafaring years.

Other emotional and physical incompatibilities explain further why Newton did not care to join with the Methodists. "The weightiest difficulty," he said, was his dislike of the "fiery" spirit of some evangelists with whom he would be associated. Also, the deprivations of his youth had diminished his endurance on the road. He wrote Wesley:

> I have not strength of body or mind sufficient for an itinerant preacher; my constitution has been broken for some years. To ride a horse in the rain, for more than above thirty miles in a day, usually discomposes and unfits me for anything.[68]

In 1761, Newton heard Wesley in Liverpool preach on perfection, his most controversial doctrine. Wesley believed it possible for a Christian to become completely sanctified. At first, Newton merely expressed in his diary disagreement with Wesley's position: "I would rather pray for and press to nearer advances towards it than fight and dispute against it; . . . yet after all I expect to be saved as a sinner, and not as a saint!"[69] Referring to the apostolic aim "that we may present every man perfect in Christ" (Colossians 1:28). Newton observed:

---

[66]Curnock and Telford, eds. *Journal of the Rev. John Wesley* 4:373.

[67]Bull, comp., *John Newton*, 107.

[68]Donald Demaray, *The Innovation of John Newton* (Lewiston NY: Edwin Mellen, 1988) 89, 305.

[69]Bull, comp. , *John Newton*, 110.

This is not sinless perfection. The more grace a man has the quicker sensibility he has about sin; nor is it the perfection of an angel, but of a child, who has all the parts of a man, but is not a man. A perfect Christian is one who has all the parts of a Christian—the head, the heart, the hands, if we may so speak—he has faith, love, humility, and the like.[70]

Four years later, Newton frankly informed Wesley that he thought the doctrine of perfection Wesley had long preached was "a dangerous mistake" and "subversive of the very foundations of Christian experience." Those words are as strong as any Newton ever used in disputing a theological issue. Newton believed in continual moral perfect*ing*, not in arriving at a static perfect*ion*. Moreover, he found a Methodist minister in Liverpool who claimed to have attained perfection to be "one of the most disagreeable persons" he ever met among those who professed to be Christians.[71] To assume that one had fully achieved maturity and needed no more growth in holiness was counter to what he understood the Bible to teach.

In response, Wesley reaffirmed that Christians could be saved "from all sin" in this life when they love God "with an *undivided heart*."[72] Perhaps prompted by this exchange, Wesley published "A Plain Account of Christian Perfection" in 1766 and recommended that Newton examine the full statement of his position on possible sinlessness.[73]

In 1760, Newton published six sermons in Liverpool. In the preface he explained that he composed them for pulpit delivery.[74] He used them while supplying the pulpits of some Presbyterian churches and was pleased with the results. Becoming the pastor of a congregation independent of the Church of England increasingly appeared to be the place where his talents would be appreciated. The tug toward becoming a dissenting minister was probably influenced by the earlier desire of his mother. He wrote Clunie about visiting in non-Anglican churches in Yorkshire: "That is a flourishing country indeed, like Eden, the garden of the Lord, watered on every side by the streams of the gospel. . . . It is

---

[70]Bull, comp., *John Newton*, 371.
[71]Hindmarsh, *John Newton and the English Evangelical Tradition*, 132.
[72]John Telford, ed., *The Letters of the Rev. John Wesley*, 8 vols. (London: Epworth, 1931) 4:298-99.
[73]Telford, ed., *Letters of John Wesley* 5:5.
[74]Newton, *Works* 2:13.

very refreshing to go from place to place and find the same fruits of faith, love, joy, and peace."[75] That same year Newton wrote to Jennings:

> It is likely you have heard of the event of my application for orders. I pursued it as far, and raised as much interest as I could, from York to Chester to Canterbury, but it has pleased the Lord to overrule my design and I have given it up. I have not been able to purge myself from a suspicion of enthusiasm and am rejected as an improper if not a dangerous person.[76]

"Enthusiasm" was a term of approbation among Anglicans who considered it bad taste to become excited about religion. In 1755, Thomas Green, vicar of Wymeswould, wrote *A Dissertation on Enthusiasm, Shewing the Danger of Its Late Increase*. To some extent he was targeting irrational fanaticism, but it was mainly a broadside against all Methodists and Moravians. Green asserted: "Enthusiasm is destructive to the cause of true religion. . . . Persons of an enthusiastic turn of mind . . . are generally of an unsettled disposition, spurred on with a desire of travelling and encountering difficulties in order to make converts." With Whitefield especially in mind, he stated, "This nation has already smarted severely from the mischief it has occasioned."[77]

Nominal church membership was expected for English ladies and gentlemen, but showing passionate devotion was not good manners. Keeping calm and suppressing exuberance was presumed to be a by-product of enlightenment. Eighteenth-century essayist Oliver Goldsmith stated that the Anglican clergy were the best educated in Europe, yet they were not respected by the English populace. "Their discourses from the pulpit are generally dry, methodical, and unaffecting; delivered with the most insipid calmness," he said.[78] Leonard Binns writes about this period in England: "The overintellectualization of religion had robbed it of life, not only for the uneducated, but even for those who had some learning."[79]

---

[75]Bull, comp., *John Newton*, 119.

[76]Hindmarsh, *John Newton and the English Evangelical Tradition*, 91.

[77]Thomas Green, *A Dissertation on Enthusiasm, Shewing the Danger of Its Late Increase* (London: J. Oliver and T. Payne, 1755) vi, ix, 90, 204.

[78]Peter Cunningham, ed. *The Works of Oliver Goldsmith* (New York: Putnam, 1908) 7:124.

[79]Leonard Binns, *The Early Evangelicals* (Greenwich CT: Seabury, 1953) 56.

Newton recognized that the word "enthuse" was altogether appropriate for an incarnational religion; indeed, it literally means having God (*theos*) within (*en*). On the role of intellect in Christianity, he said:

> The truths of Scripture are not like mathematical theorems. . . . True religion is not a science of the head, so much as an inward and heartfelt perception, which . . . brings every thought into a sweet and willing subjection to Christ by *faith*. Here the learned have no real advantage above the ignorant; both see when the eyes of the understanding are enlightened; till then, both are equally blind.[80]

While Newton had disdain for the shoutings and paroxysms that were occasionally associated with Methodist meetings, he thought it was deadly to attempt to drain emotion from religion. Even so, his test of good preaching was not emotional highs by those assembled, but understanding, followed by acting on the message. Unlike some revivalists, Newton did not focus on the ecstasy that they associated with conversion. Congregationalist Jonathan Edwards conducted a famous revival, which Newton knew about, at his church in Northampton, Massachusetts. It was accompanied by a burst of intense but short-lived excitement. Realizing that "misguided zeal" may attend sudden but unsustained awakenings, Newton cautioned: "There are many more blossoms upon a tree in spring than there will be apples in autumn. Yet we are glad to see blossoms, because we know that if there are no blossoms there can be no fruit."[81]

The Newtons were especially sensitive to the ridicule of Mary's family. The Catletts had accepted Newton when he was a slaver but could not stomach his friendliness with Methodists. They were upset that members of their middle-class family might have to mingle socially with the lower class. Newton tried to assure them that he and Mary did not plan to cut their ties with respectable people even though some of their Christian friends did not belong to polite society. He sent Mary an ambivalent message that displayed his struggle with secular values: "I am far from proposing that you shall keep company with washerwomen in this world. Hereafter, I doubt not, we shall be glad to join with such." He added: "I much more fear our being cowardly, than imprudent."[82]

---

[80]Newton, *Works* 1:347.
[81]Newton, *Letters*, 4.
[82]Martin, *John Newton*, 168.

Mary's family was also concerned that the Newtons would receive in any ministerial position only a small fraction of the remuneration they had enjoyed from Newton's cushy post in Liverpool.[83] In 1761 he had sharp words for Jack Catlett:

> I am not mad. . . . No circumstance of my life was ever conducted upon so much deliberation and advice. . . . As you would hardly allow me the claim of an infallible spirit, I suppose you do not pretend to one yourself; and without such a spirit you have no right to be sure that I judged wrongly in the part I was about to act. Remember *my thinking differently from you is no proof that I was mistaken.* . . . I do not like disgrace or poverty, but I fear God more than either.[84]

Newton's viewpoint on the significance of money in marriage is set down in a letter he wrote to a poor single minister who asked for advice:

> Methinks I hear you say, . . . to preach or marry for money, that be far from me. I commend you. However, though the love of money be a great evil, money itself, obtained in a fair and honourable way, is desirable upon many accounts, though not for its own sake. Meat, clothes, fire, and books, cannot easily be had without it. . . . They who set the least value upon money have, in some respects, the most need of it. . . . You could, perhaps, endure hardships alone, yet it might pinch you to the very bone to see the person you love exposed to them. Besides, you might have a John, a Thomas, and a William, and half a dozen more to feed. . . . But is it not written, "The Lord will provide?" It is; but it is written again, "Thou shalt not tempt the Lord thy God." Hastily to plunge ourselves into difficulties, upon a persuasion that he will find some way to extricate us, seems to me a species of tempting him. Many serious young women have a predilection in favour of a minister of the Gospel; and, I believe, among such, one or more may be found as spiritual, as amiable, as suitable to make you a good wife, with a tolerable fortune to boot, as another who has not a penny.[85]

---

[83]Newton, *Works* 4:147.
[84]Bull, comp., *John Newton*, 109.
[85]Newton, *Works* 1:517-18.

Even while Newton was still with the customs office, Mary's medical expenses appear to have been a financial drain. He wrote his brother-in-law in 1762 about his and his wife's condition:

> Her constitution is tender and feeble. . . . Our health is like our wealth—in a mediocrity. The God whom we serve does not see it good for us to be rich, but I trust he will give us what is needful and best, and I hope we do not envy those who ride in coaches.[86]

Newton was especially sensitive to Mary's adjustment as he entered the ministry. When pondering a shift in career and dwelling, he wrote her a letter while with her in Liverpool that contained these lines:

> Though it is not necessary, it always gives me pleasure, to repeat how truly I love you, how much my happiness depends upon you, and that I never taste pleasure more sincerely myself than when I am instrumental to the promoting of yours. And that, on the contrary, I account it among my most painful trials if, either through inadvertence or necessity, I occasion you any uneasiness.[87]

Had it not been for Mary's counsel, Newton said, he would have accepted work in a dissenting church. She gave him patience to await years for an appointment as a Church of England priest in spite of rejections by both Anglican archbishops as well as by other bishops. The Newtons felt that they would lose some "honour and comfort" if they turned away from the denomination to which Mary had always belonged.[88] English social leaders expressed scorn toward ministers who were not members of the church that included the nobility.[89]

Newton then became acquainted with Thomas Haweis, who, like Wesley, devoted himself to evangelical Christianity while a student at Oxford. Because of his Methodist sympathies, he lost his clergy position at St. Mary Magdalen in Oxford but had succeeded in becoming the Anglican chaplain at Lock Hospital in London.[90] On hearing some of

---

[86]Bull, comp., *John Newton*, 115.
[87]Newton, *Works* 4:152.
[88]Bull, comp., *John Newton*, 113.
[89]Newton, *Works* 4:155.
[90]A. S. Wood, "The Influence of Thomas Haweis on John Newton," *Journal of Ecclesiastical History* 4 (October 1953): 188.

Newton's seafaring tales, Haweis encouraged him to write down the remarkable episodes of his life. Newton sent him fourteen letters containing his brief autobiography, and Haweis arranged the letters for publication with the anonymous title *An Authentic Narrative of Some Remarkable and Interesting Particulars in the Life of *****.*[91] The manuscript was as much an account of Newton's spiritual odyssey as of his past adventures. Because the identification of the author was soon widely known, the book helped greatly to launch Newton into a new career.

Wesley wrote appreciatively to Newton about the *Authentic Narrative* soon after it was published, and several years later he recorded in his journal: "Today I gave a second reading to that lively book, *Mr. Newton's Account of His Own Experience.* There is something very extraordinary therein; but one may account for it without a jot of predestination."[92] Wesley did not care for the numerous deliverances Newton attributed to Providence, but he was probably impressed that they both referred to themselves with the same biblical metaphor, "a brand plucked out of the fire". Wesley so associated himself with the expression that he included it in the epitaph he wrote for himself.[93]

Haweis shared *Authentic Narrative* with William Legge, the second Earl of Dartmouth, who had the highest nobility of any evangelical Englishman, and who was a patron of Lock Chapel.[94] At the beginning of his autobiography, Newton compared his background to that of Paul who "had been a terror to the church" and who "thought little of the mischief he had hitherto done." Even so, he believed God's grace was bestowed on him and that he was called "to preach that faith which he so lately strove to destroy."[95] Recognizing the accomplishments of the apostle, Dartmouth thought Newton also had promise of great usefulness.

Dartmouth was among the wealthy landed gentry, and he owned much of Buckinghamshire. As a close friend of George III, he became one of the most powerful statesmen in the nation. Due to his influence, the king gave four times Dartmouth's own generous gift for a college on the

---

[91]John Newton and Thomas Haweis, *An Authentic Narrative of Some Remarkable and Interesting Particulars in the Life of ***** : Communicated in a Series of Letters to the Rev. Mr. Haweis, Rector of Aldwinckle, Northamptonshire, and by Him (at the Request of Friends) Now Made Public* (London: R. Hett for J. Johnson, 1764).

[92]Telford, ed., *Letters of John Wesley* 4:292; Curnock and Telford, eds., *Journal of the Rev. John Wesley* 5:333.

[93]Curnock and Telford, eds., *Journal of the Rev. John Wesley* 4:90.

[94]Bull, comp., *John Newton*, 117.

[95]Newton, *Works* 1:9; Galatians 1:23.

New England frontier. Eleazer Wheelock had solicited them for funds to expand a school for native Americans that had been started in 1743. Dartmouth became interested in civilizing and converting them after meeting Sampson Occum, who had been educated at the school and had visited Britain as an Indian evangelical preacher. On hearing Occum testify about his religious experience, Newton considered it to be a mirror image of his own.[96] In 1769, a charter of the king bestowed "the name Dartmouth College for the education and instruction of youth of the Indian tribes . . . in all liberal arts and science, and also of English youths and any others."[97]

### The Olney Parson

Simultaneously with getting to know about Dartmouth's interests, Newton informed Haweis that he was seriously considering an invitation to become a Presbyterian pastor in Yorkshire. But Haweis knew that a curate was needed for the Anglican Church of St. Peter and St. Paul in the town of Olney, seventy miles north of London. The patron of that parish church happened to be Dartmouth, so Haweis suggested to him that he appoint Newton to the work.[98] At that time, Church of England parsons were selected by nobles, while bishops were appointed by the monarch.

For five years Newton had studied to become an Anglican priest but had been rejected repeatedly until Dartmouth intervened. When Newton approached the bishop of Lincoln, John Green, for an ordination examination, the prelate shifted to an approving stance on reading Dartmouth's letter of recommendation.[99] British historian George Trevelyan describes the situation in a waggish way: "Lord Dartmouth made interest in high episcopal quarters to obtain the ordination of John Newton, who was too much in earnest about religion to be readily entrusted with a commission to teach it, except as a matter of favour to a great man."[100]

Newton candidly disclosed to the bishop his reservations about Anglican doctrine: "I observe a few expressions in the burial and baptis-

---

[96]Newton, *Works* 4:320.

[97]David McClure and Elijah Parish, *Memoirs of the Rev. Eleazer Wheelock* (Newbury: Norris, 1811) 184.

[98]Bull, comp., *John Newton*, 121.

[99]Newton, *Works* 4:156.

[100]George Macaulay Trevelyan, *The American Revolution* (New York: McKay, 1964) 92.

mal offices, and in the catechism, which I cannot fully approve. But I can assent to the whole in such a manner as is due to any writings of human authority, which are not pretended to be written by infallible inspiration."[101] Newton disputed the requirement that all clergy candidates believe that nothing in the *Book of Common Prayer* is contrary to the "Word of God." He felt at liberty to omit from the funeral service the clause that a body being committed to the grave had a "sure and certain hope of the resurrection."

Newton later clarified why he found the baptismal service deficient: "The rubric tells us gravely that those who die in infancy may be saved if baptized; I believe they may be and are saved whether baptized or not."[102] Again, he said: "Infants of all nations and kindreds, without exception, . . . who have done nothing in the body of which they can give an account, are included in the election of grace."[103] He did not think that the Bible warrants assuming that salvation is dependent on a Christian clergyman performing a ritual over a dying infant to wash away inherited sin. On this matter his position was that of Calvin, who, in opposition to the medieval church, asserted: "God declares that he adopts our babies as his own before they are born. . . . How much injury the dogma that baptism is necessary for salvation . . . has entailed!"[104]

To a minister of an independent church who inquired why Newton remained in the established church, he gave a lengthy reply. He expressed admiration for the *Book of Common Prayer*, saying, "I question if any thing in the English language (our version of the Bible excepted) is worthy of being compared with it for simplicity, perspicuity, energy, and comprehensive fullness of expression."[105] Yet Newton affirmed that he in no way considered himself bound to follow the liturgy it contained without modification. Although nonconformists criticized the use of prescribed forms, Newton noticed that many of those who profess to pray extemporaneously "go so much in a beaten path that they who hear them frequently can tell, with tolerable certainty, how they will begin, when they are about the middle, and when they are drawing towards the close of their prayer."[106]

---

[101]Bull, comp. , *John Newton*, 117.
[102]Bull, comp., *John Newton*, 317.
[103]Newton, *Works* 3:379.
[104]Calvin, *Institutes of the Christian Religion* 4.15.20.
[105]Newton, *Works* 3:405.
[106]Newton, *Works* 3:406.

Newton recognized that Scottish churchmen, who rejected bishops, considered the episcopal form of government to be "a mark of antichrist." As a "latitudinarian," Newton did not think that any one form was exclusively sanctioned by early church practice. He thought the New Testament suggested that church officials, rather than congregations, decided policies.[107] In denominations where there is local congregational autonomy, the more wealthy, who usually compose the church board, often expect that the preaching conform to their values. In such circumstances, Newton noted, it is difficult for a minister to maintain his integrity.[108]

After ordination and before moving from Liverpool, Newton was proud to have been invited to preach for the first time in St. George's Church, of which Manesty and other city dignitaries were members. Wearing his new cassock and gown, he spoke to a large congregation, and afterward noted: "Some were pleased, but many disgusted. I was thought too long, too loud, too much *extempore*."[109] Yet, he was happy to find that he and Mary continued to be generally appreciated in Liverpool. He wrote Clunie about the departure of the Newtons from the city, "When we came away I think the bulk of the people, of all ranks and parties, were very sorry to part with us."[110]

Newton's friendship with Dartmouth quickly developed. Dartmouth was not a member of the Olney congregation and had no interest in interfering with ideas expressed from the pulpit. Having preceded Mary to Olney, Newton reflected in a letter to her on his indebtedness to his wealthy patron:

> He has . . . been wonderfully kind in giving me so many opportunities of his company and engaging me so often to his house. . . . His humility is so striking and unaffected that I am rather edified than elated every time I see him. . . . There is nothing of the recluse, sour, self-tormenting spirit which has so often disgusted you among the Methodists. . . . One thing I hope, at Olney we shall not find such barren tedious Sabbaths as have been our usual appointment at Liverpool. I trust if the Lord sends me there he will enable me to preach the glad tidings of salvation.[111]

[107]Newton, *Works* 3:420-23.
[108]Newton, *Works* 3:430.
[109]Bull, comp., *John Newton*, 122.
[110]Martin, *John Newton*, 202.
[111]Martin, *John Newton*, 201.

According to Newton, "the gospel seed was first sown" in Olney by Whitefield in 1739. After stopping for the second time in the town, Whitefield had made this journal entry:

> Great numbers were assembled together; but on account of it being a rainy day, it was judged inconvenient to preach in the fields. I therefore stood upon an eminence in the street, and preached from thence with such power as I have not for some time experienced. Though it rained all the time, yet the people stood very attentive and patient. All, I really believe, *felt*, as well as *heard*, the Word, and one was so pricked to the heart, and convinced of sin, that I scarce saw the like instance.[112]

Newton felt fortunate that Moses Browne, his predecessor at Olney, had been an evangelical. He had also been appointed by Dartmouth, but could not afford to remain there and support his dozen children. While Newton was curate, Browne became the nonresident vicar of Olney. This caused him to visit there occasionally, but his main employment was as chaplain at Morden College. Newton was soon to describe his congregation as

> where the gospel has been many years known, and is highly valued by many. We have a large Church and congregation, and a considerable number of lively, thriving believers, and, in general, go on with great comfort and harmony. I meet with less opposition from the world than is usual where the Gospel is preached. This burden was borne by Mr. Browne for ten years, and in that course of time some of the fiercest opposers were removed, some wearied, some softened.[113]

Not long after Newton began preaching in the insignificant town of Olney, he learned through Mary's family that he could find employment at an Anglican church in Hampstead. The Catletts pointed out that the position was closer to old friends in Chatham and London, the congregation was of a superior social class than at Olney, and the stipend was much higher. Newton turned it down even though he recognized that his Olney salary would hardly supply his basic needs.[114]

---

[112]*George Whitefield's Journals* (London: Banner of Truth Trust, 1960) 274.
[113]Newton, *Works* 1:500.
[114]Edward Bickersteth, *Memoirs of the Rev. John Newton* (New York: Episcopal Society, 1858) 140.

The usual priests in the Church of England were quite different from Newton. In the eighteenth century, "few of them had any genuine vocation for holy orders; they entered them as a matter of course because no other opening was provided, or because there was a family living waiting for them; or, if of lowly origin, because they hoped to improve their position in life."[115] Newton entered the priesthood with a considerable reduction in comforts and income, but with a deep religious conviction and a high sense of pastoral responsibility. He recognized that in his former employments he had been lost, unable to settle into what should have been his mission in life, but now he had at last found his true calling in the parish ministry.

Newton served as deacon for only two weeks before being advanced to the ecclesiastical rank he would retain for the rest of his life. On April 17, 1764 he noted, "This day ordained priest by the bishop of Lincoln."[116] On returning to Olney the next day, he wrote: "Lord, I would dedicate myself to thee. Be thou my sun and shield. Let thy glory be my only aim, and thy presence my exceeding great reward."[117] Newton revealed to Mary his ambivalent feelings as he launched into his new work:

I now almost stagger at the prospect before me. I am . . . to take the charge of a large parish, to answer the incessant demands of stated and occasional services, to preach what I ought, and to be what I preach. Oh! what zeal, faith, patience, watchfulness, and courage, will be needful for my support and guidance! My only hope is in the name and power of Jesus.[118]

After preaching the six sermons that he had prepared years earlier, Newton worried that his ideas for sermons might soon become exhausted. Then, while walking by the Ouse River, he pondered the centuries the stream had been flowing and how long it would continue. This caused him to think of God as a fountain that will never run dry, from whom inspiration flows.[119]

As he began his new work, Newton had no savings because Manesty's shipping company, in which he had invested, went bankrupt.[120] The compensation he received at Olney was much lower than his

[115]Binns, *The Early Evangelicals*, 103.
[116]Bull, comp., *John Newton*, 124.
[117]Bull, comp., *John Newton*, 125.
[118]Newton, *Works* 4:158.
[119]Newton, *Letters*, 173.
[120]Bull, comp., *John Newton*, 135.

Liverpool income, so the Newtons lived in genteel poverty. Dartmouth introduced Newton to John Thornton, who had been converted to evangelical Christianity by Whitefield. Although he may have been the most opulent merchant in Britain, he lived modestly in London. He gave away most of his riches from trading with Russia, fulfilling Jesus' directive that disciples should clothe the naked, assist the sick, and feed the hungry.[121] Thornton wrote Newton: "Be hospitable, keep an open house for such as are worthy of entertainment—help the poor and needy. I will statedly allow you two hundred pounds a year, and readily send whenever you have occasion to draw for more."[122] This meant that Newton received from that Good Samaritan several times his annual salary to assist folks in miserable circumstances. Newton also benefited from the books Thornton supplied, and from his practice of taking clergy as guests on holidays.[123] David McClure and Elijah Parish, recognizing Thornton's support as the first treasurer of English Trust that established Dartmouth College, described his generosity as "like a river, pouring its waters through various countries, copious and inexhaustible. . . . Deep, silent and overwhelming, it still rolled on, nor even ended with his life."[124]

Dartmouth underwrote the converting of Whitefield's Savannah orphanage into a college. When he offered Newton its presidency in 1765, Newton wrote Mary: "My love of Olney and your hatred of the water are the chief reasons which moved me to say I would not accept it."[125]

In 1767, Dartmouth had a large stone vicarage constructed for the Newtons, enabling them to provide frequent entertainment for parishioners and visitors. On moving in, he prayed: "Once [I] wandered naked and barefoot, without a home, without a friend; and now for me who once used to be on the ground, and was treated as a dog by all around me, Thou hast prepared a house suitable to the connection Thou has put me into."[126] When the house was decorated, Newton had a panel painted for his study on the third floor to remind him of the contrast between his pleasant new residence and his servitude two decades earlier in Africa. Two Bible verses were placed above the mantelpiece (and can still be found there): " 'Since thou wast precious in my sight, thou hast been honourable,' BUT 'Thou shalt remember that thou wast a bondman in the

---

[121]Matthew 25:35-36.
[122]Cecil, "Memoirs of John Newton" 1:38.
[123]Martin, *John Newton*, 220.
[124]McClure and Parish, *Memoirs of the Rev. Eleazer Wheelock*, 71.
[125]Bull, comp., *John Newton*, 141.
[126]Bull, comp., *John Newton*, 159.

land of Egypt, and the Lord thy God redeemed thee' " (Isaiah 43:4; Deuteronomy 15:15). Hindmarsh observes, "This plaque illustrates what recurred in his diary, how Newton's biography took on a kind of sacramental quality, as outward and visible events were contemplated at regular intervals as signs of inward and spiritual grace."[127]

There is significance in Newton quoting the word "redeemed" from the Old Testament. There it referred to emancipation from physical bondage. In the New Testament it became a basic metaphor for liberation from evil. When the adult Newton first began to take Christianity seriously, he came to know Christian redemption only as deliverance from spiritual bondage. But during his years as a clergyman he slowly came to see that just as sin is a kind of slavery so physical slavery is a kind of sin. He came to recognize the need for both human and divine assistance to effect the liberation of African slaves.

The close friendship between Dartmouth and Newton continued and Newton's pastoral communications addressed to Dartmouth were later published as "Letters to a Nobleman."[128] Newton suggested that he and Dartmouth shared similar status in asking, "What are we, that the Most High should thus notice us?"[129] Dartmouth may have been among those he had in mind when he made this diary entry in 1764: "What an admirable thing is the grace of God—adapted to every state of life! It makes the rich humble, and the poor happy."[130] Newton engaged in no fawning toward this powerful person.

Olney was a secluded and squalid town in Buckingham along the serpentine river Ouse. "The people here are mostly poor," Newton said; "the country low and dirty."[131] Olney men farmed while their wives and children spent long hours in monotonous lace making. After placing pins on a pillow in an intricate way, the worker used many bobbins to produce a fine woven pattern. The industrial revolution contributed to the grinding poverty in Olney because cottage work was being shifted to factories, and machine-decorated cloth was cheaper to produce. As the demand for lace lessened, the prospect for starvation increased.

The lace industry was brought from France by Huguenot refugees after the devastating Saint Bartholomew's Day Massacre in 1572. Buckingham became a haven for those Calvinist nonconformists. Mean-

---

[127]Hindmarsh, *John Newton and the English Evangelical Tradition*, 234.
[128]Newton, *Works* 1:258-342.
[129]Newton, *Works* 1:311.
[130]Bull, comp., *John Newton*, 133.
[131]Bickersteth, *Memoirs of the Rev. John Newton*, 142.

while, Olney was only twelve miles from Bedford, the home of John Bunyan and a stronghold of Baptists. At the time of the seventeenth-century
civil war, the region supported the Parliament rather than the Crown.

Newton found a number of his members to be of great faith, even
though unlearned:

> Some who know no more of what passes without the bounds of
> the parish, than of what is doing beyond the Ganges, and whose
> whole reading is confined to the Bible, have such a just under-
> standing of the things of God, and of the nature and difficulties
> of the Christian life, that I derive more instruction from their
> conversation than from all my books.[132]

The problem of communicating to people lacking in intellectual curiosity was a challenge to Newton. He described the situation in this way:
"A large majority of our congregations are, I fear, sermon-proof—they
come to the house of God, and return like a door upon the hinge."[133] He
wrote about this difficulty to a university student preparing for the
ministry:

> It is not easy for persons of quick parts duly to conceive how
> amazingly ignorant and slow of apprehension the bulk of our
> congregations generally are. . . . Perhaps nine out of ten know
> little more of what we say than if we were speaking Greek. . . .
> [Written sermons are] too remote from common conversation to
> be comprehended by narrow capacities; which is one chief reason
> for the preference I give . . . to *extempore* preaching. When we
> read to the people, they think themselves less concerned in what
> is offered than when we speak to them point blank. . . . [We
> should] fix our eyes upon someone of the auditory whom we
> judge of the least capacity; if we can make him understand, we
> may hope to be understood by the rest.[134]

The main theme of Newton's preaching is revealed in his letters. At
the beginning of his ministerial career he wrote Haweis: "Grace, free
grace must be the substance of my discourse—to tell the world from my
own experience that there is mercy . . . for the most hardened."[135] In

---

[132]Newton, *Works* 3:443.
[133]Barlass, *Sermons and Correspondence*, 560.
[134]Newton, *Works* 1:545.
[135]Hindmarsh, *John Newton and the English Evangelical Tradition*, 112.

another letter he summed up what he believed to be basic: "Love of God and man is the essence of religion and of the law. Without holiness no one shall see God, but eternal life awaits those who persevere in well-doing, though this reward is not of debt but of grace."[136] Again he said: "Man is made capable of three births—by nature he enters the present world—by grace into spiritual light and life—by death into glory."[137]

Regarding the New Testament affirmation that "grace and truth came by Jesus Christ,"[138] Newton commented, "All the grand peculiarities of the gospel centre in this point."[139] Pertaining to the penitent thief who was crucified alongside Jesus, he wrote: "The grace of God has shone so bright . . . that it has dazzled the eyes even of good men. . . . Here was salvation bestowed upon one of the vilest sinners, through faith in Jesus, without previous works, or a possibility of performing any."[140]

In a 1775 letter, Newton described congregational worship as responding to a royal invitation to go to court:

> Is it not strange, that though we are all in the same place, and the King in the midst of us, it is but here and there one can see him at once! However, in our turns, we are all favoured with a glimpse of him, and have cause to say, How great is his goodness! How great is his beauty! We have the advantage of the queen of Sheba, a more glorious object to behold, and not so far to go for the sight of it. . . . If a day in his courts be better than a thousand [elsewhere], what will eternity be in his presence![141]

Some of Newton's charm came from his seafaring past, expressed in his appearance and speech. He felt more authentic when not in clerical garb, which he drolly called "my sheep's clothing." The Olney townfolks usually saw a small man with a big nose smoking a pipe and wearing a blue sea jacket.[142]

Maritime figures of speech resonate in Newton's communications: "In such a world as this, where we are every moment liable to so many unforseen and unavoidable contingencies, a man without religion may be

---

[136]Hindmarsh, *John Newton and the English Evangelical Tradition*, 116.
[137]Cecil, "Memoirs of John Newton" 1:65.
[138]John 1:17.
[139]Newton, *Works* 2:282.
[140]Newton, *Works* 2:287, 289.
[141]Newton, *Works* 1:519.
[142]Joseph Belcher, *Historical Sketches*, 298.

compared to a ship in a storm, without either rudder, anchor, or pilot."[143] He compared the overconfident Christian to "a ship with much sail spread, and but little ballast" that "goes on well while the weather is fair, but is not prepared for a storm." For instance, Peter protested to Jesus, "Though all men forsake thee, yet will not I"; he displayed, Newton discerned, unawareness that his character was unprepared for the stresses ahead.[144] In another letter, Newton again drew on his knowledge of sailing the high seas:

> The Christian calling . . . is easy and clear in theory, but not without much care and difficulty to be reduced to practice. Things appear quite otherwise, when felt experimentally, to what they do when only read in a book. Many learn the art of navigation by the fireside at home, but when they come to sea . . . they find that the art is only to be thoroughly learnt upon the spot.[145]

Hindmarsh writes of Newton:

> Storms, compass, port, rules of navigation, shipwreck, enemy ships—all these and more served as Bunyanesque images of his Christian experience. . . . He related outward events to his inward condition, reviewed his past history in the light of present resolves, and tested available metaphors for their capacity to explain the state of his soul.[146]

Hindmarsh also notes: "It was important to Newton not only that his theology could be coordinated with his experience, but also that it was rational and biblical."[147] Taking a scholar's approach to the Bible, he illustrated from the prophetic books how the King James translators sometimes missed "the beauty and clearness of the original . . . [by] not attending to the genius of the Hebrew poetical language, which is considerably different from the prose."[148] When a friend wrote Newton to inquire about an apparent inconsistency between biblical teachings, he acknowledged that some words seem to have a different meaning as the context is changed. Convinced that biblical doctrine is consistent, he recommended that a search be made for the general sense that is clearly

---

[143]Newton, *Works* 1:392.

[144]Newton, *Works* 4:491-92.

[145]Newton, *Works* 4:314.

[146]Hindmarsh, *John Newton and the English Evangelical Tradition*, 31.

[147]Hindmarsh, *John Newton and the English Evangelical Tradition*, 78.

[148]Newton, *Works* 4:344.

and repeatedly affirmed and then obscure texts should be interpreted in that light.[149] "As many locks . . . are opened with equal ease by one master key," Newton stated, "so there is a certain comprehensive view of scriptural truth which opens hard places, solves objections, and happily reconciles, illustrates, and harmonizes many texts."[150]

For annual festivals that drew large crowds to Olney, Newton found a fresh but biblical way of making his message more attractive. Using Isaiah's image that compared God's message to a marketplace commodity (Isaiah 55:1-2), Newton described to Dartmouth his unconventional way of appealing to visitors:

> On the evening of our fair days I usually preach, which I call opening my booth. Sometimes I invite them to buy the truth or to come and see; sometimes I depreciate the wares and objects of the fair, and endeavour to convince them that all is vanity and vexation of spirit in comparison to what is set forth to view and to sale, without money or price, in the ordinances of the gospel.[151]

On such occasions Newton may have preached, as Whitefield did, wherever a crowd could be assembled. He said that if the gospel is "preached in simplicity, and honoured by a meek, inoffensive behaviour in those who profess it—it does not much signify whether they meet in a church, a chapel, or a barn."[152]

Newton preached twice on Sundays and frequently during the week, but he viewed its effect as just the first step toward the goal of personal change of his congregants. Hindmarsh writes:

> Through the preaching of the gospel he sought to awaken sinners; then, through pastoral visiting he aimed to observe, and through counselling to hasten, the work of grace in particular cases, testing its genuineness before finally announcing his hope that this or that person had been truly converted.[153]

Although Newton sometimes wrote out his sermons, he did not use a manuscript or notes in the pulpit. When overly busy, he prepared his

---

[149]Newton, *Works* 1:83.
[150]Newton, *Works* 1:108.
[151]Hindmarsh, *John Newton and the English Evangelical Tradition*, 194.
[152]Newton, *Letters*, 10.
[153]Hindmarsh, *John Newton and the English Evangelical Tradition*, 188.

sermon on the way from the vicarage to the church. In response to a theological student's inquiry about his methods of preaching, Newton wrote: "As to preparation, I make little use of books, excepting the Bible and concordance. Though I preach without notes, I most frequently write more or less upon the subject. . . . I believe the best and most useful parts of my sermon occur *de novo* while I am preaching."[154] He elaborated on the latter idea in his interpretation of a story about Jesus:

> I went this morning into the pulpit, as having only a small piece of bread, and of fish, to set before the multitude. But, through mercy, it multiplied in the distribution, and, I hope, there was a comfortable meal for those who were present, and some fragments left that will not be lost.[155]

Recognizing that long sermons were counterproductive, Newton entered in his diary this confession: "I spoke near an hour, and perhaps should have been shorter if I had had more to say. . . . I had no settled view of my subject." To a clergyman who preached two-hour sermons, he advised:

> There is still in being an old-fashioned instrument called an hourglass which . . . used to be the measure of many a good sermon. . . . I cannot wind up my ends to my own satisfaction in a much shorter time. . . . We can seldom stretch our attention to spiritual things for two hours together without cracking it . . . and when weariness begins, edification ends.
>
> Perhaps it is better to feed our people like chickens, a little and often, than to cram them like turkeys, till they cannot hold one gobbet more. Besides, overlong sermons break in upon family concerns, and often call off the thoughts from the sermon to the pudding at home, which is in danger of being overboiled. They leave likewise but little time for secret or family religion, which are both very good in their place, and are entitled to a share in the Lord's Day.[156]

Newton criticized not only the length of sermons but also protracted prayers:

---

[154]Newton, *Works* 1:81.
[155]Newton, *Works* 4:166.
[156]Newton, *Works* 1:547-48.

The chief fault of some good prayers is that they are too long; . . . it is better . . . that the hearers should wish the prayer had been longer than spend half or a considerable part of the time in wishing it was over. . . . It sometimes happens, both in praying and in preaching, that we are apt to spin out our time to the greatest length, when we have in reality, the least to say.[157]

In the Olney sanctuary, Newton was delighted with the presence of 175 children who made "a pretty show in the chancel." He said: "In speaking to the children, I sometimes speak to the bystanders, without seeming to intend it; and who knows but a random shot may now and then hit the mark?"[158] Bernard Martin observes: "Judging by the letters, novels, and diaries of the period there were not many adults who sought the society of children. Newton did; and he understood them. . . . He had quite a reputation with children for the Chinese junks he could make out of paper."[159] Newton told how his preaching to adults was influenced by his informal manner with children: "With them I was obliged to stoop in order to be understood; and I soon found that the familiar style I was obliged to use to children was the most proper to engage the attention of grown people."[160]

The children's instruction that he supervised was a large part of their education. Virtually all the training of any kind they had previously received pertained to lace making or farming. The Society for Promoting Religious Knowledge among the Poor, to which Newton belonged, helped supply books, such as Isaac Watts's hymnbook for children and *Sermons to Young Persons* by Philip Doddridge.[161] Newton enjoyed explaining to them parables of Jesus and illustrating the story of the prodigal by his own life. He gave monetary awards for those who responded well to catechetical instruction and who learned by heart some hymns and Bible passages. After some time he was able to bring in a schoolmaster for the children.[162]

For those young people, Newton composed this charming poem:

---

[157]Newton, *Works* 1:154.

[158]Bickersteth, *Memoirs of the Rev. John Newton*, 136.

[159]Martin, *John Newton*, 263.

[160]Demaray, *The Innovation of John Newton*, 182.

[161]Isaac Watts, *Divine Songs: Attempted in East Language for the Use of Children* (London: M. Lawrence, 1715); Philip Doddridge, *Sermons to Young Persons*, 3rd ed. (London: M. Fenner, 1743).

[162]Hindmarsh, *John Newton and the English Evangelical Tradition*, 196-98.

Once on a time a paper kite
Was mounted to a wondrous height,
Where, giddy with its elevation,
It thus expressed self-admiration:
"See how soon crowds of gazing people
Admire my flight above the steeple;
How would they wonder if they knew
All that a kite like me can do!
Were I set free, I'd take a flight,
And pierce the clouds beyond their sight;
But, ah! like a poor prisoner bound,
My string confines me near the ground,
I'd brave the eagle's towering wind,
Might I but fly without a string."
It tugged and pulled, while thus it spoke,
To break the string—at last it broke.
Deprived at once of all its stay,
In vain it tried to soar away;
Unable its own weight to bear,
It fluttered downward through the air;
Unable its own course to guide,
The winds soon plunged it in the tide.
Ah! foolish kite, thou hadst no wing,
How couldst thou fly without a string?
My heart replied, "O Lord, I see
How much this kite resembles me!
Forgetful that by thee I stand,
Impatient of thy ruling hand;
How oft I've wished to break the lines
Thy wisdom for my lot assigns!
How oft indulged a vain desire
For something more, or something higher!
And, but for grace and love divine,
A fall thus dreadful had been mine."[163]

Newton gave the moral of "The Kite" poem in his biblical subtitle,
"Pride must have a Fall,"[164] and sent it to Thornton with this explanation:

I have now and then perhaps once in a year what I call a wise
dream. . . . One of this sort I had two nights ago. I dreamed that

---

[163]Newton, *Works* 2:603.
[164]Cf. Proverbs 16:18.

a fable was told me by some person, which seemed to convey
such a lesson to me, that in order to preserve it, I put it into a
hasty kind of verse.[165]

Unlike the typical Anglican clergyman of his generation, who tended
to identify with the respectable and to champion the status quo, Newton
took seriously the gospel admonition about helping the poor. The charity
he dispensed on behalf of Thornton composed most of Olney's social
welfare, but he also effectively encouraged the few haves in his parish to
assist the many have-nots. Trevelyan describes the establishment preacher
of the eighteenth century: "His sermons, carefully composed, were read
from the pulpit as literary exercises, meant to flatter the taste of the
elegant."[166] Historian William Willcox also remarks about this period:
"Organized Christianity was of and for the propertied class"; consequently the poor "had little more contact with religion than if they had been
living in the Dark Continent."[167]

The most neglected gospel teaching, according to Newton, was Jesus'
counsel that his disciples open their homes to the poor, the crippled, and
the blind, rather than to kinspersons and friends in comfortable circumstances (Luke 14:12-14). He interpreted the hyperbole in this way: "I do
not think it unlawful to entertain our friends; but if these words do not
teach us that it is in some respects our duty to give a preference to the
poor, I am at a loss to understand them." He also commented to the well-
off: "Your friends have houses of their own, and money to pay at an inn
if you do not take them in, but the poor need relief."[168] Newton, like
Paul, knew "both how to be abased and . . . how to abound" in material
things (Philippians 4:12), and thought himself wealthy because he had
received an abundance of love. He wanted the Olney people to realize
that they could not be completely poverty stricken if they possessed
God's love.

The issue was raised with Newton as to whether there is a distinction
of ranks in the Kingdom of God. He rejected notions of social exclusivity,
saying:

---

[165]Demaray, *The Innovation of John Newton*, 235.

[166]George Macaulay Trevelyan, *Illustrated English Social History* (London:
Longmans, 1951) 3:64.

[167]William Willcox, *The Age of Aristocracy* (Lexington MA: Heath, 1976) 172. His
presumption that Africans were without religion illustrates that the darkest thing
about the "Dark Continent" has been Caucasian ignorance of it.

[168]Newton, *Works* 1:75.

One man like Mr. Whitefield is raised up to preach the gospel with success through a considerable part of the earth; another is called to the humbler service of sweeping the streets. . . . I see not why he may not be as great a man in the sight of God, as he who is followed and admired by thousands. . . . If you and I were to travel in search of the best Christian in the land, . . . it is more than two to one we should not find the person in a pulpit, or any public office of life; perhaps some old woman at her wheel, or some bedridden person, hid from the knowledge of the world . . . would strike our attention more than any of the doctors or reverends with whom we are acquainted.[169]

Newton found visitations important in making his sermons relevant to the "poor, afflicted, ignorant, and illiterate" parishioners of Olney. "They were taught of God *before I saw them*," he observed. "I was their official teacher from the pulpit; but I taught them chiefly by what I first learned from them in the course of the week, by visiting and conversing with them from house to house."[170]

As a conscientious visitor, Newton ministered to the victims of smallpox that ravaged Olney for some of the years he was there. He wrote Thornton: "I have buried three out of a house more than once. I had frequently five or six such families to visit in a day; but through mercy never had my health better than when so many were dying around me."[171] His pastoral ability is displayed in this consoling letter to someone who had been critically ill:

I am glad to hear you are better; I hope the Lord has no design to disable you from service, but rather (as he did Jacob) to strengthen you by wounding you; to maintain and increase in you that conviction which, through grace, you have received, of the vanity and uncertainty of every thing below: to give you a lively sense of the value of health and opportunities, and to add to the treasury of your experience new proofs of his power and goodness, in supporting, comforting, and healing you.[172]

---

[169]Newton, *Works* 4:333.
[170]Newton, "Diary" 6/3/1767.
[171]Demaray, *The Innovation of John Newton*, 90.
[172]Newton, *Works* 1:507.

Due to Whitefield and Browne having prepared the ground and planted the gospel, and to Newton's continuation of the preaching combined with compassionate care, the work at Olney flourished. He reported, "The people flock in from four, six, or more miles about the country, to hear the Word."[173] The large attendance necessitated the addition of a balcony in the Olney church that increased the seating capacity to about two thousand, which would accommodate most of the population of the area.[174] Once a month the sacrament of the Lord's Supper was administered, but the worship services centered in the sermons. In 1772, Newton wrote:

> It has been . . . a time of grace and revival. . . . We have had as many awakened within about three months past as for two or three years before. . . . Though I think there never was a people less disposed to think themselves qualified to teach their ministers, yet they have often taught me without intending it.[175]

In writing Liverpool friends, Newton compared the congregation he was feeding to a pastoral scene:

> We are quiet and happy at Olney. We know nothing about disputes or divisions. If you pass a flock of sheep in a pasture towards evening, you may observe them all very busy in feeding. Perhaps here and there one may just raise his head and look at you for a moment, but down he stoops again to the grass directly. He cannot fill his belly by staring at strangers.[176]

The freedom that Newton felt in Olney did much to make his life pleasant and productive there. He wrote:

> My superiors in the church leave me at full liberty to preach and manage within my own parish as I please. The bishop usually comes into the neighbourhood once in three years. . . . Except for about four days in three years, I know no more of a superior than if I was an archbishop myself.[177]

---

[173]Bickersteth, *Memoirs of the Rev. John Newton*, 140.
[174]Bickersteth, *Memoirs of the Rev. John Newton*, 137.
[175]Bull, comp., *John Newton*, 179.
[176]Bull, comp., *John Newton*, 165.
[177]Barlass, *Sermons and Correspondence*, 545.

Parish work kept Newton so busy that it is surprising he found time to edify those who lived elsewhere. Haweis persuaded him to write a church history "to trace the gospel spirit, with its abuses and oppositions, through the several ages of the Church." He was aware that Newton's knowledge of ancient classical writers equipped him to provide a historical context for understanding the development of Christianity. Newton only completed the first part, on the New Testament era, which was published in 1769 with the title *A Review of Ecclesiastical History*.[178]

The philosophy of history contained in Augustine's *City of God* as well as in Calvin's treatices can be detected when Newton wrote: "The spirit of the firstborn, Cain, appears to have influenced the whole human race: the peace of nations, cities, and families, has been continually disturbed by the bitter effects of ambition, avarice, revenge, cruelty, and lust."[179] Newton illustrates this depravity with an account of the pagan Romans who were taking Paul for trial before Caesar (Acts 27:42):

> The soldiers would have killed all the prisoners, right or wrong, rather than one of them should have a possibility of escaping; and in this, without doubt, they consulted their own safety, and the spirit of their laws. . . . Could there be a greater proof of cruelty and injustice found amongst the most barbarous nations, than to leave prisoners, who possibly might be innocent, exposed to the wanton caprice of their keepers?[180]

On the other hand, in his *Ecclesiastical History*, Newton commented that there is goodness in people, even though it falls short of perfection. "The best are sometimes blameable," he stated. "Warm and active tempers, though influenced, in the main, by the noble ambition of pleasing God in all things, are apt to overshoot themselves, and to discover a resentment and keenness of spirit which cannot be wholly justified." Newton noted such weakness in Peter even though he was the "prince of the apostles."[181]

When someone labeled Newton a Calvinist, he declared that was analogous to saying that "because Calvin had seen the sun, and has mentioned it in his writings, we build our knowledge of its light and

---

[178]Bull, comp., *John Newton*, 120. John Newton, *A Review of Ecclesiastical History* (London: Edward and Charles Dilly, 1770).

[179]Newton, *Works* 2:273.

[180]Newton, *Works* 2:274.

[181]Newton, *Works* 2:309.

influence upon his testimony." Newton went on to say that it is more accurate to say that he received his religion from the New Testament than from Calvin.[182] Like Augustine, Calvin, and Wesley, Newton had a triple base of authority: sacred history, reason, and experience. He admired texts by certain Protestant interpreters while emphasizing that certain books of the New Testament provided the best grounding in theology. "I should prefer the epistles of St. Paul as a summary," he said, "to any human systems I have seen."[183] Newton elaborated:

> If the world so pleased, I had rather be called a Peterist or a Paulist, than a Calvinist; but reproachful as the last term is deemed by fashionable folks, I must not be ashamed of it, because I believe Calvin to have been an eminent servant of God, and his writings, especially his latter writings, are scriptural, judicious, and accurate. As a Latin writer, I think he deserves a place among the best modern classics. . . . It is much more easy to pity or despise Calvin, than to equal or even to emulate him.[184]

What essentially does it mean to be a Calvinist? Philosopher Vergilius Ferm provides this concise definition: "Calvinistic thought is a system in which God is made the center of all that is and happens, God's will pervading human and cosmic events, and upon whom man is utterly and cheerfully dependent."[185] That accurate description does not emphasize the judgment of God, because John Calvin's teaching focused more on divine mercy.[186]

In an elusive manner, Newton identified the stream of Protestantism to which he belonged. "I am what they call a Calvinist," he said; "yet there are flights, niceties, and hard sayings to be found among some of that system, which I do not choose to imitate."[187] Martin writes:

> Newton never for a single day forgot his own spiritual experience. It was more vivid and real to him than any dogma. He wanted everyone to share it, and to share the abundant life and

---

[182]Newton, *Works* 3:320-21.
[183]Newton, *Works* 2:486.
[184]William Roberts, *Memoirs of the Life and Correspondence of Mrs. Hannah More*, 2 vols. (New York: Harper & Brothers, 1835) 1:448.
[185]"Calvinism," *Dictionary of Philosophy*, ed. Dabobert D. Runes, New Students Outline Series 119 (repr.: Ames IA: Littlefield, Adams, 1958).
[186]Calvin, *Institutes of the Christian Religion* 2.8.21.
[187]Newton, *Works* 1:503.

joy that came from it. If he must be given a theological and an ecclesiastical label then he would be Calvinist and Church of England; but he was impatient of theological dispute and tolerant of other denominations.[188]

When the *Gospel Magazine* was attacking Wesley and other Arminians in 1771, Newton contributed to the journal this letter:

Of all people who engage in controversy, we who are called Calvinists are most expressly bound by our own principles to the exercise of gentleness and moderation. . . . If our zeal is embittered by expressions of anger, invective, or scorn, we may think we are doing service to the cause of truth, when, in reality, we shall only bring it into discredit. . . . Whatever it be that makes us trust in ourselves that we are comparatively wise or good, so as to treat those with contempt who do not subscribe to our doctrines, or follow our party, is a proof and fruit of a self-righteous spirit. . . . What will it profit a man if he gains his cause, and silences his adversary, if, at the same time, he loses that humble, tender frame of spirit in which the Lord delights?[189]

Newton's ambivalence toward Calvinism emerged again in his comments to a minister:

I am an avowed Calvinist; the points which are usually comprised in that term, seem to me so consonant to Scripture, reason, and experience. . . . What is by some called high Calvinism, I dread. I feel much more union of spirit with some Arminians, than I could with some Calvinists. . . . Though I never preach a sermon in which the tincture of Calvinism may not be easily discerned by a judicious hearer, yet I very seldom insist expressly upon those points.[190]

The "once saved, always saved" doctrine of high Calvinism troubled Newton because it minimized human responsibility. Unlike those who believed that once "elected" there would be "perseverance of the saints" evermore, Newton acknowledged with the Methodists that there are "backsliders," those who had professed their faith but were no longer expressing it in word or deed. Newton defined the "backslider" as "one

---

[188]Martin, *John Newton*, 212.
[189]Newton, *Works* 1:159.
[190]Newton, *Works* 4:369.

who has formerly known the goodness of God, has rested in his love, and rejoiced in his salvation, . . . but, at length, by an unguarded conduct . . . has grieved the good Spirit of God." His "backsliding" word picture came from the King James Version, and he illustrated it from the lives of King David and the apostle Peter.[191] In his diary, Newton also occasionally called himself a backslider.

Whitefield, a Calvinistic and evangelical Anglican, was the role model for the type of churchman Newton aspired to be—except for his outdoor preaching style. In 1765, he invited Whitefield to Olney where, a generation earlier, Whitefield had twice visited but had been denied a pulpit. In responding, Whitefield expressed joy that Newton was now a minister and stated: "Gladly shall I come whenever bodily strength will allow me to join my testimony with yours in Olney pulpit, that God is love. As yet I have not recovered from the fatigues of my American expedition."[192] However, Whitefield was unable to meet with Newton again. Newton asserted: "I love young preachers, for they are sprightly, warm, and earnest. I love old preachers, for they are solid, savoury, and experimental. So I love them all, and am glad to hear all as occasion offers. But I own I like the old wine best."[193] The elderly evangelist that Newton loved best was Whitefield.

In 1770, after Whitefield's death in New England, Newton preached a memorial sermon at Olney on a text from John 5:35 that originally referred to John the Baptist. He reminisced on getting up to hear Whitefield preach to a large congregation at sunrise, and gave him this tribute:

> I have not read or heard of any person, since the days of the apostles, of whom it may be more emphatically said, "He was a burning and a shining light." . . . The state of religion when he first appeared in public was very low in our established church. . . . The doctrines of grace were seldom heard from the pulpit and the life and power of godliness were little known. . . . What a change has taken place throughout the land within a little more than thirty years! . . . How much of this change has been owing to God's blessing on Mr. Whitefield's labors is well known to many who have lived through this period. . . . His zeal was not like wildfire, but directed by sound principles, and a sound

---

[191]Newton, *Works* 1:80, 91; 2:214-15, 222, 502.
[192]Bull, comp., *John Newton*, 125.
[193]Bull, comp., *John Newton*, 225.

judgement. . . . I never met anyone who could imitate him with success. Those who attempted, generally made themselves disagreeable.[194]

After twenty-two years of marriage, Newton wrote Mary: "I am often tongue-tied, and can speak more readily to anybody than to you."[195] However, he had no trouble writing at great length to Mary, whose written responses were brief but unfortunately were not preserved. When Mary visited her newly wedded sister, Newton wrote: "Do they love like us? No, they cannot yet. For love at first is a child, and grows stronger by age."[196] Commenting further on that love, Newton wrote, "It was once an acorn but it has now spreading branches and a deep root like an old oak." Also, he enscribed:

Since the Lord gave me the desire of my heart in my dearest Mary, the rest of the sex are no more to me than the tulips in the garden. . . . I have a vile heart, capable of every evil; and, in myself, am as prone to change as a weathercock. But, with respect to you, he has been pleased to keep me fixed, as the north pole, without one minute's variation for twenty-four years.[197]

Later that same year, Newton sent these sentiments to a couple on their wedding day:

Marriage is undoubtedly the most important concern with respect to this world in which we can engage. . . . Success depends not upon appearances, for they are changeable. . . . We see too many instances of people who come together, with all seeming advantages, and yet, from unforeseen causes, the affection which promised to be permanent, gradually subsides into indifference, and perhaps terminates in disgust. . . . I am now far advanced in the twenty-fifth year of marriage; and though I set out blindfold, and was so far infatuated by an idolatrous passion, . . . yet the Lord . . . did not deal with me as I deserved. When I look back . . . as a husband, I cannot but say, my lot in life has been most happy. Few, I think, can have been more favoured; and to the

---

[194]Luke Tyerman, *The Life of the Rev. George Whitefield* (New York: Randolph, 1877) 2:625.
[195]Newton, *Works* 4:176.
[196]Martin, *John Newton*, 224.
[197]Newton, *Works* 4:183.

best of my recollection I never wished, for a single minute, it were possible to exchange situation with any person upon earth. . . . My dear friends, you will now acquire a new set of feelings; how sickness, or pain, or trouble, affects you in your own persons you know, but how you will be affected by them in the person of a husband or wife, you have yet to learn.[198]

After twenty-five years of marriage, the Newtons received an additional fulfillment to their lives by becoming parents of an orphaned niece, Betsy Catlett. About that adoption, Newton said:

The Lord has given us a child whom we love as our own. . . . We think it an advantage, rather than otherwise, that she was born (if I may so say) to us, above five years old, which saved us all the trouble and expense of pap and cradle; it is a great mercy to us that he has given her an amiable and manageable disposition, so that she is quite a companion; we love to please her, and she studies to please us.[199]

When Betsy was attending a boarding school at the age of twelve, she developed a morbid fear of death. In an effort to help her overcome depression, Newton wrote:

Cheerfulness is no sin, nor is there any grace in a solemn cast of countenance. . . . Do not indulge a hard thought of him [Jesus], as though he were severe and stern, and ready to take advantage of you. Form your ideas of him from the accounts the evangelists give you, that he was meek and lowly when upon earth, full of compassion and gentleness, ready to pity, to heal, to help, and to teach all who come to him; and they will tell you that he had, in particular, a great love for children.[200]

Writing was such a satisfaction to Newton that he encouraged his adopted daughter to improve her correspondence:

I want a good long letter; I care not what it is about, so that you write easily. You read sometimes; cannot you find something in your books to tell me of? You walk sometimes, and without doubt look about you. Take notice of anything that strikes your

---

[198]Newton, *Works* 4:363.
[199]Newton, *Works* 4:291.
[200]Newton, *Works* 4:382.

eye; make some reflection or observation upon it, and then put up your thoughts very safely in a corner of your memory, that you may send them to me the next time you write.[201]

In 1783 also he wrote Betsy that "a hardhearted, unfeeling, selfish Christian, is a contradiction." In that letter, he also commented on the Revolutionary War:

> Had we lived in America . . . we should have seen towns, villages, and houses in flames; have heard the groans of widows and orphans around us; have had everything we call our own torn from us, and perhaps have been glad to hide ourselves in the woods, to save ourselves. Such has been the lot of thousands in the course of the war.[202]

In spite of residing in a rural area, Newton's network of evangelicals grew. Hindmarsh writes: "The Olney vicarage hosted what must have seemed one continual religious conversation, as students, laymen, and clergy of various denominations came from around the country to stay as houseguests for a night or, in some cases, several weeks."[203] Newton wrote some doggerel about an anticipated visit with William Bull, a Baptist minister:

> A theosophic pipe with brother B.,
> Beneath the shadow of his favorite tree;
> And then how happy I! how cheerful he![204]

Newton also frequently visited many parishes in the region, warming beds and pulpits while he was there. He probably was the most scholarly and widely traveled person in the region. His diary shows that he often participated in meetings at places other than Olney, even though his week included at least one church meeting for adults or children on most days there.

Newton displayed his acceptance of the religious parties in Olney by arranging to have Baptists, Congregationalists, and Anglicans meet together three times at the beginning of the year, when a minister from each denomination would preach.[205] This would surely have pleased his

---

[201]Newton, *Works* 4:397.

[202]Newton, *Works* 4:393.

[203]Hindmarsh, *John Newton and the English Evangelical Tradition*, 194.

[204]Bull, comp., *John Newton*, 255.

[205]George Redford, ed., *The Autobiography of the Rev. William Jay* (New York:

patron, for, as Trevelyan puts it, "Dartmouth's breadth of charity and ardour of conviction were bounded by no ecclesiastical barriers."[206]

During the latter phase of Newton's ministry in Olney, he got to know a young minister who later would have great influence. He was Thomas Scott, an Anglican with Unitarian leanings, who lived in a town near Olney. He associated irrational zeal with those who preached without a manuscript. After a pharmacist recommended Newton's preaching, he sampled one of his services. Although Newton did not know this visitor was present, Scott's report showed that he had a guilty conscience:

> Mr. N. looked full on me . . . and when he named his text, to my great astonishment it was this: . . . [Paul said], "Thou enemy of all righteousness, wilt thou not cease to pervert the right ways of the Lord?" As I knew that he preached *extempore*, I took it for granted that he had chosen the text purposely on my account.

Some time later, Newton walked a long way from Olney to visit more than once a dying couple in Scott's parish that the neighboring priest had neglected. This caused him to acknowledge that although Newton's pulpit method was "uncouth," his practice was more in accord with ministerial duty than his own. Scott then wrote Newton, presenting what he thought to be irresistibly convincing arguments against his evangelical outlook. Newton responded in a moderate manner and did not try to force his views on his younger colleague. Scott then observed, "He returned a very friendly and long answer to my letter in which he carefully avoided the mention of those doctrines which he knew would offend me." After several letter exchanges, Scott wrote, "His discourse comforted and edified me, and my heart . . . became susceptible of affection for him."[207]

Under Newton's inspiration, Scott reexamined the Greek New Testament. He soon accepted evangelical ideas that he had ridiculed, and they became close friends. Newton wrote in his diary in 1778, after asking Scott to preach: "My heart rejoiced and wondered, O my Lord, what a teacher art Thou! How soon, clearly and solidly is he established in the knowledge and experience of Thy gospel, who but lately was a disputer against every point."[208] After hearing Scott preach, he noted,

---

Carter, 1855) 309.

[206]Trevelyan, *American Revolution*, 96.

[207]Thomas Scott, *The Force of Truth: An Authentic Narrative* (New York: Dodge, 1814) 26, 35, 81.

[208]Newton, "Diary" 2:209.

"What liberty, power, and judgment in so young a preacher!"[209] Newton introduced Scott to a group of clergy as the one whom he hoped "would prove the Jonathan Edwards of Old England."[210] Scott told of his interactions with Newton in his widely circulated book, *The Force of Truth*. Newton made efforts to have Scott replace him when he left Olney, which succeeded after a brief interlude. But Scott's lack of Newton's tact caused him trouble, and after a few years he moved on to London.

The interactive skills of Newton were well illustrated in his friendship with Scott. For example, he responded to Scott's criticisms of the trinitarian creed in this disarming manner: "Your integrity greatly pleases me. . . . I set a great value upon your offer of friendship, which I trust will not be interrupted on either side by the freedom with which we mutually express our difference of sentiments." Again, Newton wrote Scott, "Your objections neither displease nor weary me . . . for I have formerly made the like objections myself."[211] In his personal counseling, Newton said that he attempted to balance agreeableness with faithfulness to the gospel:

> They are singularly favoured whom the Lord is pleased to guide and to keep in the *golden mean*. What we call a polite and cultivated behaviour, is certainly no real bar to that faithfulness we owe to God or man; and if maintained under a strict Scriptural restraint, may greatly soften prejudices, and conciliate the goodwill even of unawakened hearers in a considerable degree. . . . The probable good effects of a very faithful testimony in the pulpit have been wholly defeated by too successful endeavours to be agreeable out of it. The world will often permit a minister to think, and perhaps to preach, as he pleases, provided he will come as near them as possible in a sociable conformity. . . . If, like Achilles, you have a vulnerable heel, I apprehend you more in danger of suffering loss by the smiles than by the frowns of men.[212]

For other examples of Newton's winsome advice, consider first this letter to a minister on the occasion of his ordination:

---

[209]Bull, comp., *John Newton*, 233.
[210]Hindmarsh, *John Newton and the English Evangelical Tradition*, 154.
[211]Newton, *Works* 1:343, 348, 352.
[212]Newton, *Works* 4:366.

It is a poor affair to be a stageplayer in divinity, to be able to hold a congregation by the ears, by furnishing them with an hour's amusement, if this be all. But the man who is what he professes to be, who knows what he speaks of, in whom the truth dwells and lives, who has not received the gospel from books, or by hearers only, but in the school of the great Teacher, acquires a discernment, a taste, a tenderness, and a humility, which secures to him the approbation of the judicious, qualifies him for the consolation of the distressed, and even so far opens his way to the hearts of the prejudiced, that if they refuse to be persuaded, they are often convicted in their own consciences, and forced to feel that God is with the preacher. . . . The grand principle of gospel oratory is simplicity. Affectation is displeasing in all persons, but in none is it so highly disgusting as in a preacher.[213]

To another minister who was discouraged over his lack of success, Newton wrote:

Faithfulness and diligence is our part; the rest is the Lord's. I suppose you are quite as acceptable as Jeremiah was in Jerusalem. . . . He was not very popular, but he was plain and honest. . . . It seems you think other people preach better than you. I hope you will always think so; if you should be mistaken, it is a fault on the right side.[214]

In a 1770 letter, Newton showed that he had come to realize that becoming a Christian is typically a gradual affair:

The Lord compares the usual method of his grace to the growth of corn (Mark 4:26-29), which is perfected by a slow and almost imperceptible progress. The seed is hidden for a time in the soil, and when it appears, it passes through a succession of changes— the blade, the stalk, the ear, and it is brought forward amidst a variety of weather; the dew, the frost, the wind, the rain, the sun, all concur to advance its maturity, though some of these agents are contrary to each other, and some of them, perhaps, seem to threaten the life of the plant. Yet when the season of harvest returns, the corn is found ready for the sickle.[215]

---

[213]Newton, *Works* 4:447-48.
[214]Newton, *Works* 4:335.
[215]Newton, *Works* 3:450.

In interpreting the parable for Thornton, Newton described the first stage as when a Christian's "faith is weak, but his heart is warm," and the likelihood of failure is great because of self-will. In the second stage, confrontation with temptation teaches compassion. Then there is the final stage of continual awareness of one's weakness and humbly accepting God's will. The recipient of grace is finally "full of mercy and good works, without partiality, and without hypocrisy."[216] Thus, the organic analogy tells of the never ending development in which a theocentric outlook replaces an egocentric one.

Toward the end of his Olney years, a fire destroyed a dozen thatched-roofed houses in town. Newton responded by opening a relief fund and by providing words of comfort. One expression of the latter is contained in this recollection:

> I once visited a family that had suffered a great loss by fire. I found the mistress of the house in tears. I said, "Madam, I wish you joy." She answered, "What! do you wish me joy of the fire?" "No, Madam, I wish you joy that you have treasure laid up which the fire cannot reach." This turn stopped the grief; she wiped away her tears and smiled.[217]

Newton advised against following the custom of putting candles in windows on Guy Fawkes Day because of the devastation a month earlier. However, a defiant drunken mob came to the vicarage with the intent to smash windows and he had to bribe them to prevent damage. Some friends suggested that this threat came because "he had been too familiar with an ignorant people; too generous in meeting their material wants; and too apt to encourage them to speak at the Great House and cottage prayer meetings."[218] This disheartening experience made Newton realize that his influence in Olney was waning.

Words that Newton wrote to a recently ordained minister reflected the difficulties he was having in Olney:

> A distant view of the ministry is generally very different from what it is found to be when we are actually engaged in it. The young soldier, who has never seen an enemy, may form some general notions of what is before him; but his ideas will be much

[216]Newton, *Works* 1:117-23.
[217]Newton, *Letters*, 65-66.
[218]Martin, *John Newton*, 270.

more lively and diversified when he comes upon the field of battle. If the Lord was to show us the whole beforehand, who that has a due sense of his own insufficiency and weakness would venture to engage? . . . The ministry of the gospel . . . is a bitter sweet; but the sweetness is tasted first; the bitterness is usually known afterwards, when we are so far engaged that there is no going back. Yet, . . . grace is sufficient for us; and if he favours us with a humble and dependent spirit, a single eye, and a simple heart, he will make every difficulty give way, and mountains shall sink into plains before his power.[219]

As soon as Thornton, patron of London's St. Mary Woolnoth Church, learned of the death of the rector who had not been evangelically oriented, he wrote Newton to offer him the position.[220] A letter that Thornton wrote in 1774 to accompany gifts sent to Dartmouth College shows why he would favor Newton:

Orthodox opinions delivered in a cold and formal way, without application, seem to have a tendency to lull the hearers asleep. . . . It is a sad thing indeed to profess, and not possess the grace of the gospel, in a measure as is too common among us. . . . May the blessed Jesus keep us simple hearted.[221]

Newton expressed to Bull his reservations over taking a pastorate in a metropolis:

London is the last situation I should have chosen for myself. The throng and hurry of the busy world, and noise and party conten-tions of the religious world, are very disagreeable to me. I love woods and fields and streams and trees—to hear the birds sing and the sheep bleat. I thank the Lord for His goodness to me here. Here I have rejoiced to live—here I have often wished and prayed that I might die. I am sure no outward change can make me happier, but it becomes not a soldier to choose his own post.[222]

---

[219]Newton, *Works* 1:90.
[220]Cecil, "Memoirs of John Newton" 1:43.
[221]McClure and Parish, *Memoirs of the Rev. Eleazer Wheelock*, 311-12.
[222]Bull, comp., *John Newton*, 239.

# 4

# How Sweet the Sound

When Newton was a bachelor, he composed ditties that fellow sailors appreciated, resulting in light verse such as this:

What different senses of that word, a wife!
It means the comfort or the bane of life.
The happiest state is to be pleased with one,
The next degree is found in having none.[1]

After marriage, he retained the muse but for a more serious purpose. On his silver wedding anniversary, he penned these sentiments:

With mutual love, and peace, and health,
And friends, we have been blest;
And if not what the world calls *wealth*,
We have *enough* possessed. . . .

Like checkered cloth, the warp with love
And comfort has been spread;
But cares and crosses interwove,
Have furnished half the thread. . . .

Yet every cross a mercy is,
A blessing every thorn.[2]

## Hymnist Predecessors

As a parish priest, Newton turned his talent to making verses that could be sung in worship. He became part of a long English folksong tradition that can be traced to Caedmon (fl. 658–680), the father of English poetry. That seventh-century Anglo-Saxon herdsman put biblical teachings into simple songs to assist the memory of fellow Anglo-Saxons.[3] The more

---

[1]Josiah Bull, comp., *John Newton of Olney and St. Mary Woolnoth: An Autobiography and Narrative*, compiled chiefly from his diary and other unpublished documents (London: Religious Tract Society, 1868) 250.

[2]Newton, *Works* 4:214.

[3]Bede, the Venerable, *The Ecclesiastical History of the English Nation from the Coming of Julius Caesar into this Island, in the Sixtieth Year before the Incarnation of*

immediate predecessors of Newton in the eighteenth-century evangelical movement were Isaac Watts, Charles Wesley, and Philip Doddridge. Those musical mentors composed songs that gave congregations the opportunity to offer enthusiastic worship in contemporary terms.

In the typical routine of the Church of England in Newton's day, metrical psalms were sung perfunctorily. "The great majority of services were lifeless formalities with no power to arouse the religious sense or to elevate it if already present," Leonard Binns observes.[4] Evangelical Anglican William Romaine did not help this situation by his undeviating Calvinism. In his *Essay on Psalmody*, published in 1775,[5] he urged that church singing should be limited to paraphrases of words from the Bible. He attributed the lack of vitality in congregations to neglect of the metrical psalms, and depreciated Isaac Watts's hymns by calling them "Watts's whyms." Newton's perception was the opposite of that of Romaine; he associated congregational revival with the introduction of nonpsaltry songs.[6]

Breaking with the prevailing dull singing in English churches, Watts thought congregational songs should freely express current feelings and not be limited to King David's spiritual experiences. He lamented: "While we sing the praises of our God in his church, we are employed in that part of worship which . . . is nearest akin to heaven; 'tis a pity that this . . . should be performed the worst upon earth."[7] Watts assumed that "religion never was designed to make our pleasures less."[8]

The musical mentors of Newton opted for both psalm paraphrases and new hymns. Watts continued to give prominence to the psalms, which is evidenced by paraphrases such as "Joy to the World" (Psalm 98); "Jesus Shall Reign Where'er the Sun" (Psalm 72); and "Our God, Our Help in Ages Past" (Psalm 90). Watts's best-known hymn, "When I Sur-

---

*Christ, till the Year of Our Lord 731* (London: J. Batley and Meighan, 1723) 4, 24.

[4]Leonard Binns, *The Early Evangelicals* (Greenwich CT: Seabury, 1953) 107.

[5]*An Essay on Psalmody. A Collection out of the Book of Psalms, Suited to Every Sunday in the Year* (London: n.p., 1775).

[6]Bruce Hindmarsh, *John Newton and the English Evangelical Tradition* (New York: Oxford University Press, 1996) 264.

[7]Isaac Watts, *Hymns and Spiritual Songs. In Three Books. I. Collected from the Scriptures. II. Compos'd on Divine Subjects. III. Prepared for the Lord's Supper. With an Essay towards the Improvement of Christian Psalmody, by the Use of Evangelical Hymns in Worship, as Well as the Psalms of David* (London: J. Humphreys for John Lawrence, at the Angel in the Poultrey, 1707) preface.

[8]Gordon Rupp, *Religion in England 1688–1791* (Oxford: Clarendon, 1986) 514.

vey the Wondrous Cross," sets to music themes from Paul's gospel (for example, Galatians 6:14; Philippians 3:7-8). Countering the widespread assumption of ascetics that religion should be a killjoy, Watts wrote hymns such as "There Is a Land of Pure Delight" that combine gladness with sincerity. "Come, Holy Spirit, Heavenly Dove," another of Watts's hymns, has a stanza that criticizes contemporary congregational singing:

In vain we tune our formal songs,
In vain we strive to rise;
Hosannas languish on our tongues,
And our devotion dies.[9]

Some of the thousands of hymns composed by Charles Wesley, John's younger brother, also had an impact on Newton. Many, such as "Soldiers of Christ, Arise" and "Jesus, Lover of my Soul" abound with biblical imagery. Some, such as "Hark, the Herald Angels Sing" and "Christ the Lord Is Risen Today," celebrate events in the life of Jesus. "O for a Thousand Tongues to Sing" and "O for a Heart to Praise my God" are typical of Wesley's attention to changing one's inner life so as to have the emotional and moral experience of salvation.

Newton was also influenced by Philip Doddridge of Northampton, a disciple of Watts and a Congregational minister. Some of Doddridge's writings were known well by Newton, who most likely was familiar with his hymnbook. Posthumously published in 1755, Doddridge's hymnal[10] contained selections such as "Awake, My Soul, Stretch Every Nerve" and "O God of Bethel." Donald Demaray shows how Doddridge's hymns "helped pave the way" for Newton; he also traces phrases such as "amazing grace" and "how sweet the sound" that appear in the lyrics of both men.[11]

---

[9]"Come, Holy Spirit, Heavenly Dove," stanza 3, from Watts's *Hymna and Spiritual Songs* (1707). An alternate version of this stanza (as in some modern hymnals) reads: "Hosannas languish on our tongues, / and our devotion dies. / Waken our souls to joyful songs; / let pure devotion rise."

[10]Philip Doddridge, *Hymns Founded on Various Texts in the Holy Scriptures,* ed. Job Orton (Salop [Shropshire], England: J. Eddowes, J. Cotton, et al., 1755).

[11]Donald Demaray, *The Innovation of John Newton* (Lewiston NY: Edwin Mellen, 1988) 212.

## The Ministry of Song

Composing hymns was an activity integral to Newton's ministry. His diary discloses that hymn singing put him, as well as his congregation, into the proper mood: "Preached to the young people in the evening. . . . I went to church remarkably dull—but in singing the hymn before sermon I felt a softening of spirit, and was favored in preaching with remarkable liberty."[12] He recognized that hymns were a pleasant medium for conveying religious values. Having witnessed the effectiveness of singing in the revivals of Whitefield and Wesley, he wanted to appropriate their ways of communicating gospel warmth. Newton may have perceived that hymns of Charles Wesley, such as "Love Divine, All Loves Excelling" and "Rejoice, the Lord Is King," were as effective as the sermons of Charles's brother John in launching the evangelical revival. Bruce Hindmarsh discerningly writes: "The hymn was an apt literary form for the expression of Newton's spiritual ideals, since like the familiar letter it allowed him to treat a substantial theological subject without the loss of personal, or even autobiographical, immediacy."[13]

Newton followed Watts in composing hymns to encapsulate sermons as well as to reinforce them with an emotional thrust. He found that a musical expression of evangelical theology was an excellent way to cultivate both mind and heart. Indeed, his versified sermonettes may have had more impact in Olney than his pulpit discourses. For simplicity of images, here is a sample:

> More of thy presence, Lord, impart,
> More of thine image let me bear;
> Erect thy throne within my heart,
> And reign without a rival there.[14]

Newton composed with the commoners in mind while hoping that the elite would also appreciate his lyrics. In an unassuming manner, he explained:

> Though I would not offend readers of taste by a willful coarseness, and negligence, I do not write professedly for them. If the

---

[12]Newton, "Diary" 2:1.

[13]Hindmarsh, *John Newton and the English Evangelical Tradition*, 257.

[14]*The Olney Hymns* 1:32 (taken from Newton's *Works* and using the classifying numbers he gave).

Lord whom I serve has been pleased to favor me with that mediocrity of talent, which may qualify me for usefulness to the weak and poor of his flock without quite disgusting persons of superior discernment, I have reason to be satisfied.[15]

The Protestant Reformers' democratic mode of worship was emphasized by Newton. He focused on congregational singing rather than on the choir performances that had been the customary mode of medieval Christianity. Like the Wesleys, he encouraged all members to belt out songs lustily. With the Hebrews, the evangelicals affirmed: "Let us sing unto the Lord; let us make a joyful noise to the rock of our salvation" (Psalm 95:1).

Not being sanctuary oriented, Newton favored religious songs that could be easily shared apart from a church setting. They were an integral part of his pastoral activity in and around Olney. He arranged cottage meetings where a few neighbors gathered to sing, pray, and talk. Families were also advised to engage in a private expression of faith by having a daily time for worship. Newton suggested that parents alternate in leading in extemporaneous prayer, Bible reading, and hymn or psalm singing.[16]

Newton's hymns were both devotional and informative of the common biblical tradition. Some hymns contributed to private prayer and meditation, others helped in the healing of those wounded by the stresses of life, while still others encouraged affection for one another. They enabled ordinary Christians to practice their faith with the proper disposition. As Newton put it: "Religion does not consist in doing great things, for which few of us have frequent opportunities, but in doing the little necessary things of daily occurrence with a cheerful spirit, *as to the Lord*."[17]

For hymn sings, teaching sessions, and prayer meetings throughout the week, Newton obtained from Lord Dartmouth the use of a vacant mansion Dartmouth owned in Olney. At that social center Newton also gave a long series of addresses on Bunyan's *Pilgrim's Progress*, the favorite nonbiblical book for British Christians.

To commemorate the official opening of the "Great House" in 1769, Newton composed this hymn:

---

[15]Newton, *Works* 2:463.

[16]Newton, *Works* 1:87-88.

[17]David Jeffrey, ed., *A Burning and a Shining Light* (Grand Rapids MI: Eerdmans, 1987) 38.

O Lord, our languid souls inspire,
For here, we trust, thou art!
Send down a coal of heavenly fire,
To warm each waiting heart.

Dear Shepherd of thy people, hear,
Thy presence now display;
As thou hast given a place for prayer,
So give us hearts to pray.

Within these walls let holy peace,
And love, and concord dwell;
Here give the troubled conscience ease,
The wounded spirit heal. . . .

And may the gospel's joyful sound
Enforced by mighty grace,
Awaken many sinners round,
To come and fill the place.[18]

Youth gathered at the Great House to make use of Watts's catechism and his hymnbook for children, which contained no psalm paraphrases. Newton supplied the Olney children with both, motivated by the deep impression they made on him as a boy.[19] In particular, he recalled the "good pattern" that one of the songs provided him:

I'll not willingly offend,
Nor be easily offended;
What's amiss (in myself) I'll try to mend,
And endure what can't be mended.[20]

Many of Watts' hymns for children had a grace motif, as this one illustrates:

There is a gospel of rich grace,
Whence sinners all their comfort draw;

---

[18]*Olney Hymns* 2:43. These four stanzas are stanzas 1, 2, 4, and 7 of the original seven stanzas of "O Lord, Our Languid Souls Inspire." In some later versions, stanzas 1 and 2 are transposed, and the hymn thus has the title "Dear Shepherd of Thy People, Hear." To commemorate the beginning of weekly "prayer meetings" in the Olney Great House, William Cowper also composed a hymn: "Jesus, Where'er Thy People Meet."

[19]Edward Bickersteth, *Memoirs of the Rev. John Newton* (New York: Episcopal Society, 1858) 136.

[20]Newton, *Letters*, 19.

Lord, I repent, and seek thy face;
For I have often broke thy law.[21]

Newton was at home in various denominational groups and liked spiritual expressions that promoted Christian solidarity. Pertaining to his Sunday evening sermons, he noted: "I usually make one hymn a week to expound at the Great House."[22] When he had no new hymn of his own to present, he commented on those of others. He noted: "At the Great House spoke from a hymn in the *Gospel Magazine*, 'The God of Abraham Praise.' "[23]

To find the appropriate rhyme and rhythm, as well as the proper economy of words for articulating complex religious experiences, Newton gave artistic care to his craft. "I usually make a hymn weekly and sometimes it costs me so much thought and study that I hardly do anything else," he stated.[24] In one diary entry he acknowledged that it had taken him "a good part" of several days to choose the right phrases for one of his hymns.[25] Alfred, Lord Tennyson confirmed that plain compositions are not simply created:

A good hymn is the most difficult thing in the world to write. In a good hymn you have to be commonplace and poetical. The moment you cease to be commonplace and put in an expression at all out of the common, it ceases to be a hymn.[26]

Newton's hymns feature the "grace" keyword of his theology, which was also the hallmark Paul used for opening and closing each of his letters. The emphasis upon Pauline themes in Newton's hymns harmonizes with his sermons: in the eighty-four Newton sermons that have been published, there are more references to Paul's letters than even to all the

---

[21]Isaac Watts, *Divine Songs: Attempted in Easy Language for the Use of Children* (London: Printed for M. Lawrence, 1715) 15.

[22]Newton, "Diary" 2:32.

[23]Newton, "Diary" 2:79. That hymn was a "Christianized" paraphrase (ca. 1770) by Thomas Olivers (1725–1799) of the traditional Jewish doxology or *Yigdal* ("may He be magnified"), based on Moses Maimonides' thirteen Articles of Faith, and as paraphrased and set to music (ca. 1404) by the liturgical poet Daniel ben Judah Dayyam. (In most modern hymnals, the 1885 paraphrase by Max Landsberg and Newton Mann is used rather than that of Olivers.)

[24]Newton, "Diary" 2:52.

[25]Newton, "Diary" 2:53.

[26]Hallam Tennyson, *Alfred Lord Tennyson* (New York: Macmillan, 1897) 754.

Gospels combined.[27] Newton said: "Though [I am] not . . . what I wish or hope to be, and not what I once was—I think I can truly say with the apostle, 'By the grace of God I am what I am' " (1 Corinthians 15:10).[28] He marveled that the depraved Saul (later called Paul), who was portrayed in the Bible as "breathing out threatenings and slaughter against the disciples of the Lord" (Acts 9:1), had received God's unconditional acceptance. As Newton put it in one of his hymns: "How soon the Saviour's gracious call / Disarmed the rage of bloody Saul."[29] Newton vied with Paul for the title "chief of sinners" (1 Timothy 1:15), as he sang: "Though of sinners I am chief, / He has ranked me with his saints."[30] Reflecting on Paul's life, Newton commented that if one wanted in his own day a parallel example of "grace in softening the hardest heart," he knew of "no case more extraordinary" than his own.[31]

The depth psychology in a letter Paul wrote at Corinth provided Newton self-understanding. In 1774, he appropriated Paul's analysis of his divided self (Romans 7) in this imaginative manner:

> Did you ever see my picture? I have it drawn by a masterly hand. And though another person . . . sat for it, it is as like me as one new guinea is like another. The original was drawn at Corinth. . . . What is remarkable, it was drawn long before I was born. . . . According to the different light in which you view the picture, I appear to rejoice and to mourn, to choose and refuse, to be a conqueror or a captive. In a word, I am a double person; a riddle; it is no wonder if you know not what to make of me, for I cannot tell what to make of myself. . . . I find the hardest things easy, and the easiest things impossible; but while I am in this perplexity, you will observe in the same piece a hand stretched forth for my relief, and may see a label proceeding out of my mouth with these words—"I thank God, through Jesus Christ my Lord" (Romans 7:25). The more I study this picture, the more I discover some new and striking resemblance, which convinces me that the painter knew me better than I knew myself.[32]

---

[27]Demaray, *The Innovation of John Newton*, 108.
[28]Bull, comp., *John Newton*, 334.
[29]*Olney Hymns* 3:79.
[30]*Olney Hymns* 1:51.
[31]Newton, *Works* 1:9.
[32]Newton, *Works* 4:287-88.

When providing clarifying notes for *Pilgrim's Progress*, Newton again quoted from that same autobiographical chapter in Paul's letters:

The Pilgrim complains of the law in his members warring against the law of his mind, which made the chief Apostle cry out, "O wretched man that I am, who shall deliver me from this body of death." This is more or less the complaint and burden of all God's children: the remains of sin cleave to their best performances.[33]

A prayer of Newton that sums up his life from wretch to rectory contains overtones of Paul's experience:

Perhaps Thy grace may have recovered some from an equal degree of apostasy, infidelity, and profligacy; but few of them have been redeemed from such a state of misery and depression as I was in, upon the coast of Africa, when Thy unsought mercy wrought for my deliverance. That such a wretch should not only be spared and pardoned, but reserved to the honor of preaching Thy gospel, which he had blasphemed and renounced, . . . this was wonderful indeed.[34]

Newton admired the breadth of the "apostle to the Gentiles." He saw that Paul, after receiving undeserved acceptance by God, recognized true religion as neither in the custody of a particular ethnic group who were biblically literate nor the special possession of a superior class or gender. Rather: "There is neither Jew nor Greek, there is neither bond nor free, there is neither male nor female: for ye are all one in Christ Jesus" (Galatians 3:28). Newton asked, "May we not say with the apostle, 'Grace be with all that love the Lord Jesus Christ in sincerity?' [Ephesians 6:24] I think that is a latitudinarian prayer."[35]

For Newton, as for Paul (Colossians 3:1-3), "the resurrection" pertained as much to spiritual life before death, as after death:

"I am," saith Christ, "your glorious head,"
(May we attention give)
"The resurrection of the dead,
The life of all that live." . . .

---

[33]John Bunyan, *Pilgrim's Progress* (Exeter NH: Williams, 1819) 48.

[34]Richard Cecil, "Memoirs of John Newton," in *The Works of the Rev. John Newton*, 2 vols., ed. Richard Cecil (Philadelphia: Hunt, 1831) 1:52.

[35]Newton, *Letters*, 107.

Fulfill thy promise, gracious Lord,
On us assembled here;
Put forth thy Spirit with the word,
And cause the dead to hear. . . .

Thy power and mercy first prevailed,
From death to set us free;
And often since our life had failed,
If not renewed by thee.[36]

Newton applied Ezekiel's vision of a resurrection of disassembled corpses (Ezekiel 37:1-14) to pew fillers in a church. To twit a clerical colleague who was confronted with an unresponsive congregation, he wrote:

> I am not well pleased with the account you give of so many dry bones. It increases my wonder that you could so readily exchange so much plump flesh and blood as you had about you for a parcel of skeletons. I wish they may not haunt you, and disturb your peace. I wish these same dry bones do not prove thorns in your sides and in your eyes. You say, now you have to pray and prophesy, and wait for the four winds to come and put life into these bones.[37]

Lines from four hymns show that Newton identified with biblical preachers who attempted to bring about a revival of people who lacked spiritual vitality:

Lord, we have tried and tried again,
We find them dead, and leave them so. . . .

Where are those we counted leaders,
Filled with zeal, and love, and truth?
Old professors, tall as cedars,
Bright examples to our youth! . . .
Some, alas! we fear are blighted,
Scarce a single leaf they show. . . .

Hear, ye dry bones, the Saviour's word!
He, who when dying gasped, "Forgive!"
That gracious, sinner-loving Lord,
Says, "Look to me, dry bones, and live." . . .

---

[36]*Olney Hymns* 1:116.
[37]Newton, *Works* 1:489.

Who can describe the pain
Which faithful preachers feel,
Constrained to speak in vain,
To hearts as hard as steel!
Or who can tell the pleasures felt,
When stubborn hearts begin to melt![38]

In examining some of Newton's hymns individually, his currently best-known one is a good place to start because it sounds the dominant motif of many of his compositions:

Amazing grace! (how sweet the sound)
That saved a wretch like me!
I once was lost, but now am found,
Was blind, but now I see.

'Twas grace that taught my heart to fear,
And grace my fears relieved;
How precious did that grace appear
The hour I first believed!

Through many dangers, toils and snares,
I have already come;
'Tis grace has brought me safe thus far,
And grace will lead me home.

The Lord has promised good to me,
His word my hope secures:
He will my shield and portion be
As long as life endures.

Yes, when this flesh and heart shall fail
And mortal life shall cease,
I shall possess, within the vail,
A life of joy and peace.

The earth shall soon dissolve like snow,
The sun forbear to shine;
But God, who called me here below,
Will be forever mine.[39]

Newton indicated that "Amazing Grace" was composed after he reflected on David's prayer: "Who am I, O Lord God . . . that thou hast

---

[38]*Olney Hymns* 2:13; 2:51; 2:15; 2:26.
[39]*Olney Hymns* 1:41.

brought me hitherto? . . . And yet . . . thou . . . hast regarded me according to the estate of a man of high degree" (1 Chronicles 17:16-17). When the Jewish king was promised a dynasty that would be established forever, he was astounded that God would make a covenant with him that would have a monumental effect in salvation history. Newton saw David, like himself, as one who had been forgiven for past iniquity and had received God's gracious favor.

The parenthesis in the opening line of "Amazing Grace" emphasizes the theme just announced, and the sharp contrasts that follow disclose the cause of the initial exclamation. Those antitheses are drawn from the leading motifs of two prime gospel stories. The Gospel of Luke contains a series of parables with a lost and found theme. In the first of these a shepherd calls his friends together and says, "Rejoice with me, for I have found my sheep which was lost" (Luke 15:6). Jesus compared that scene with God's joy over the repentance of those who become aware that they are displaced in the divine scheme and who strive to return to where they belong.

Newton was also heartened by the story in John's Gospel of a person born blind who, after being healed by Jesus, testifies, "Whereas I was blind, now I see" (John 9:25). The restoration of physical sight metaphor was first made famous by Plato in a dialogue about intellectual enlightenment. In his cave allegory, Plato described "a whole nation of blind men, and one or two persons should go amongst them, and profess that they could see."[40] For Newton, the metaphor pertained to Christian enlightenment by God: "Men, by nature, are stark blind with respect to this light; by grace, the eyes of the understanding are opened." Those with restored vision would be attacked as "disturbers of the public peace" until grace transforms others into seers. The enlightenment is progressive, as with the blind man in Mark's Gospel who first saw "men as trees walking" (Mark 8:24). Newton said, "This light is like the dawn, which, though weak and faint in its first appearance, shineth more and more unto the perfect day."[41]

Stanzas of "Amazing Grace" contain not only antitheses but many monosyllables that reiterate the main theme. Of the 146 total words, 125 have a single syllable. A pilgrim's progress across a lifespan is described: grace is received for coping with memories of difficult past situations, for facing *present* hazards, and for moving into the earthly and heavenly *future*. Accordingly, Newton entitled this hymn, "Faith's Review and

---

[40]Plato, *Republic* 517.
[41]Newton, *Works* 1:167-70.

Expectation." Fifteen first-person pronouns—I, me, my, mine—are used by Newton, not to boast of the uniqueness of his experience, but, rather, to call attention to the faith journey of every Christian, from the earliest ones onward. The genius of the hymn is that its personal words bind the experience of the singer with the radical transformations of some biblical personalities and the hymnwriter. Madeleine Marshall and Janet Todd state this in another way: "Newton's best hymns proceed from his total identification of himself with his people, for whom he then stands and whom he can then instruct in the basics of the faith, placing them in a world full of providential signs."[42]

In 1769, about the same time "Amazing Grace" was composed, Newton stated what he meant by "grace":

> The grace of God has a real influence upon the whole man. It enlightens the understanding, directs the will, purifies the affection, regulates the passions, and corrects the different excesses to which different persons are by constitution or habit inclined. . . . It will dispose us to see instruction, make us open to conviction, and willing to part with our prejudices, so far and so soon as we discover them; but it will not totally and instantaneously remove them.[43]

A sense of personal unworthiness and a marveling over God's grace remained ever fresh for Newton. In 1785, his diary contains this prayer: "I . . . stand as a striking instance of the riches of Thy mercy that can pardon scarlet and crimson sins, and the power of Thy grace that can soften the hardest hearts and subdue the most inveterate habits of wickedness." That same year he wrote a friend:

> It is part of my daily employment to look back to Africa, and to retrace the path by which the Lord has led me, for about forty-seven years, since he called me from infidelity and madness. My wonderful unsought deliverance from the hopeless wickedness and misery into which I had plunged myself, taken in connexion with what he has done for me since, seem to make me say, with peculiar emphasis, "Oh to grace how great a debtor!"[44]

---

[42]Madeleine Marshall and Janet Todd, *English Congregational Hymns in the Eighteenth Century* (Lexington: University Press of Kentucky, 1982) 148.
[43]Newton, *Works* 2:309.
[44]Demaray, *The Innovation of John Newton*, 251.

The line quoted by Newton is from a hymn composed in 1758 ***NOT 1760*** by Robert Robinson, a Baptist minister and a disciple of Whitefield. Living near Olney, at Cambridge, Robinson was probably an acquaintance of Newton. The context of the line illustrates that "grace" was sometimes the leitmotif of hymns by Newton's contemporaries:

Come, Thou Fount of every blessing,
Tune my heart to sing Thy grace;
Streams of mercy, never ceasing,
Call for songs of loudest praise. . . .

O to grace how great a debtor
Daily I'm constrained to be!
Let that grace now, like a fetter,
Bind my wandering heart to Thee. . . .[45]

"Amazing Grace" has wide appeal because it affirms that no matter what one has done, God's steadfast love is always there and free for the taking. Hindmarsh writes:

That this hymn has become now nearly a folksong in many countries, suggests that Newton's capacity to universalize his own experience was indeed one of his distinctive traits as a hymnwriter. . . . To write in simple words which retain . . . scriptural resonances and the evocation of the common human condition, without simply falling into stock epithets and dead metaphors, defines a particularly demanding poetic task.[46]

Beginning in the nineteenth century, a stanza by an unknown composer has often been substituted for the original last stanzas of "Amazing Grace:"

When we've been there ten thousand years
Bright shining as the sun,
We've no less days to sing God's praise
Than when we first begun.[47]

---

[45]First four lines of stanzas 1 and 3 of Robinson's "Come, Thou Fount of Every Blessing." The hymn first appeared in *A Collection of Hymns Used by the Church of Christ in Angel Alley, Bishopgate* (1759) as four eight-line stanzas.
[46]Hindmarsh, *John Newton and the English Evangelical Tradition*, 278.
[47]This verse appears in a version of the anonymous hymn "Jerusalem, My Happy Home" in several nineteenth-century American hymnals, e.g., in *The*

The sentiments of this alternative stanza might not have been acceptable to Newton, for he followed the theology of Augustine, the preeminent church father, who taught that eternity is a timeless different dimension and therefore has no calendar measure. Also, the dazzle of creatures in the heavenly court ("bright shining . . . ") is not in accord with the humility Newton thought befitting. He associated life after death with penetrating the "vail," a now obsolete term meaning "veil," an opaque covering. Once "within the vail," the real nature of the immortal life will no longer be concealed and true joy and peace will be experienced. Newton alludes to the final vision of the Bible that portrays the "glory of God" lighting the heavenly community so that the sun is not needed.[48] The "bright shining" is therefore not due to the radiance of the redeemed.

The simple melody of "Amazing Grace," as well as its plain lyrics, help explain why it has become a favorite of millions. The hymn is now known by a plantation tune ("New Britain") that may have originated among slaves in the southern United States. The tune is based on a pentatonic scale (with interval collection corresponding to that of the black piano keys), which was common to much early American folk music. After being sung by rural folks in camp meetings, Newton's words and the New Britain melody perhaps first appeared together in James P. Carrell's *Virginia Harmony* (Harrisonburg, 1831).[49] The present version of the tune is probably to be credited to E. O. Excell, first published as number 235 in his *Make His Praise Glorious* (1900). In 1972, a bagpipe version by the Royal Scots Dragoon Guards resulted in the melody topping the charts of records sold in Britain and Australia.

Mary Rourke and Emily Gwathmey comment on the impact of the words and music of "Amazing Grace":

In 1947 gospel singer Mahalia Jackson helped move it toward anthem stature when she recorded it. Her version of the hymn was often played on the radio to comfort the country as it continued to recover from the losses of World War II. In the

---

*Baptist Songster* (1929, #38). This anonymous stanza has become, routinely, the fifth or sixth verse of "Amazing Grace" in most hymnals, at least since E. O. Excell's *Coronation Hymns* (1910) where apparently it first appeared as part of "Amazing Grace."

[48]Revelation 21:23.

[49]"Amazing Grace" has appeared with more than two dozen different tunes in the United States alone. The current tune, "New Britain," may have first appeared in Shaw and Spilman's *Columbian Harmony* at "45 on the top" in 1829.

1960s Martin Luther King, Jr. brought the hymn to greater public attention when he and his associates sang it as they led civil rights marches.[50]

In 1977, when Honoria Bailor-Caulker, chief of the Shenge district of Sierra Leone, was invited to speak to the American Anthropological Association, she surprised the academics by leading them in singing "Amazing Grace" before beginning her talk. She then pointed out that this "national hymn of the United States" was written by Newton, who had been trader in her tribal area. She explained:

> He took a lot of his merchandise from Shenge and assembled them in a slave pen on Plantain Island—just offshore from Shenge; ships would then come and take them away to America. Plantain Island was the last piece of Africa on which the slaves had stood. Today it is the first thing the Shenge people see through the church doorway on Sundays, as they turn from their prayers and leave our small church.

Caulker did not intend to place a load of guilt on white slavers who pretended to be Christian. She admitted that her family was also involved:

> Yes, the Caulkers were slavers. . . . Their territory included Plantain and Banana Islands. These islands were busy slave-trading centres, regularly visited by ships from Europe; the Caulkers grew rich and powerful on the slave trade. We bought the slaves that others brought from up-country and sold them to the ships.[51]

Two centuries passed from the time "Amazing Grace" was written until it attained stellar status. In 1950, hymnologist Albert Bailey discussed several of Newton's outstanding hymns but did not mention "Amazing Grace."[52] Also at that time, neither John Johansen, writing in the United States, nor Marcus Loane, K. L. Parry, or Albert Parsons, writing in England, include "Amazing Grace" in their lists of Newton's best-known hymns.[53] In 1951, Erik Routley commented on twenty-five of

---

[50]Mary Rourke and Emily Gwathmey, *Amazing Grace in America* (Santa Monica CA: Angel City, 1996) 112.

[51]John Reader, *Africa* (New York: Knopf, 1998) 378-79.

[52]Albert Bailey, *The Gospel in Hymns* (New York: Scribner's, 1950) 128.

[53]*Olney Hymns* 1:23; Marcus Loane, *Oxford and the Evangelical Succession* (London: Lutterworth, 1950) 113; K. L. Parry, *Companion to Congregational Praise* (London: Independent, 1953) 475; Albert Parsons, *John Newton* (London: Church

his hymns in a chapter devoted to Newton's hymns, but omitted "Amazing Grace."[54] In the first edition of the *Oxford Dictionary of Quotations* (1941), lines from some of Newton's hymns were included, but not until the third edition (1979) was "Amazing Grace" included. Also, not until its fifteenth edition (1980) was a stanza from the hymn included in Bartlett's *Familiar Quotations*.

During the past generation, "Amazing Grace" has enjoyed phenomenal popularity in mainstream America. It is sung at both happy and sad occasions, at weddings and at funerals. Television has shown world viewers the singing of "Amazing Grace" at memorial services for victims of a variety of man-made and natural disasters. The 1989 *United Methodist Hymnal*, the 1990 *Presbyterian Hymnal*, and the internet *CyberHymnal* <http://www.cyberhymnal.org> include a translation of the first stanza in five native American languages; in addition, *CyberHymnal* includes the most popular five verses in Afrikaans.

The next Newton deserving close attention is "Glorious Things of Thee Are Spoken," long recognized as his best, from both literary and theological standpoints. When sung with the stately tune "Austria," composed by Newton's contemporary Franz Haydn, it is unexcelled in hymnal quality. Routley comments: "It communicates the gaiety and toughness of Christianity. No hymn more jubilantly disposes of the legend that the Christian faith puts a premium on vagueness, ineffectiveness, otherworldliness and the accent of the stage parson."[55] A careful analysis of four of its stanzas is worthwhile:

Glorious things of thee are spoken,
Zion, city of our God!
He, whose word cannot be broken,
Formed thee for his own abode.
On the Rock of Ages founded,
What can shake thy sure repose;
With salvation's walls surrounded,
Thou mayest smile at all thy foes.

See! the streams of living waters
Springing from eternal love;
Well supply thy sons and daughters,
And all fear of want remove:
Who can faint while such a river

Book Room) 1948) 3, 16.
[54]Erik Routley, *I'll Praise My Maker* (London: Independent, 1951) 145-78.
[55]Erik Routley, *Hymns and the Faith* (London: Murray, 1955) 227.

Ever flows their thirst t'assuage?
Grace, which like the Lord, the Giver,
Never fails from age to age.

Round each habitation hov'ring,
See the cloud and fire appear!
For a glory and a cov'ring,
Showing that the Lord is near;
Thus deriving, from our banner,
Light by night and shade by day;
Safe they feed upon the manna
Which he gives them when they pray. . . .

Saviour, if of Zion's city
I through grace a member am,
Let the world deride or pity,
I will glory in Thy Name.
Fading is the worldling's pleasure,
All his boasted pomp and show;
Solid joys and lasting treasure
None but Zion's children know.[56]

As with many of Newton's hymns, "Glorious Things" is a sermon in song and is dependent upon the singer's recollection of biblical images. The hymn displays well Newton's grasp of biblical theology. Realizing that the Bible was the only book known by many in his Olney congregation, he drew exclusively from that literary source. The hymn's two opening lines are from a psalm: "The Lord loveth the gates of Zion. . . . Glorious thing are spoken of thee, O city of God" (Psalm 87:2-3). That psalm also inspired the title of Augustine's magnum opus, *The City of God*, Europe's most widely known book apart from the Bible. "Zion," an ancient name for Jerusalem and environs, became in the New Testament a designation for the ideal city of the future.[57] Lines 3 and 4 of stanza 1 are based on another psalm that declares: "The Lord hath sworn in truth unto David; he will not turn from it. . . . The Lord hath chosen Zion; he hath desired it for his habitation" (Psalm 132:11, 13). Line 5 alludes to Paul's allegorical reference to Christ as the rock struck by Moses (1 Corinthians 10:4), and calls attention to the hymn entitled "Rock of Ages" written by Augustus M. Toplady (1776), a ministerial correspondent of Newton. The next line is informed by the concluding parable of the Sermon on the Mount that tells of the wise man who "built his house

---

[56]*Olney Hymns* 1:60.
[57]Galatians 4:26; Revelation 21:2-3.

upon a rock" that withstood floods and winds (Matthew 7:24-25). The last two lines of the first stanza allude to Judeans singing, "We have a strong city; salvation will God appoint for walls" (Isaiah 26:1).

The second stanza is based on sentiments of Isaiah, who prophesied: "Look upon Zion, the city of our solemnities: thine eyes shall see Jerusalem a quiet habitation. . . . There the glorious Lord will be unto us a place of broad rivers and streams" (Isaiah 33:20-21). That stanza also alludes to the psalm that stimulated Luther to compose "A Mighty Fortress Is Our God": "There is a river, the streams whereof shall make glad the city of God," and therefore there is no reason to "fear, though the earth be removed" (Psalm 46:4, 2). As with the first stanza, Newton skillfully interwove a motif from the Hebrew Bible with a gospel theme. He alluded to Jesus' words to a Samaritan woman: "Whosoever drinketh of the water that I shall give him shall never thirst, . . . [it] shall be in him a well of water springing up into everlasting life" (John 4:14).

In the third stanza, imagery from the Israelite Exodus is used to express divine providence. Marvelous manna was supplied for food and a mysterious cloud for guidance. Newton was especially indebted to Isaiah's treatment of that Exodus motif: "The Lord will create upon every dwelling place of Mount Zion . . . a cloud and smoke by day, and the shining of a flaming fire by night" (Isaiah 4:5). In spite of the many biblical references in the hymn, the theme is so integrated that it does not appear to be a stringing together of disparate verses.

The last stanza compares Newton's former disgraceful maritime career with his present life. In one of his letters, as we have seen, Newton boasted of the exalted position he had on a slave ship. Now a middle-aged village priest with little pay or secular power, he found more of worth in his presumed citizenship in a community of his Liberator or "Saviour." He humbly accepted the shift from being sovereign to being subject.

All of Newton's best-known hymns are punctuated with the grace of God. In a subtle way it can be found in "How Sweet the Name of Jesus Sounds":

How sweet the name of Jesus sounds
In a believer's ear!
It soothes his sorrow, heals his wounds,
And drives away his fear.

It makes the wounded spirit whole
And calms the troubled breast;
'Tis manna to the hungry soul,
And to the weary, rest.

Dear name! the rock on which I build,
My shield and hiding place;
My never-failing treasury, filled
With boundless stores of grace.

By thee my prayers acceptance gain,
Although with sin defiled;
Satan accuses me in vain,
And I am owned a child.

Jesus! My Shepherd, Husband, Friend,
My Prophet, Priest, and King;
My Lord, my Life, my Way, my End,
Accept the praise I bring.

Weak is the effort of my heart,
And cold my warmest thought;
But when I see thee as thou art,
I'll praise thee as I ought.

'Till then I would thy love proclaim
With every fleeting breath;
And may the music of thy name
Refresh my soul in death.[58]

In "Amazing Grace" and "Glorious Things," so many of the biblical images were drawn from the Hebrew Bible that a rabbi might find them acceptable for synagogue singing. By contrast, "How Sweet the Name" is distinctively Christian even though it contains several Old Testament images. Newton printed over the hymn this line from the Song of Songs: "Thy name is as ointment poured forth" (Song of Songs 1:3). He assumed that the "ointment" is for healing, so the first two stanzas stress the therapeutic effects of the Jesus mantra. Two Bible verses are in the background of Newton's lines: a Psalmist who sang of God, "He healeth the broken in heart, and bindeth up their wounds" and Isaiah who assured that the Lord will "cause the weary to rest" (Psalm 147:3; Isaiah 28:12). Newton may have composed this hymn in 1776 when a large and painful tumor on his thigh was operated on successfully.[59]

Beginning with the third stanza, there is a shift to first-person intimacy. Stanza 5 gives ten biblical images for Jesus. Newton's notoriousness as a sailor for finding pleasure "in blaspheming the name and person of Jesus"[60] sets in sharp relief his emphasis here on praising that name with a variety of titles. Showing adoration to Jesus as "Husband" is the most unusual figure Newton used. He accepted the allegorical interpretation that the church has traditionally given the Song of Songs.[61] Accordingly, the Song expresses the mutual love between Jesus, the groom, and the Christian, his bride. Hymnbook editors who have found the nuptial metaphor jarring have tendentiously replaced it with "brother" or "guardian." A question by Louis Benson suggests, but does not justify, why the change has been made: "If men are to go to church at all, how can they address Christ as their husband?"[62]

To sing at the close of a worship service, Newton composed these lines:

May the grace of Christ our Saviour,
And the Father's boundless love,
With the Holy Spirit's favour,
Rest upon us from above![63]

This hymn, a paraphrase of Paul's trinitarian benediction (2 Corinthians 13:14), displays Newton's typical emphasis upon God's lovingkindness. In contrast to some of the evangelical hymns of his day, apparently aimed at frightening people into religious commitment, Newton's lyrics avoid stressing God's wrath. He told of a woman in prison who was indifferent when a preacher tried to motivate behavioral change by threats of hell but who was responsive when he spoke of God's love.[64] For Newton, love was the essence of the gospel. He exclaimed: "Great is the power of love! It makes hard things easy, and bitter sweet. . . . But this noblest principle of the soul never can exert itself with its full strength, till it is supremely fixed upon its proper object. The love of Christ has a constraining force indeed!"[65] Newton testified that he attempted to live out in his daily life what he sang, by being gentle and forgiving to everyone.

---

[60]William Barlass, *Sermons and Correspondence* (New York: Eastburn, 1818) 560.

[61]William Phipps, "The Plight of the Song of Songs," *Journal of the American Academy of Religion* (March 1974): 82-94.

[62]Louis Benson, *Studies of Familiar Hymns* (Philadelphia: Westminster, 1926) 134.

[63]*Olney Hymns* 3:101.

[64]Bernard Martin, *John Newton: A Biography* (London: Heinemann, 1950) 321.

[65]Newton, *Works* 3:197.

Stanzas from a number of other Newton hymns also sound a grace note:

Physician of my sinsick soul,
To thee I bring my case,
My raging malady control,
And heal me by thy grace. . . .

The help of men and angels joined,
Could never reach my case;
Nor can I hope relief to find,
But in thy boundless grace. . . .

Can I be the very same,
Who lately durst blaspheme thy name,
And on thy gospel tread?
Surely each one who bears my case,
Will praise thee, and confess thy grace
Invincible indeed! . . .

See the rich pastures of his grace,
Where, in full streams, salvation flows!
There he appoints our resting place,
And we may feed, secure from foes.

There, 'midst the flock, the Shepherd dwells,
The sheep around in safety lie;
The wolf, in vain, with malice swells,
For he protects them with his eye. . . .

Though once a man of grief and shame,
Yet now he fills a throne,
And bears the greatest, sweetest name,
That earth or heaven have known.

Grace flies before, and love attends
His steps wherever he goes;
Though none can see him but his friends,
And they were once his foes. . . .

Grace tills the soil, and sows the seeds,
Provides the sun and rain;
Till from the tender blade proceeds
The ripened harvest grain.
'Twas grace that called our souls at first;
By grace thus far we're come:
And grace will help us through the worst,
And lead us safely home. . . .

Joy is a fruit that will not grow
In nature's barren soil;
All we can boast till Christ we know,
Is vanity and toil.

But where the Lord has planted grace,
And made his glories known
There fruits of heavenly joy and peace
Are found, and there alone.[66]

Stanzas from some of Newton's other hymns also deserve notice:

Approach, my soul, the mercy seat,
Where Jesus answers prayer;
There humbly fall before his feet,
For none can perish there. . . .

Oh wondrous love! to bleed and die,
To bear the cross and shame,
That guilty sinners, such as I,
Might plead thy gracious name. . . .

How bitter that cup,
No heart can conceive,
Which he drank quite up,
That sinners might live!
His way was much rougher,
And darker than mine;
Did Jesus thus suffer,
And shall I repine?

Since all that I meet
Shall work for my good,
The bitter is sweet,
And the med'cine is food;
Though painful at present,
Will cease before long,
And then, oh how pleasant!
The conqueror's song! . . .

By various maxims, forms and rules,
That pass for wisdom in the schools,
I strove my passion to restrain;
But all my efforts proved in vain.

---

[66]*Olney Hymns* 1:83; 1:115; 1:121; 2:94; 3:13; 3:86; 1:42.

But since the Saviour I have known,
My rules are all reduced to one;
To keep my Lord, by faith, in view,
This strength supplies, and motives too.

I see him lead a suffering life,
Patient, amidst reproach and strife;
And from his pattern courage take
To bear, and suffer, for his sake.[67]

In his hymn "Jacob's Ladder," Newton relates to incarnational theology a Hebrew patriarch's dream of mediating angels:

Well does Jacob's ladder suit
To the gospel throne of grace;
We are at the ladder's foot,
Every hour, in every place.
By assuming flesh and blood,
Jesus heaven and earth unites;
We, by faith, ascend to God,
God to dwell with us delights.[68]

That hymn alludes to the encouragement Christians are given in the New Testament to "come boldly unto the throne of grace" (Hebrews 4:16). Also contained in the hymn are two images from the opening chapter of John's Gospel, one being the declaration that "the Word was made flesh, and dwelt among us (and we beheld his glory)" (John 1:14). The other image is of Jesus connecting heaven and earth: "Ye shall see heaven open, and the angels ascending and descending upon the Son of man" (John 1:51).

Seasonal hymns were given some attention by Newton. To celebrate the autumn harvest he wrote a hymn with this opening stanza:

See! the corn again in ear!
How the fields and valleys smile!
Harvest now is drawing near
To repay the farmer's toil.
Gracious Lord, secure the crop,
Satisfy the poor with food;
In thy mercy is our hope,

---

[67]*Olney Hymns* 3:12; 3:37; 1:134.
[68]*Olney Hymns* 1:9.

We have sinned, but thou art good.[69]

Newton composed an Advent hymn in which he marveled at the meaning of Emmanuel, "God with us":

Sweeter sounds than music knows
Charm me, in Emmanuel's name;
All her hopes my spirit owes
To his birth, and cross, and shame.

When he came the angels sang
"Glory be to God on high!"
Lord, unloose my stammering tongue,
Who should louder sing than I?[70]

Newton wrote thirty hymns to commemorate the new year, from which this sample comes:

Bless, O Lord, the op'ning year,
To each soul assembled here;
Clothe thy word with power divine,
Make us willing to be thine. . . .

Where thou hast thy work begun,
Give new strength the race to run;
Scatter darkness, doubts and fears,
Wipe away the mourner's tears.[71]

One hymn, probably the earliest in the collection, was composed by Newton when he was writing his autobiography before going to Olney.[72] It alludes to his involvement in the *Greyhound* disaster:

Tis past—the dreadful stormy night
Is gone, with all its fears;
And now I see returning light,
The Lord, my Sun, appears.[73]

Newton's nautical background also helps explain why he composed lyrics on "Paul's Voyage" and "The Disciples at Sea." His experiences of

---

[69]*Olney Hymns* 2:36.

[70]*Olney Hymns* 2:37.

[71]*Olney Hymns* 2:9.

[72]It can be found in a July 1763 letter to Haweis that is now part of the Newton collection at the Firestone Library in Princeton.

[73]*Olney Hymns* 3:21.

oceanic shifts between the tranquil and the terrifying enabled him to allegorize effectively in these hymns:

> If, for a time, the air be calm,
> Serene and smooth the sea appears,
> And shows no danger to alarm
> The unexperienced landsman's fears.
>
> But if the tempest once arise,
> The faithless water swells and raves.
> Its billows, foaming to the skies,
> Disclose a thousand threatening graves. . . .
>
> As some tall rock amidst the waves
> The fury of the tempest braves,
> While the fierce billows, tossing high,
> Break at its foot, and, murm'ring die.
>
> Thus, they who in the Lord confide,
> Though foes assault on every side,
> Cannot be moved or overthrown,
> For Jesus makes their cause his own. . . .
>
> The storm increased on every side,
> I felt my spirit shrink.
> And soon, with Peter, loud I cried,
> "Lord, save me, or I sink."[74]

In June 1775, Newton called a special prayer meeting after receiving news of armed clashes in the area of Concord, Massachusetts, that resulted in numerous British soldiers and colonists being killed.[75] He lamented: "Poor New England! once the glory of the earth, now likely to be visited with fire and sword. . . . Their sins as a people are not to be compared with ours."[76] He composed at that time a hymn entitled "On the Commencement of Hostilities in America." In one stanza he expressed his fear that the conflict might erupt into a civil war among kinfolks:

> Already is the plague begun,
> And, fired with hostile rage,
> Brethren, by blood and interest one,

---

[74]*Olney Hymns* 2:87; 1:120; 1:87.
[75]Newton, "Diary" 2:9.
[76]Newton, *Works* 1:495.

With brethren now engage.[77]

On the theme of acceptable and unacceptable political or religious ardor, Newton penned:

Zeal is that pure and heavenly flame
The fire of love supplies;
While that which often bears the name,
Is self, in a disguise.

True zeal is merciful and mild,
Can pity and forbear;
The false is headstrong, fierce, and wild,
And breathes revenge and war. . . .

Dear Lord, the idol, self, dethrone,
And from our hearts remove;
And let no zeal by us be shown,
But that which springs from love.[78]

Newton had personal interest in the War of Independence because his half-brother, Harry, was serving with the Royal Navy at Boston.[79] After a 1776 British defeat in the Massachusetts colony, he wrote another Englishman: "I am not a politician, much less an American; but I fear the Lord has a controversy with us. I cannot but tremble at the consequences of our present disputes."[80] In December 1777, Newton prayed: "Thou, King of Nations, art doing Thy pleasure with regard to America and I fear Thy hand is lifted up against this sinful nation. There was a short exultation lately for General Howe's victory, but soon denied by the news of Burgoyne's surrender with his army [at Saratoga, New York]."[81]

Although Newton sympathized with the protests of the colonists, he did not think it right for either side to take up arms. "The slaughter of thousands, whether called Britons or Americans, is awful," he opined.[82] He was uneasy that some questioned his patriotism inasmuch as Lord Dartmouth was serving at the beginning of the hostilities as the secretary of state for the American colonies. He wrote his patron to assure him that

---

[77]*Olney Hymns* 2:64.
[78]*Olney Hymns* 3:70.
[79]Martin, *John Newton*, 264.
[80]Newton, *Works* 4:372.
[81]Newton, "Diary" 2:198.
[82]Martin, *John Newton*, 266.

he had remained loyal to the British government.[83] As the war continued, Newton was chagrined that "more millions must be spent and more blood spilt before we can submit to give up attempting what in my view is now becoming not only improbable but impossible."[84] In his diary, he jotted: "America gone—surely Thou hast a controversy with this sinful land [of England]."[85] In a 1778 hymn, he portrayed the war as a vampire "spreading desolation . . . through a once much favoured land":

> War, with heart and arms of steel,
> Preys on thousands at a meal;
> Daily drinking human gore,
> Still he thirsts and calls for more.[86]

In the midst of that grim war, the Cherry Fair in Olney was a light occasion at which a caged lion was a main attraction. William Cowper found its royal appearance magnificent, and wrote about it to William Unwin:

> A lion was imported here at the fair, seventy years of age, and was as tame as a goose. Your mother and I saw him embrace his keeper with his paws and lick his face. Others saw him receive his head in his mouth, and restore it to him again unhurt, . . . a practice hardly reconcilable to prudence unless he had a head to spare.[87]

Newton told how that local spectacle prompted him to introspection:

> Last week we had a lion in town; I went to see him. He was wonderfully tame, as familiar with his keeper, as docile and obedient as a spaniel. Yet the man told me he had his surly fits, when they durst not touch him. No looking glass could express my face more justly than this lion did my heart. I could trace every feature. As wild and fierce by nature, yea, much more so; but grace has, in some measure, tamed me. I know and love my Keeper, and sometimes watch his looks, that I may learn his will. But, oh! I have my surly fits too; seasons when I relapse into the

---

[83]Hindmarsh, 202.
[84]Martin, *John Newton*, 294.
[85]Newton, "Diary" 2:232.
[86]*Olney Hymns* 2:5.
[87]Robert Southey, ed. *The Life and Works of William Cowper* (London: Bohn, 1854) 2:228.

savage again as though I had forgotten all. I got a hymn out of this lion.[88]

This is the lyric that came out of that experience:

A lion, though by nature wild,
The art of man can tame;
He stands before his keeper, mild
And gentle as a lamb. . . .

But man himself, who thus subdues
The fiercest beasts of prey;
A nature more unfeeling shows,
And far more fierce than they.

Though by the Lord preserved and fed,
He proves rebellious still;
And while he eats his Maker's bread,
Resists his holy will. . . .

Yet we are but renewed in part,
The lion still remains;
Lord, drive him wholly from my heart,
Or keep him fast in chains.[89]

The lion hymn must have delighted as well as inspired members of the Olney congregation who had also been fascinated with the visiting lion. Isaiah had also associated the transformation of leonine traits with characteristics of the peaceful messianic kingdom (Isaiah 11:6). Newton's diary indicates that he felt that he was far away from that ideal era: "I find not one corruption of my vile heart is dead, though some seem now and then asleep."[90]

Newton is appropriately called a "parson" because he was the person at the center of Olney life. The songs sung and the words spoken in his church provided a mixture of entertainment and worship for the village. Hymn singing was one of the few pleasures of those underprivileged folks. To enable them to identify with gospel episodes, Newton was especially interested in composing hymns like this:

Encouraged by thy word

---

[88]Newton, *Works* 1:596.
[89]*Olney Hymns* 2:93.
[90]Martin, *John Newton*, 265.

Of promise to the poor,
Behold a beggar, Lord,
Waits at thy mercy's door!
No hand, no heart, O Lord, but thine,
Can help or pity wants like mine.[91]

Again, in a hymn entitled "The Good Samaritan," Newton compared the experiences of a Bible character to those of a singer in desperate straits:

Oh! I remember well the day,
When sorely wounded, nearly slain,
Like that poor man I bleeding lay,
And groaned for help, but groaned in vain.

Men saw me in this helpless case,
And passed, without compassion, by;
Each neighbour turned away his face,
Unmoved by my mournful cry.[92]

Newton's use of horticultural metaphors was in sync with the English nature poets of his era. In one hymn, the convert is a seed "planted by God's own hand"; rather inelegantly, the "under gardener" adds "fresh manure," meaning pulpit admonitions, to produce "fruits of grace."[93] The garden images continue:

Honey though the bee prepares,
An envenomed sting he wears;
Piercing thorns a guard compose
Round the fragrant, blooming rose. . . .

Yet, through the Redeemer's love,
These afflictions blessings prove;
He the wounding stings and thorns
Into healing medicines turns.[94]

From his Olney experiences, Newton encapsulated songs of lamentation as well as of joy. In 1777, a blazing fire destroyed some cottages and could have devastated the whole town had not the wind direction changed. Out of that trauma, Newton enabled his community to sing:

---

[91]*Olney Hymns* 1:81.
[92]*Olney Hymns* 1:99.
[93]*Olney Hymns* 1:103.
[94]*Olney Hymns* 1:56.

Wearied by day with toils and cares,
How welcome is the peaceful night!
Sweet sleep our wasted strength repairs,
And fits us for returning light.

Yet when our eyes in sleep are closed,
Our rest may break ere well begun;
To dangers ev'ry hour exposed
We neither can forsee or shun. . . .

The shout of "fire!", a dreadful cry,
Impressed each heart with deep dismay;
While the fierce blaze and red'ning sky,
Made midnight wear the face of day.

The throng and terror who can speak?
The various sounds that filled the air!
The infant's wail, the mother's shriek,
The voice of blasphemy and prayer!

But prayer prevailed, and saved the town;
The few, who loved the Saviour's name,
Were heard, and mercy hasted down
To change the wind, and stop the flame.[95]

Marshall and Todd tell of the place of Newton's compositions in the history of Protestantism:

> Newton's excellences hinted at a new age of hymnology. Both his charitable interest in common human affairs and his integrating vision of the providential meaning of life implied the irrelevance of that dualism which splits the realms of spirit and flesh. . . . The features of his best hymns suggest a new appreciation of life in this world as life in the Spirit. This integration signaled both a return to an earlier day of belief, unchallenged by the secular Enlightenment, particularly to the dynamic Calvinism of the Puritans, and the transition to a new era in which common humanity would be idealized and the visionary would appreciate history.[96]

---

[95]*Olney Hymns* 2:69.
[96]Marshall and Todd, *English Congregational Hymns in the Eighteenth Century*, 117.

### Cowper's Collaboration

Germane to an understanding of Newton's musical contribution is an awareness of William Cowper's (1731–1800) difficult life and a discussion of some of his hymns. Cowper's early life was similar to that of Newton, for his adored mother died when he was six and his distant father dispatched him to boarding school, where he had a miserable experience. Later Cowper fell in love with a young woman, but her father did not approve of a marriage. Following that disappointment, Cowper had difficulty becoming certified in a profession.

Soon after being asked to defend his qualifications to become a lawyer, Cowper suffered from a mental breakdown. He did not succeed in his clumsy attempts to kill himself by poison, knife, and rope. After being in an asylum for eighteen months, Morley and Mary Unwin, who lived in Huntingdon, took him in as a paying guest. When Newton paid a consolation visit to Mary after her clergy husband was killed by falling off a horse, he became acquainted with Cowper. On learning that Mary Unwin and Cowper were planning to relocate, Newton recommended Olney. Attracted more by the thought of being near the Newtons than by the town, Cowper and his caregiver lived in the Olney vicarage for several months after their 1767 move. Then they settled in a house by the market square (now the Cowper-Newton Museum) that was separated from the vicarage by an orchard behind their gardens. In order to have a backyard shortcut to facilitate frequent visits, they paid a guinea annually for permission to cross what they called the "Guinea Field."

Binns comments on the chemistry between Newton and Cowper:

> What could they have in common, the virile ex-sea captain and the delicate, nervous ex-lawyer, the self-taught curate and the refined scholar and man of exquisite taste? In actual fact they had many things in common, and not least that enduring bond, a strong sense of humour. That Cowper should learn of a man of Newton's immense strength of character, when once he had given him his confidence, seems natural enough; but the relationship between them was by no means one-sided, for Cowper's mind when unclouded by disease was strong and vigorous. Newton, for his part, though seemingly rough and uncouth, was tender and sympathetic at heart; he had, too, an intense love of classical literature, which though it was self-acquired, went

deeper than that of many professed scholars. But the closest link between them was their similar outlook in religion.[97]

Mental healing continued as Newton's friendship with Cowper developed. In his epic poem entitled *The Task*, written two decades later (1783–1785), he told about the grace of Christ that Newton communicated:

> I was a stricken deer that left the herd
> Long since; with many an arrow deep infix'd.
> My panting side was charged, when I withdrew,
> To seek a tranquil death in distant shades.
> There was I found by One who had Himself
> Been hurt by the archers. In his side he bore,
> And in his hands and feet, the cruel scars.
> With gentle force soliciting the darts
> He drew them forth, and healed and bade me live.[98]

As congeniality developed, Cowper became Newton's unofficial lay assistant in the Olney parish. It was therapeutic for him to accompany the pastor as he made his rounds to visit the sick and distribute alms. Newton told of the respect the simple people gave to the one they called "Sir Cowper":

> He was soon known in many places, and everywhere admired by competent judges as a gentleman and a scholar. He was a great blessing to the Lord's poor and afflicted people at Olney in the still higher and more important character of an eminent and exemplary Christian. For he had drunk deeply into the spirit of his Lord; he loved the poor, often visited them in their cottages, . . . counselled and comforted them in their distresses, and those seriously disposed were often cheered and animated by his prayers.[99]

Not long after Cowper came to Olney, Newton conceived of a joint hymn-writing project that would serve their church while helping Cowper gain more mental stability. Newton was already familiar with these stanzas of a hymn that Cowper had composed before they met:

Thro' all the storms that veil the skies

---

[97]Binns, *The Early Evangelicals*, 262.
[98]Southey, *The Life and Works of William Cowper* 6:54.
[99]Bull, comp., *John Newton*, 189.

And frown on earthly things;
The Sun of Righteousness he eyes
With healing in His wings.

Struck by that light, the human heart,
A barren soil no more,
Sends the sweet smell of grace abroad,
Where serpents lurked before.[100]

Recognizing Cowper's poetic gifts, Newton encouraged him to
express more of his evangelical thought in lyrics, and they stimulated one
another. Demaray says of the synergism between these men that

> It is often pointed out that Newton, by enlisting Cowper to help
> him write the Olney hymns, started Cowper on the road to fame.
> Seldom, however, is it observed that Cowper exercised an
> influence on Newton's hymns. . . . Newton says, "Mr. Cowper
> . . . is a better judge [of poetry] than myself."[101]

Simplicity of style was Cowper's most significant contribution to
Newton's hymnody, according to Demaray.[102] Newton virtually ceased
writing hymns after separating from Cowper and Olney.

In one of the first hymns Cowper composed, he lifted an image from
the verse, "Enoch walked with God" (Genesis 5:24), to convey his
desperate quest for companionship and serenity:

Oh! for a closer walk with God,
A calm and heavenly frame;
A light to shine upon the road
That leads me to the Lamb! . . .

The dearest idol I have known,
Whate'er that idol be,
Help me to tear it from thy throne,
And worship only thee.[103]

Cowper's iconoclastic stanza probably resulted from his affection for
Mary Unwin, who was extremely ill in 1767 when he composed it. He
then called her his "chief blessing" and hoped that her critical condition

---

[100]*Olney Hymns* 3:44.
[101]Demaray, *The Innovation of John Newton*, 217.
[102]Demaray, *The Innovation of John Newton*, 221.
[103]*Olney Hymns* 1:3.

would improve his religion: "Oh that it may have a sanctified effect, that I may rejoice to surrender up to the Lord my dearest comforts."[104] The stanza may also have been influenced by Newton, who was long obsessed with a dread that his spousal adoration was excessive. Cowper may have read some of Newton's letters to Mary, for Newton had no objection to her seeing them. Overtones of Cowper's stanza can be detected in this love letter of Newton: "There was a time (what a mercy that the Lord did not tear my idol from me!) when you had that place in my heart which is only due to Him, and I regarded you as my chief good."[105]

The happiest of Cowper's hymns is entitled "Joy and Peace in Believing." The first stanza is a statement of trust in God who provides therapy to the sufferer. The last stanza of the picturesque lyric is based on Habakkuk 3:17-18, where confidence is expressed in God's salvation in spite of natural calamity:

Sometimes a light surprises
The Christian while he sings;
It is the Lord, who rises
With healing in his wings.
When comforts are declining,
He grants the soul, again,
A season of clear shining,
To cheer it after rain. . . .

Though vine nor fig tree neither
Their wonted fruit shall bear,
Though all the fields should wither,
Nor flocks nor herds be there;
Yet God the same abiding,
His praise shall tune my voice;
For while in him confiding,
I cannot but rejoice.[106]

One of Cowper's hymns has been offensive to many, though popular with fundamentalists. Crude images are concentrated in the first stanza:

There is a fountain filled with blood
Drawn from Immanuel's veins;

---

[104]James King, ed., *The Letter and Prose Writings of William Cowper* (Oxford: Clarendon, 1979) 1:186.
[105]Newton, *Works* 4:115.
[106]*Olney Hymns* 3:48.

And sinners plunged beneath that flood,
Lose all their guilty stains.[107]

The hymn pictures a wrathful God who has been placated by Jesus, the sacrificial victim. By this means, offending humans can be washed in his blood and cleansed. Ostensibly, this stanza combines texts from the two parts of the Bible. A Hebrew prophet tells of a coming day of purification when "there shall be a fountain opened to the house of David and to the inhabitants of Jerusalem for sin and for uncleanness" (Zechariah 13:1). Subsequently, a Christian seer tells of saints who have "washed their robes, and made them white in the blood of the Lamb" (Revelation 7:14). Overtones of an ancient pagan Roman ritual can also be detected in the imagery: initiates who gathered in a pit became immortal by being drenched by the blood of a bull that was being slaughtered on a platform overhead. The human pollutedness reflected in the hymn may display Cowper's unhealthy self-abasement, and he may have been in the twilight of lucidness when he composed this hymn.

By comparison, without using grotesque images, Newton powerfully affirmed the sacrifice of Jesus in a hymn. He alluded to his own experience:

In evil long I took delight,
Unawed by shame or fear,
Till a new object struck my sight,
And stopped my wild career.

I saw one hanging on a tree
In agonies and blood,
Who fixed his languid eyes on me,
As near his cross I stood.

Sure, never till my latest breath
Can I forget that look;
It seemed to charge me with his death,
Though not a word he spoke. . . .

Thus, while his death my sin displays
In all its blackest hue;
(Such is the mystery of grace,)
It seals my pardon too.

With pleasing grief and mournful joy
My spirit now is filled,

---

[107]*Olney Hymns* 1:79.

That I should such a life destroy,
Yet live by him I killed.[108]

Newton's theme is similar to that of the African-American spiritual, "Were You There When They Crucified My Lord?" In his *Ecclesiastical History*, Newton commented that when Christians contemplate that greatest travesty of justice they commonly "condemn the treachery of Judas, the cowardice of Pilate, the blindness of the people, and the malice of the priests." Many who blame those persons surrounding Jesus flatter themselves by thinking: "If we had seen his works and heard his words, we would not have joined with the multitude in crying, 'Crucify him.' " Newton doubted if those who pride themselves on their superior virtue would have been less perverse than Jesus' contemporaries.[109]

Another Cowper hymn dealing with Jesus' sacrificial life tells how he provides a model of steadfastness that can reduce complaints of his followers:

Lord, who hast suffered all for me,
My peace and pardon to procure,
The lighter cross I bear for thee,
Help me with patience to endure. . . .

Let me not angrily declare
No pain was ever sharp like mine;
Nor murmur at the cross I bear,
But rather weep, remembering thine.[110]

When Cowper composed his best-known hymn—"God Moves in a Mysterious Way"—he may have had in mind Newton's story of God saving his life during a storm at sea. Newton entitled what was probably Cowper's last hymn, "Conflict: Light Shining out of Darkness":

God moves in a mysterious way,
His wonders to perform;
He plants his footsteps in the sea,
And rides upon the storm. . . .

Ye fearful saints, fresh courage take,
The clouds ye so much dread

---

[108]*Olney Hymns* 2:57.
[109]Newton, *Works* 2:292.
[110]*Olney Hymns* 3:28.

Are big with mercy, and shall break
In blessings on your head.

Judge not the Lord by feeble sense,
But trust him for his grace;
Behind a frowning providence
He hides a smiling face.[111]

This hymn ponders the perplexity of the way in which God's sovereign will is expressed. The images drawn from the Hebrew scriptures picture the Israelite God outdoing the storm-god Baal in riding upon the clouds with majesty (2 Samuel 22:7020). Cowper's theme is this: be brave, because God can use seeming disasters for a good purpose. Bailey comments on the hymn: "Poetry and an attitude of faith can make even Calvinism comforting!"[112] Johansen provides an unverified story pertaining to the hymn:

During an especially grievous visitation of his mental distress Cowper gave his coachman orders to drive to the River Ouse. The night was dark, and the driver missed his way either by accident or on purpose; and Cowper found himself back at his own house. By that time the cloud had lifted from his mind, and he celebrated the Providence of God in this hymn.[113]

Cowper's mental turmoil is also well expressed in this composition:

The billows swell, the winds are high,
Clouds overcast my wintry sky;
Out of the depths to thee I call,
My fears are great, my strength is small. . . .

Though tempest-tossed, and half a wreck,
My Saviour through the floods I seek;
Let neither winds nor stormy main
Force back my shattered bark again.[114]

Newton had encouraged Cowper and Mary Unwin to wed: "They were congenial spirits, united in the faith and hope of the gospel, and

---

[111]*Olney Hymns* 3:15.
[112]Bailey, *The Gospel in Hymns*, 133.
[113]John Johansen, *The Olney Hymns* (Springfield OH: Hymn Society of America, 1956) 18.
[114]*Olney Hymns* 3:18.

their intimate and growing friendship led them in the course of four or five years to an engagement for marriage . . . but was prevented by the terrible malady which seized him."[115] Newton was referring to Cowper's paranoia of 1773, when he believed Mary had poisoned his food. He fled to the vicarage and Newton permitted him to live there, along with Mary, for fifteen months.[116]

At that time the suicidal condition returned that Cowper had confronted before coming to Olney. It may have been triggered by the last of a series of bereavements in Cowper's family. In addition to his father and five siblings who had died earlier, he now lost his beloved brother John. Newton wrote a hymn, perhaps at this time, that paraphrases assurances from the Hebrew Bible, especially as recorded in Isaiah 54:4-11:

Fear thou not, nor be ashamed,
All thy sorrows soon shall end:
I who heaven and earth have framed
Am thy husband and thy friend:
I the High and Holy One,
Israel's God, by all adored,
As thy Saviour will be known,
Thy Redeemer and thy Lord. . . .

When my peaceful bow appears,
Painted on the wat'ry cloud;
'Tis to dissipate thy fears,
Lest the earth should be o'erflowed:
'Tis an emblem too of grace,
Of my cov'nant love a sign:
Though the mountains leave their place,
Thou shalt be forever mine.

Though afflicted, tempest-tossed,
Comfortless awhile thou art,
Do not think thou canst be lost,
Thou art graven on my heart:
All thy wastes I will repair,
Thou shalt be rebuilt anew;
And in thee it shall appear
What a God of love can do.[117]

---

[115]Bull, comp., *John Newton*, 192.
[116]James King, *William Cowper* (Durham NC: Duke University Press, 1986) 88.
[117]*Olney Hymns* 1:63.

The Newtons' compassion was unusual, for "lunatics" were then generally shunned and treated with scornful laughter and confinement in a "madhouse." Newton's diary shows that for week after week in 1773 he was unable to get much accomplished other than providing care for Cowper. Affection and lack of rigidity from the Newtons helped Cowper recover his sanity and enter into his most productive period as a poet even though he did not continue on the joint hymn-writing project. David Jeffrey writes:

> Cowper notably represents Newton's patient nurturing of a person who was emotionally unstable to a degree that might have caused his complete destruction in less gentle hands, and for whom a lesser pastor would probably not have found time. . . . But out of his emotional fragility—in which he was sometimes up, sometimes down to the very abyss of despair—came a fine flowering of poetry and hymns of faith, and when we look at these in the light of his broken life we see how he is, as much as his pastor Newton, a trophy of "amazing grace." Against every probability, he became England's most celebrated poet in the latter years of his life.[118]

From the time Cowper came to live in Olney, three years after Newton had arrived there, they were constant companions. Newton paid him this tribute:

> In humility, simplicity, and devotedness to God, in the clearness of his views of evangelical truth . . . and the uniform and beautiful example by which he adorned them, I thought he had but few equals. He was eminently a blessing both to me and my people by his advice, his conduct, and his prayers. The Lord who had brought us together so knit our hearts and affections, that for nearly twelve years we were seldom separated for twelve hours at a time, when we were awake and at home. The first six I passed in daily admiring and trying to imitate him; during the second six I walked pensively with him in the valley of the shadow of death.[119]

Newton had assumed Cowper was going to have a larger share in contributing to the hymnbook but he was prevented "by a long and

---

[118]Jeffrey, ed., *A Burning and a Shining Light*, 36.
[119]Bull, comp., *John Newton*, 158.

affecting indisposition" that began in 1773. To express his disappointment over this situation, Newton borrowed the lament of a psalmist in Babylonian captivity who was not in a singing mood (Psalm 137). Although Newton actually played no musical instrument, he said, "I hung my harp upon the willows."[120] After coping with this setback and feeling that "the Saviour" had reenergized him, Newton wrote this dialogue hymn:

> My harp untuned and laid aside,
> (To cheerful hours the harp belongs,)
> My cruel foes, insulting, cried,
> "Come, sing us one of Zion's songs." . . .
>
> "Though for a time I hide my face,
> Rely upon my love and power;
> Still wrestle at a throne of grace,
> And wait for a reviving hour.
>
> "Take down thy long neglected harp,
> I've seen thy tears, and heard thy prayer;
> The winter season has been sharp,
> But spring shall all its wastes repair."
>
> Lord, I obey; my hopes revive;
> Come, join with me, ye saints, and sing;
> Our foes in vain against us strive,
> For God will help and healing bring.[121]

On his own, Newton then decided to go ahead and organize for publication Cowper's 68 compositions along with 280 of his own. Newton was overly prolific, some of his poems being little more than platitudinous doggerel. In writing Mrs. Thornton, he excused the stylistic infelicities of his hymns: "They were composed for the use of a very plain people. My poor folks at Olney are simple and devout, but they know little of the meaning of the word taste."[122]

In his preface to the hymn collection, Newton stated that one reason for the publication was to promote "the faith and comfort of sincere Christians." His main interest was not to convert outsiders but to assist Christians in expressing their beliefs. Alluding to Cowper, he stated that his other reason was "to perpetuate the remembrance of an intimate and

---

[120]Newton, *Works* 2:463.

[121]*Olney Hymns* 2:52.

[122]Demaray, *The Innovation of John Newton*, 238, 244.

endeared friendship."[123] Each lyric Cowper contributed was identified by the letter "C," and his fame began after *Olney Hymns* was issued in 1779.

When Newton completed his years as pastor in Olney, Cowper and Mary Unwin remained there. Forlorn Cowper wrote this poem, entitled "To the Rev. Mr. Newton":

> That ocean you have late surveyed,
> Those rocks I too have seen;
> But I, afflicted and dismayed,
> You tranquil and serene.
>
> You from the flood-controlling steep
> Saw stretched before your view,
> With conscious joy, the threatening deep,
> No longer such to you.
>
> To me, the waves that ceaseless broke
> Upon the dangerous coast,
> Hoarsely and ominously spoke
> Of all my treasure lost.
>
> Your sea of troubles you have past,
> And found the peaceful shore;
> I, tempest-tossed and wretched at last,
> Come home to port no more.[124]

Newton's satisfaction with what he had contributed to the hymnal is displayed in this comment: "The hymns, . . . taken altogether, contain a full declaration of my religious sentiments."[125] Its publication came as a fitting end to his ministry in Buckinghamshire and he appropriately dedicated it to his "dear friends in the parish and neighbourhood of Olney, for whose use the hymns were originally composed." However, Newton intended that the hymns be used more widely than in his and in other Anglican congregations. Rising above sectarianism, he struck an ecumenical note in his preface: "As the workings of the heart of man, and of the Spirit of God, are in general the same, in all who are the subjects of grace, I hope most of these hymns, being the fruit and expression of my own experience, will coincide with the views of real Christians of all denominations."[126]

---

[123]Newton, *Works* 2:463.
[124]Southey, *The Life and Works of William Cowper* 6:199.
[125]Newton, *Works* 3:466.
[126]Newton, *Works* 2:464.

Thornton, who had encouraged Newton to gather up his hymn compositions, launched their publication by underwriting the first thousand copies of *Olney Hymns*. The collection was divided into sections with the longest one consisting of hymns written on sermon texts, arranged by biblical books. By drawing imagery from most of the books of the Bible, Newton displayed its centrality in his thought. Approximately half of his total compositions were based on scriptural texts. A few of these hymns, as we have noted, have become accepted as among the best loved of all religious songs, in large part because of their scriptural quality. Other sections of the hymnbook were organized around themes such as praise to God, comfort amid conflict, and seasons of the year. Leigh Bennett aptly attributes the lasting influence of the Newton hymns to a mixture of his "rich acquaintance with Scripture, knowledge of the heart, directness and force, and a certain sailor imagination."[127]

During the century after Newton's collection was first published, hundreds of thousands of copies were distributed both inside and outside the Anglican communion. Sung in informal settings, the hymns provided a corrective in the Church of England, where veneration for dignity tended to depreciate warmth of expression. Louis Benson says of the hymnbook: "It was the Evangelical theology put into rhyme for singing, but even more for reading and remembering. It became an Evangelical handbook, printed over and over in England and America, and it exerted an immense influence."[128] The Wesley family appreciation of the Olney hymnwriter was manifested when Newton served as one of Charles Wesley's pallbearers.

A half-century after *Olney Hymns* was first published, James Montgomery, the renowned Scottish hymnist, wrote: "The collection has become a standard-book . . . of every evangelical denomination. . . . Newton was a poet of very humble order, yet he has produced . . . proofs of great versatility in exercising the one talent of this kind entrusted to him."[129] Roman Catholic hymnist Frederick Faber wrote in 1849 of the strong hold the Olney collection had even over members of his church. He described its charm in this way:

> Less than moderate literary excellence, a very tame versification, indeed often the simple recurrence of a rhyme is sufficient; the

---

[127]John Julian, ed., *Dictionary of Hymnology* (New York: Scribner's, 1892) 803.
[128]Louis Benson, *Studies of Familiar Hymns* (Philadelphia: Westminster, 1926) 135.
[129]James Montgomery, *Olney Hymns* (Glasgow: Collins, 1829) xxix, xliii.

spell seems to lie in that. Catholics are not unfrequently found poring with a devout and unsuspecting delight over the verses of the Olney Hymns.[130]

Hymnologist David Music writes that "the 'golden age'—one of the most productive and significant periods in British hymnwriting—may be said to have reached its zenith when *Olney Hymns* were published."[131] Olney became known and continues to be known internationally mainly by the two hymnwriters who lived there—Newton and Cowper. Some of the hymns were translated into Gaelic, Latin, German, and Italian.[132] Memorized by the young, these hymns continue to serve many Christians as they cope with the challenges of life.

---

[130]Frederick Faber, *Jesus and Mary: or, Catholic Hymns* (London: Burns, 1849) xii.

[131]Kristen Forman, *The New Century Hymnal Companion* (Cleveland OH: Pilgrim Press, 1998) 98.

[132]Demaray, *The Innovation of John Newton*, 272.

# 5

## Now I See

### The St. Mary Woonoth Rector

"I am about to form a connection for life with one Mary Woolnoth, a reputed London saint in Lombard Street," Newton wittily wrote a friend in regard to his decision to change pastorates. "To wed Molly is in some respects pleasing, but then to be divorced from Olney will be in many respects painful."[1] After fifteen years as a town parson at Olney, Newton became rector of a church in the center of London's financial district. Architect Nicholas Hawkemoor directed its construction after the great fire of London, and it is still described as "very sumptuous."[2]

Newton's ministerial career, starting in Olney and ending in London, illustrates the spread of the evangelical movement, first among the poorer and less educated folk and then among the wealthier and more educated. Although there were only 142 houses in the London parish of less than one square mile, it was distinguished by having the lord mayor and other prominent citizens as parishioners. An evangelical could not have asked for a more prestigious and influential post. Newton's personal economic concerns became a thing of the past because he now received several times his Olney salary.

Somewhat overwhelmed by the significance of his new position, Newton reflected:

> That one of the most ignorant, the most miserable, and the most abandoned of slaves should be plucked from his forlorn state of exile on the coast of Africa, and at length be appointed minister of the parish of the first magistrate of the first city in the world . . . is a fact I can contemplate with admiration, but never sufficiently estimate.[3]

---

[1]Josiah Bull, compiler, *John Newton of Olney and St. Mary Woolnoth: An Autobiography and Narrative*, compiled chiefly from his diary and other unpublished documents by the Rev. Josiah Bull (London: Religious Tract Society, 1868) 238.

[2]John Betjeman, *The City of London Churches* (London: Pitkin, 1974) 26.

[3]Richard Cecil, "Memoirs of John Newton," in *The Works of the Rev. John Newton*, 2 vols., ed. Richard Cecil (Philadelphia: Hunt, 1831) 1:45.

Many were attracted to St. Mary Woolnoth to hear the noted "gospel preacher." Soon after he arrived in London, some congregants complained that strangers were crowding them out of their small sanctuary. The churchwarden proposed that Newton occasionally let other clergy fill the pulpit without public announcement in advance, because outsiders might not throng the church if they were unsure whether Newton would be preaching.[4] "Sermon tasting was among the delights that in that age attracted visitors to the metropolis," writes Gordon Rupp.[5] Newton also made the round of London churches to hear other preachers—as much as was possible for a person with a heavy preaching schedule. He reported, "Whatever else be dear in London, the gospel is good, cheap, and in great plenty."[6]

To introduce his approach to ministering, Newton's first sermon in his new parish was on "speaking the truth in love" (Ephesians 4:15). The Pauline text, he said, contains "that combination of integrity and benevolence which constitute the character of a true Christian."[7] The sermon set forth the honesty with which he planned to approach personal and social issues confronting his congregation. Newton felt that he, unlike many ministers, was freer to preach the full gospel because his parishes had been "bestowed by private patronage."[8] He had not been pressured by Lord Dartmouth and John Thornton at Olney, nor by Thornton alone at London, to support their biases.

Newton wrote a nonconformist that the *Book of Common Prayer* was not as constricting as some rules that dissenters had established for their denominations:

> By assenting to our church ritual, I give up less of my own private judgment, for the sake of peace, than I should by espousing the rules and practices of any dissenting churches I am acquainted with. . . . The administration of our church governance is gentle and liberal. I have, from the first, preached my sentiments with the greatest freedom. . . . I have done some things which have not the sanction of general custom; but I have never met with the smallest check, interference, or displeasure from any of

---

[4]Bull, comp., *John Newton*, 246.
[5]Gordon Rupp, *Religion in England 1688–1791* (Oxford: Clarendon, 1986) 516.
[6]Bruce Hindmarsh, *John Newton and the English Evangelical Tradition* (New York: Oxford University Press, 1996) 310.
[7]Newton, *Works* 3:517.
[8]Newton, *Works* 2:249.

my superiors in the church. . . . Indeed, I have often thought that I have as good a right to the name of Independent as yourself.[9]

Newton deeply missed his friends in Olney and the rural vistas there. Having injured his shoulder several months after moving to London, he wrote William Cowper and Mary Unwin: "A removal from two such dear friends is a dislocation . . . analogous to what my body felt when my arm was forced from its socket. I live in hopes that this mental dislocation will one day be happily reduced likewise, and that we shall come together again *as bone to its bone.*"[10] Newton nostalgically asked Cowper to send paintings to decorate his study. He was willing to forgo Raphaels and Titians but he needed "a few mountains and valleys, woods, streams, and ducks, to ornament the walls."[11] On the other hand Newton was aware that he could enjoy in London greater contact with other evangelicals in London than was possible in Olney:

I seem now to prefer it to the country. My apparent opportunities for usefulness are doubtless much enlarged, and here, as in a centre, I have liberty to see most of my friends, who are fixed in different and distant places, but are, upon one occasion or other, usually led to London in the course of the year.[12]

When Newton came to London, he was one of the two evangelical pastors of Anglican churches, the other being William Romaine, who served St. Andrews-by-the-Wardrobe. Newton recalled, "I have known him as a preacher of the gospel since about the year 1750." He described him as "inflexible as an iron pillar in publishing the truth, and unmoved either by the smiles or the frowns of the world. He is the most popular man we have had since Mr. Whitefield."[13] Romaine was attracted to Whitefield when they were fellow students at Oxford; subsequently both became powerful preachers. As Anglican priests, they, like Newton, blended Calvinism with evangelicalism.

There were some significant differences between Romaine and Newton, London's leading evangelical Anglicans. Romaine strongly opposed dissenters and criticized their acceptance of songs other than metrical psalms in worship services. A Romaine biographer also notes:

---

[9]Newton, *Works* 3:427-28.
[10]Newton, *Works* 4:325.
[11]Newton, *Works* 4:328.
[12]William Barlass, *Sermons and Correspondence* (New York: Eastburn, 1818) 574.
[13]Newton, *Letters*, 76.

"He possessed little of those varied sympathies which made John Newton excellent as a spiritual counsellor. He was capable, too, of displays of hot temper. When he saw people talking in church he would . . . sometimes knock their heads together."[14]

More effective, perhaps, than Newton's public speaking and writing was his charisma in informal settings. In spite of his growing eminence, young people found him ever approachable. For a number of years in London he invited ministers and other friends to his house on Tuesdays and Saturdays for breakfast, prayer, and discussion. Often he entered compassionately into the struggles of those he befriended, but sometimes conversations were more playful. Newton twitted a zealous Baptist preacher by claiming there was one biblical text that he could not use. It was, "Christ sent me not to baptize, but to preach the gospel" (1 Corinthians 1:17).[15] Sometimes, beginning with the morning gathering, Newton conversed all day with a succession of visitors.

Having no delight in formalities, Newton told a correspondent about a "parochial farce" on Ascension Day, 1780. In accord with an annual tradition, he put on his robes and, carrying a flower bouquet, paraded with other church leaders around the perimeter of the St. Mary Woolnoth parish. Accompanying them were shouting boys, carrying white wands for touching corners that designated the boundaries. He gave this description: "This ostentatious service draws abundance of eyes; ladies, gentlemen, porters, and carters, all stop, and turn, and stare. After the procession, and distributing ribbons and cakes to the parishioners, we divided into two parties for dinner." The decorum of the outing was acceptable, Newton judged, but the ritual was empty, being the type of ceremony that might have been practiced by the pagan Romans.[16]

In the summer of 1780, Newton was confronted by an outburst of bigotry toward Roman Catholics. It was provoked by Parliament's extension of the 1689 Toleration Act that accepted Catholics in addition to all trinitarian Protestants. A riot led by Lord George Gordon resulted in the pillaging and burning of a number of Catholic chapels and homes. Newton was especially perturbed because some Catholic families lived within his parish. From the window of his vicarage he could see fires each night that the "no-popery" mob had set. He discerned that "most of

---

[14]"William Romaine," *Dictionary of National Biography* (New York: Macmillan, 1897).

[15]George Redford, ed., *The Autobiography of the Rev. William Jay* (New York: Carter, 1855) 308.

[16]Newton, *Works* 4:327.

those who were very loud against popery had little more regard for the true gospel than the papists themselves."[17]

Newton abhorred the "mistaken zeal" of the Protestant Association in London that was responsible for those acts of wanton destruction. He asked: "Are these the fruits of love? Is it thus we do as we would wish to be done by? Surely the Son of man came not to destroy men's lives, but to save them."[18] With particular reference to the persecution of Catholics, Newton insisted that there is "no warrant from His word to inflict pains and penalties upon any sort of people in matters pertaining to conscience."[19] When Protestant Association members asked Newton to condemn the papacy, he urged them to be more introspective in rooting out evil, "I have read of many wicked popes, but the worst pope I ever met is Pope Self."[20] To counter the prejudice against all Catholics, Newton named eminent ones, such as Blaise Pascal, who had a "deep knowledge of the workings of the Spirit of God and of the heart of man, and such masterly explications of many important passages of Scripture, as might do honour to the most enlightened Protestant."[21] Looking back later on the London riot, Newton asserted:

So far as popery may concern the civil state of the nations, I apprehend no great danger from it. . . . I cannot see why a Papist has not as good a right to worship God according to his con-science, though erroneous, to educate his children, etc., as I have myself. I am no friend of persecution or restraint in matters of conscience. The stir made in 1780, at a time when Protestants were gaining more liberty in Papist countries, I thought was a reproach to our national character. . . . I cannot see that an unprincipled or wicked Protestant is a whit better than a bigoted Papist. Yet these . . . are tolerated.[22]

From before Newton's time, and continuing until today, Protestants and Catholics have clashed in Ireland. The Scottish Presbyterians who settled in Northern Ireland, following their stringent founder, John Knox, stated in their official doctrine that the Catholic Church was a "syna-gogue of Satan"; they called the Pope "that antichrist, that man of sin,

[17]Barlass, *Sermons and Correspondence*, 592.
[18]Newton, *Letters*, 58.
[19]Barlass, *Sermons and Correspondence*, 584.
[20]Cecil, "Memoirs of John Newton" 1:65.
[21]Newton, *Works* 3:418.
[22]Newton, *Letters*, 14.

and son of perdition, that exalteth himself in the church against Christ, and all that is called God."[23] But Newton discerned that hate talk, denouncing Catholics as being worse than atheists, encouraged zealots to attack them at will and tear their children away from them.[24]

Newton reasoned that Irish Catholics should be given liberty to worship without intrusion:

> I think the Roman Catholics in Ireland were long treated like Israel in Egypt. . . . I am glad of liberty to worship God according to my light, and therefore am very willing that others should have the same liberty. Toleration, if considered as a matter of favour, is an insult upon conscience, and an intrusion on the prerogative of the Lord of conscience. . . . I should think it hard if I could not breakfast or dine without the leave of Parliament.[25]

In one of his London sermons, Newton stated that he found much truth in Jonathan Swift's acerbic criticism of fellow Britons, "We have just religion enough to make us hate, but not enough to make us love one another." Newton's biographer, Josiah Bull, commented:

> Mr. Newton was exceedingly averse to controversy. There was no pugnacity in his disposition. If he erred it was in loving too well, and not always wisely. . . . Mr. Newton was liberal and large-hearted, and . . . often spoke of the *comparative* insignificance of the secondary matters of church government.[26]

To modify what Alexander Pope said of learning, Newton might have said, "A little *religion* is a dangerous thing; / Drink deep, or taste not."[27] Because of "the spirit of party, prejudice, bigotry," Newton observed, "the feuds which obtain among religious people are pursued with greater violence."[28] Pope, who lived in London a generation before Newton, expressed well Newton's outlook on sectarian disputes when he wrote:

> For modes of faith let graceless bigots fight;
> He can't be wrong whose life is in the right;

---

[23]*The Westminster Confession of Faith* (1647) 25.5-6.
[24]Newton, *Letters*, 56-57.
[25]Bull, comp., *John Newton*, 330.
[26]Bull, comp., *John Newton*, 274.
[27]Alexander Pope, *An Essay on Criticism* (London: W. Lewis, 1711) 2.15.
[28]Newton, *Works* 3:295.

In faith and hope the world will disagree,
But all mankind's concern is charity.[29]

Richard Cecil, an Oxford-educated leader in the second generation of
evangelical clergy in the national Church, became pastor of the influential
St. John's Chapel in London a few months after Newton became the
rector of St. Mary Woolnoth. He gave this portrayal of Newton's
ecumenical and economic openness:

> Being of the most friendly and communicative disposition, his
> house was open to Christians of all ranks and denominations.
> Here, like a father among his children, he used to entertain,
> encourage, and instruct his friends, especially younger ministers,
> or candidates for the ministry. Here also the poor, the afflicted,
> and the tempted found an asylum and a sympathy which they
> could scarcely find, in an equal degree, anywhere besides.[30]

David Jeffrey also comments on the broad range of Newton's
personal magnetism:

> People came to him from far and wide for help and guidance.
> They included lords and ladies, bankers and rich merchants,
> simple cottagers, even a Mohawk Indian chief converted under
> Whitefield in America and suffering culture shock in Britain.
> They came to talk, and to be encouraged; afterward, many of
> them were to receive the continuing pastoral correspondence for
> which Newton is justly famous.[31]

During his first year in London, Newton published 156 pastoral
letters to two dozen persons that he had written in Olney. The collection
was entitled *Cardiphonia*, a Greek-based neologism meaning "heart
utterance." A letter to Dartmouth in the book indicates why the title was
appropriate. Newton pictured himself as a cardiologist in the field of
spiritual medicine. "Anatomy is my favourite branch," he explained; "I
mean the study of the human heart, with its workings and counterwork-
ings, as it is differently affected in a state of nature or of grace, in the
different seasons of prosperity, adversity, conviction, temptation, sickness,

[29]Alexander Pope, *An Essay on Man* (London: John Wright for Lawton Gilliver,
1734) 3.305-308.
[30]Cecil, "Memoirs of John Newton" 1:45.
[31]David Jeffrey, ed., *A Burning and a Shining Light* (Grand Rapids MI:
Eerdmans, 1987) 390.

and the approach of death."[32] William Cairns tells of the abiding qualities of that publication:

> *Cardiphonia* still keeps its place as a devotional classic, and one never reads far without feeling in close contact with a transparently honest, robust-minded, good man, gifted with excellent common sense, and with humour and that unwearied patience and lovingkindness whose worth Cowper had proved at Olney."[33]

Newton's charm resulted in his having a strong influence on the most outstanding woman of his time in London. Hannah More was so brilliant that she could read five languages as a teenager. While still young, her drama *Percy* was the most successful tragedy on the London stage. She served as Edmund Burke's campaign manager when that philosopher ran as a Whig for Parliament, and she became a favorite of Samuel Johnson and Horace Walpole. During the years of the American Revolution, More was among the artistic elite of London. She was a leading participant in a group known as the Bluestockings, which gave women a place in literary circles that previously had been exclusively for males only. High society liked her witty poems, but she was not satisfied with that popularity.

After Newton had published anonymously some of his letters, More wrote a friend who had given her a copy in 1781. "Thank you for *Cardiphonia*," she said, "I like it prodigiously; it is full of vital, experimental religion. . . . Who is the author? . . . I have found nothing but rational and consistent piety."[34] Reading *Cardiphonia* shifted More's interests away from the whirl of fashionable society and toward the evangelical awakening among Anglicans.

More may have been impressed that nearly one-third of the letters were addressed to women, and that Newton displayed respect for recipients regardless of gender. To one woman, he had written: "You once showed me a paper, together with the corrections and alterations proposed by a gentleman whose opinion you had asked. I thought his corrections had injured it, and given it an air of stiffness which is often

---

[32]Newton, *Works* 1:291.

[33]William Cairns, *The Religion of Dr. Johnson and Other Essays* (London: Oxford University Press, 1946) 51.

[34]William Roberts, *Memoirs of the Life and Correspondence of Mrs. Hannah More*, 2 vols. (New York: Harper & Brothers, 1835) 1:111.

observable when learned men write in English."[35] Again he wrote to the same woman:

> I perfectly agree with you, Madam, that our religious sensations and exercises are much influenced and tinctured by natural constitution; and that, therefore, tears and warm emotions on the one hand, or comparative dryness of spirit on the other, are no sure indications of the real state of the heart.[36]

In 1782, More published *Sacred Dramas*, which were Bible stories written as plays to instruct the elite. Several years later, she wrote: "Today I have been into the city to hear good Mr. Newton preach; and afterwards went and sat an hour with him, and came home with two pockets full of sermons."[37] Her visit to St. Mary Woolnoth was the beginning of a lengthy friendship and correspondence. To one of Newton's writings, More responded, "I was so pleased with the candor, good sense, and Christian spirit of it, that I never laid it out of my hands while there was a page unread."[38] Reciprocating, she sent him her bestseller, entitled *Thoughts on the Importance of the Manners of the Great to General Society*, and he commented, "The circle of politeness, elegance, and taste, unless a higher spirit and principle predominate, is to me an enchanted spot, which I seldom enter without fear, and seldom retire from without loss."[39] She later sent him a book that he especially liked, entitled *An Estimate of the Religion of the Fashionable World*.

More wrote Newton of her frustration over attempting to develop her spiritual life by retreating to a rural "hermitage," surrounded by the loveliness of nature. She found that such leisure and comfort did not separate her from worldly temptations or enable her to focus more on divine wisdom. Cultivating flowers seemed to her to contribute little to cultivating virtue. Newton responded that he as well as Cowper had also shared a love of working in rustic gardens and hiking in the woods. For him, those delights had now been sublimated:

> The noises which surround me in my present situation, of carriages and carts, and London cries, form a strong contrast to the sound of falling waters and the notes of thrushes and

---

[35]Newton, *Works* 1:447.
[36]Newton, *Works* 1:446.
[37]Martin, *John Newton*, 318.
[38]Roberts, *Memoirs of the Life and Correspondence of Mrs. Hannah More* 1:263.
[39]Roberts, *Memoirs of the Life and Correspondence of Mrs. Hannah More* 1:274.

nightingales. But London, noisy and dirty as it is, is my post. . . .
The prospect of a numerous and attentive congregation, with
which I am favoured from the pulpit, exceeds all that the
mountains and lakes of Westmoreland can afford; and *their*
singing, when their eyes tell me their voices come from the heart,
is more melodious in my ear than the sweetest music of the
woods. . . . The disorder we complain of is *internal*, and in
allusion to our Lord's words upon another occasion, I may say,
it is not that which surrounds us, it is not anything in our
outward situation (provided it is not actually unlawful) that can
prevent or even retard our advances in religion; we are defiled
and impeded by that which is within. So far as our hearts are
right, all places and circumstances which his wise and good
providence allots us are nearly equal.[40]

Reinforced by Newton in her conviction that an active life was more
fulfilling than a contemplative and retiring life, she joined with the
evangelicals who gathered in Chapham at the home of the Thorntons.
Plans were made there for bettering social conditions, because humanitarianism was an expression of their religion. Newton counseled More to
express the gospel by reforming the rich and assisting the dispossessed.
Consequently she devoted the latter part of her life to enabling impover-
ished children to acquire basic education.

More was part of the propitious movement to institute Sunday
schools that Gloucester journalist Robert Raikes began in July 1780. At
that time the state had done nothing for public education. In 1784, More
opened a Sunday and weekday charity school in a church for 140
children in the farming area of Cheddar. They were taught not only to
recite catechisms, as had long been done in Christian churches, but also
to read. The "Bishop in Petticoats" then extended education that provided
basic Bible knowledge and moral instruction to more than a thousand
other parishes. She was especially interested in the neglected families of
coal miners in the Mendip hills. From philanthropists she obtained funds
to produce and publish millions of religious fiction tracts to put into their
hands. Opposition accompanied her efforts because some industrialists
and landed gentry realized that if poor children became literate,
recruiting them for jobs where pay was a pittance would be more
difficult.

---

[40]Roberts, *Memoirs of the Life and Correspondence of Mrs. Hannah More* 1:277.

In her passion for educational reform, More published in 1799 *Strictures on the Modern System of Female Education*. Her prolific writing also included *Practical Piety; or, the Influence of the Religion of the Heart on the Conduct of the Life*. She used the funds she acquired from her literary successes to pay for the establishment of more Christian schools for the poor.

As time went on, Newton found that his style of preaching was not appreciated in London as much as in Olney. He observed, "If a minister of the Gospel is warm and earnest, he is frequently stigmatized as an enthusiast, that is, as the imposers of the name would have it understood, a person of a weak mind and disordered judgment." Newton was disappointed that many assumed reason and emotion to be immiscible in respectable pulpits.[41]

One way preachers cultivated imperturbabilty was by reading to congregants a sermon that they, or someone else, had written. Newton said:

> The prejudice in favour of reading is so strong that many people can form no expectation of sense, argument, or coherence, from a man who preaches without a book. They will require little more proof of his being unworthy of their notice, than to be told he is an *extempore* speaker. . . . [Yet, in] other parts of Christendom, a man who should attempt to read his sermon from the pulpit, would find but few hearers.[42]

Newton continued to advocate that preachers digest their thoughts beforehand and have no more than a slip of paper to remind them of principal points. "The great aim of preaching should be to make an *impression*," he asserted, "and this is more likely to be effected by speaking to your hearers than *reading* to them."[43] Recognizing the high literacy of his London parishioners, Newton gave more attention to writing down his sermon after preaching it for distribution to those who were absent.

For years Newton gave evening lectures in London on biblical history, beginning with the Israelites and finishing with the early Christian movement. Guided by his earlier published *Ecclesiastical History*, he did not get beyond the development of the church in the ancient era. Cowper regretted that Newton had not completed his church history text because he was of the opinion that its quality of prose was superior to

---

[41]Newton, *Works* 4:511.
[42]Newton, *Works* 4:563.
[43]Bull, comp., *John Newton*, 333.

that of a contemporary author who was being heralded for writing *The Decline and Fall of the Roman Empire*. He said: "I never saw a work that I thought more likely to serve the cause of truth, nor history applied to so good a purpose. . . . The style, in my judgment, [is] incomparably better than that of . . . Gibbon."[44]

Rather than following the Anglican lectionary and preaching on assigned scripture passages, Newton addressed timely topics. His sermons in 1785, during the lengthy festival commemorating the centennial of George Handel's birth, are a prime example. The Newtons may have earlier attended an oratorio by Handel that he conducted, for such performances were featured in concert halls until Handel's death in 1759. Thousands were attracted to London from across Britain for stunning performances of the *Messiah* oratorio by more than five hundred vocal and instrumental musicians. The musical spectacular was consuming the interest of the fashionable, and the soloists were receiving much applause. Newton took advantage of the peaked interest in the momumental work of art and religion by delivering at St. Mary Woolnoth, and subsequently publishing, fifty expositions on the lyrics of the *Messiah*. He was especially appreciative of Charles Jennens, the librettist for the oratorio, who culled texts from both parts of the Bible to tell of messianic prophecy and fulfillment. They started with the "Comfort Ye" text from Isaiah and continued through the Hallelujah chorus from the last book of the New Testament.

In the introductory sermon for his *Messiah* series, Newton explained:

> Conversation in almost every company, for some time past has much turned upon the commemoration of Handel; the grand musical entertainments, and particularly his oratorio of the *Messiah*, which has been repeatedly performed . . . in Westminster Abbey. If it could be reasonably hoped that the performers and the company assembled to hear the music . . . were capable of entering into the spirit of the subject, I will readily allow that the *Messiah* . . . might afford one of the highest and noblest gratifications of which we are capable in the present life. . . . I mean to lead your meditations to the language of the Oratorio, and to consider, in their order, the several sublime and interesting passages of Scripture which are the basis of that admired composition. . . . The series of these passages is so judiciously

---

[44]Robert Southey, ed. *The Life and Works of William Cowper* (London: Bohn, 1854) 3:26.

disposed, so well connected, and so fully comprehends all the principal truths of the Gospel, that I shall not attempt either to alter or to enlarge it.[45]

Newton hoped to edify his congregants about the historical Messiah of Christianity to complement the musical gratification they were receiving from the oratorio. He believed it was a sacrilege to be captivated by the glorious music while disregarding the meaning of the powerful lyrics. He said:

Of all our musical compositions, this is the most improper for a public entertainment. . . . Though the music is, in a striking manner adapted to the subject, yet, if the far greater part of the people who frequent the Oratorio are evidently unaffected by the Redeemer's love, and uninfluenced by his commands, I am afraid, it is no better than a profanation of the name and truths of God.[46]

Jennens included this text from the Book of Revelation: "The kingdoms of this world are become the kingdoms of our Lord, and of his Christ; and he shall reign forever and ever" (Revelation 11:15). In his exposition of that text, Newton concluded:

At present, the kingdoms which, by their profession, should be subjects of the Prince of Peace, are perpetually disturbing, invading, and destroying each other. . . . War is followed as a trade, and cultivated as a science. . . . How transporting the thought that a time shall yet arrive, when the love of God and man, of truth and righteousness, shall obtain through the earth. . . . But to many persons the extension of dominion and commerce appears much more desirable. The glory and extent of the British government has been eagerly pursued, . . . while the glory of the Redeemer's kingdoms, and the conversion of the heathen, are considered by the politicians and merchants of the earth as trivial concerns. . . . But it is said of MESSIAH, and of his church, "the nation and kingdom that will not serve thee shall perish."[47]

In London, Newton became convinced that the rich were even more in need of heeding the gospel than the poor. Recognizing how natural it

---

[45]Newton, *Works* 3:26-27.
[46]Newton, *Works* 3:397.
[47]Isaiah 60:12; Newton, *Works* 3:296-97.

was for those who had lost their wealth to ask for help, he was more impressed by a note he found posted at St. Mary Woolnoth, "A young man having come to the possession of a very considerable fortune, desires the prayers of the congregation, that he may be preserved from the snares to which it exposes him." When a woman asked Newton to congratulate her for having the winning lottery ticket, he, probably recalling his own former weakness for the game, responded, "For a friend under temptation, I will endeavour to pray for you."[48]

As rector of St. Mary Woolnoth, Newton could give more attention to preaching effectively because he usually had a curate to take care of routine parish business. Among those attending the church were bankers and businessmen who knew little about the gospel. Newton recognized the importance of meeting "babes in Christ" on a level they would find satisfying and lowered his sermon time to forty-five minutes.[49] To assist their digestion he fed some with "milk" rather than "meat," following the practice of Paul.[50]

Newton characterized many of the professing Christians in London in this way:

> The chief mark of their profession is their attendance upon the ordinances of worship. At other times, and in other respects, they are not easily distinguished from the world. . . . The manner in which they follow their business sufficiently proves them to be covetous. . . . For how can it be otherwise, if they had a spark of life and grace in their hearts, while they attempt to look two ways at once, and to reconcile the incompatible claims of God and mammon?[51]

Ebenezer Scrooges appear to have been numerous in Newton's affluent parish:

> Money is generally loved and valued at first, as a means of procuring other things which appeared desirable; but many who begin thus, are brought, at length, to love money for its own sake. Such persons are called misers . . . who, so far from being benevolent to others, are cruel to themselves; and, though

---

[48]Cecil, "Memoirs of John Newton" 1:46.
[49]Newton, *Works* 4:561.
[50]Cecil, "Memoirs of John Newton" 1:46.
[51]Newton, *Works* 4:495.

abounding in wealth, can hardly afford themselves the neces-
saries of life.[52]

As a member of the middle class, Newton served as mediator,
combating the rigid class distinctions that were taken for granted in
British culture. He did not allow the elite and cosmopolitan membership
of his church to distract him from his Olney-developed concerns for the
poor, most of whom were outside the boundary of his parish. Accepting
pauper and prince as having equal importance in the divine scheme, he
took his ministerial services to the infamous Newgate prison.

Newton combined concern for the needy with a frugality of clergy
lifestyle. He compared Christians who treated ministers as "avowed
epicures" to Jesus' friend Martha. Intending to show kindness, she was
inappropriately consumed with serving Jesus a sumptuous meal. Newton
desired that all who extend hospitality be "more conformable to the
simplicity of our Christian profession." When a guest, he often thought
that "this dish, unnecessary in itself, or unnecessarily expensive, might
have been well spared, and the money given to the poor." Newton dryly
commented that being served delicacies when away from home was an
unpleasant reminder of the bland fare he received at home. He referred
to Joseph Butler, the outstanding bishop of Durham, who entertained in
a modest manner even though he could afford to be wasteful and show
off his affluence.[53]

Gilbert Thomas has written about the way Newton dealt with fame:

> It is Newton's glory that, though he became a considerable
> scholar and public character in the City of London, surrounded
> by the perils of affluence and flattery, he retained unimpaired the
> wisdom and simplicity of one who had seen God's wonders in
> the deep.[54]

## Encounters with Abolitionists

While in London Newton expressed first privately and then publicly his
disdain for the slave trade. Who or what might have caused his dawning
awareness of the unchristian and inhumane nature of his previous em-

---

[52]Newton, *Works* 4:493.
[53]Newton, *Works* 4:485-86.
[54]Gilbert Thomas, *William Cowper and the Eighteenth Century* (London:
Nicholson and Watson, 1935) 201.

ployment? Neither he nor his contemporaries discussed particular agents of grace that helped change his attitude toward slavery. But it is plausible that his earlier friendship with pioneering abolitionist John Wesley influenced his gradual recognition of the humanity of black Africans.

As we have seen, Newton and Wesley had occasions for discussions in Liverpool over several years, beginning in 1757. Wesley, the elder by more than two decades, reported that Newton thought of him as a "father and a brother."[55] To compensate for the years when his spiritual formation was curtailed by living as a ship captain in isolation from Christian friends, Newton sought constantly to learn from insights that fellow evangelicals shared with him.

One immediate result of these conversations with Wesley, as we have seen, was Newton's realization of the connection between religion and ethical social practice. He had accepted the custom, winked at in Liverpool, of allowing shippers to evade paying tariff by bribing the customs officer. But Wesley made Newton aware that allowing smugglers to defraud the government was unethical, even if commonly practiced. While Wesley and Newton visited together in an English port that was booming because of the slave trade, is it not likely that they also reminisced on their separate experiences in an American slave port and talked about the relationship between the gospel and slavery?

Fifteen years before Newton helped deliver slaves to Charleston, Wesley had sailed to Savannah as a missionary to Native Americans. Georgia was the only English colony that did not permit slavery, so it was only when visiting Charleston in 1736 that Wesley observed slavery in operation.[56] In South Carolina, where slaves composed most of the population, he and his brother Charles witnessed the cruelty of slave masters, and heard plaintive melodies that would evolve into "Negro spirituals." Some slaves attended a Charleston church where Wesley was invited to preach, and he found them "very desirous and very capable of instruction."[57] Convinced by his Carolina experiences that slavery should not be tolerated by Christians, Wesley prohibited in his General Rules of

---

[55]Hindmarsh, *John Newton and the English Evangelical Tradition*, 127.

[56]William E. Phipps, "John Wesley on Slavery," *Quarterly Review* (Summer 1981): 23.

[57]John Wesley, *The Works of Rev. John Wesley, with the Last Corrections of the Author*, 14 vols. in 7, 3rd American ed., ed. John Emory (New York: Carlton & Porter, 1831) 1:40, 49.

1743 the "buying or selling the bodies and souls of men, women, and children, with an intention to enslave them."[58]

Wesley's abolitionist stance increased when he became aware of the witness of the Quakers. The Quaker State was a harbinger of abolition when the Pennsylvania assembly had inscribed on a bell a scripture verse that conveyed a theme of the Society of Friends, "Proclaim liberty throughout all the land unto all the inhabitants thereof" (Leviticus 25:10). Wesley had read *Some Historical Account of Guinea* by Anthony Benezet, a Quaker schoolmaster in Philadelphia. That 1771 publication contained slave-business data that Benezet had gathered from visitors to West Africa, sailors on slave ships, and from settlers in the West Indies. Wesley reported that Benezet's work was on that "sum of all villanies, commonly called the slave trade." Even though Wesley had observed the operation of slavery in an American colony, he was shocked by Benezet's details. "I read of nothing like it in the heathen world, whether ancient or modern," he said; "and it infinitely exceeds, in every instance of barbarity, whatever Christian slaves suffer in Mahometan [Muslim] countries."[59] In 1774, Wesley published *Thoughts upon Slavery*, which was heavily dependent on the information he obtained from Benezet. He hoped his tract would publicize more widely the cause that was stirring among Quakers in America and would be taken seriously in England by those with power to make social changes.

Aware that the Bible contains some verses that could be used to justify slavery and others to defend its abolition, Wesley's denunciation was based more on larger religious principles of justice and mercy than on specific biblical texts. Rejecting the argument that enhancing British wealth justified slave labor, he said, "Better is honest poverty, than all the riches bought by the tears, and sweat, and blood, of our fellow creatures." Wesley may have had in mind conversations with Newton, or his written account of voyages, when he directed these comments to ship captains who traded in slaves: "You have stowed them together as close as ever they could lie, without any regard either to decency or convenience. . . . When you saw the flowing eyes, the heaving breasts, or the bleeding sides and tortured limbs of your fellow creatures, were you a stone, or a brute?"

---

[58]Donald Mathews, *Slavery and Methodism* (Princeton NJ: Princeton University Press, 1965) 6.

[59]Nehemiah Curnock and John Telford, eds. *The Journal of the Rev. John Wesley, Enlarged from Original Mss., with Notes from Unpublished Diaries, Annotations, Maps, and Illustrations* (London: Epworth, 1938) 5:445.

After expressing his indignation in *Thoughts upon Slavery*, Wesley concluded his tract with a prayer filled with biblical phrases:

> O thou God of love, thou who art loving to every man, . . . thou who hast mingled of one blood all the nations upon earth; have compassion upon these outcasts of men, who are trodden down as dung upon the earth! Arise, and help these that have no helper, whose blood is spilt upon the ground like water! Are not these also the work of thine own hands, the purchase of thy Son's blood? Stir them up to cry unto thee in the land of their captivity; and let their complaint come up before thee; let it enter into thy ears! Make even those that lead them away captive to pity them. . . . Thou Saviour of all, make them free, that they may be free indeed![60]

In 1778 Wesley again wrote in a forthright manner in his "Serious Address to the People of England":

> I would to God . . . we may never more steal and sell our brethren like beasts; never murder them by thousands and tens of thousands! O may this worse than Mahometan, worse than pagan abomination be removed from us forever! Never was anything such a reproach to England since it was a nation, as the having any hand in this execrable traffic.[61]

Wesley's antislavery tract had little effect on the gentlemen and ladies who influenced governmental reforms because Methodism was scorned as a lower-class movement. Even those British leaders sympathetic to evangelicals were not in favor of eliminating the slave trade, not to mention abolishing the institution of slavery. Lord Dartmouth asserted that Britain could not permit a reduction "in any degree a traffic so beneficial to the nation."[62]

During the early years of his ministry, Granville Sharp (1735–1813) must also have influenced Newton. Sharp initiated the abolitionist movement in Britain with the publication in 1769 of his pamphlet, *A Representation of the Injustice and Dangerous Tendency of Tolerating Slavery . . . in England*. In 1772, he defended in a lawsuit James Somerset, a slave from

---

[60]Wesley, *Works* 6:289, 293.
[61]Wesley, *Works* 11:145.
[62]Quoted in Edmund Morel, *The Black Man's Burden* (New York: Modern Reader, 1969) 21.

Virginia who had been brought to England by his master. Somerset then became a fugitive but was recaptured and sold by his master for slavery in the West Indies. Sharp argued that slavery not only was a violation of English common law but also was condemned by the "higher law" of the Bible. He pointed out that the practice of returning a fugitive to the one who had purchased the person was contrary to the law of the Hebrew Bible and to standards found in the Gospels. Deuteronomy states, "Thou shalt not deliver unto his master the servant which is escaped from his master unto thee" (Deuteronomy 23:15). More important than that explicit directive is the quintessence of divine law that is contained in the Mosaic commandment to love God and love other humans as one's self—both aliens and neighbors.[63] Sharp held that Scripture cannot legitimately be used to sanction human bondage, even though some churchmen throughout history "have ventured to assert that slavery is not inconsistent with the Word of God."[64]

By a brilliant appeal to the best of English and biblical tradition, Sharp won the much-publicized Somerset case. Lord Chief Justice Mansfield declared that "the state of slavery is so odious that nothing can be suffered to support it but positive law." In the absence of such law the master had no right to force his former slave to go back to a colony from England. Although the decision did not emancipate the more than ten thousand slaves then residing in the British Isles, it was given that broader interpretation in the following decades. After the Somerset case it was no longer possible in Britain to take for granted the legality of slavery.

Proslavery advocates responded to the court ruling by attempting to denigrate the character of Africans who had become slaves. They could appeal to Edward Long who, after living in Jamaica, wrote an influential book that contained this description: "In general, they [blacks] are void of genius, and seem almost incapable of making any progress in civility or science. They have no plan or system of morality among them. Their barbarity to their children debases their nature even below that of brutes."[65] Long maintained that blacks belong to a species between the human and the ape.

In 1783, a court case involving the English ship *Zong* also raised British awareness of the inhumane slave trade. On nearing the West

---

[63]Deuteronomy 6:5; Leviticus 19:18, 34; Mark 12:28-31.

[64]David Davis, *The Problem of Slavery in the Age of Revolution 1770–1823* (Ithaca NY: Cornell University Press, 1975) 393.

[65]Edward Long, *History of Jamaica* (London: Lowndes, 1774) 2:353.

Indies, a ship captain recognized that many of his slaves were weakened by dysentery and could not be sold for a profit. Consequently, he had 132 jettisoned on the assumption that his loss would be less if an insurance claim were made for lost cargo compensation.[66] The ship owners did not win their case because the court ruled that slaves could not be defined as mere merchandise. But no one considered prosecuting the captain for mass murder.

Newton now recognized that the slave trade was inimitable to basic Christian ethics and that he must do all that he could as a pastor and as a citizen to remove the British from involvement in it. In 1785, before throwing his weight behind the antislavery campaign, Newton preached a sermon entitled "Messiah's Easy Yoke" on the need to emulate Jesus by serving one another. He reasoned:

> If we are really Christians, Jesus is our Master—our Lord—and we are his servants. . . . He cautions us against calling anyone "master" upon earth. . . . There was nothing in his external appearance to intimidate the poor and the miserable from coming to him. He was lowly or humble. . . . In this respect he teaches us by his example. "He took upon him the form of a servant" (Philippians 2:7), a poor and obscure man, to abase our pride, to cure us of selfishness.[67]

## Working with Wilberforce

In the 1780s Newton began to influence governmental reforms by advising William Wilberforce, a member of Parliament. Wilberforce had gotten to know Newton as a boy when Wilberforce was living with his uncle and aunt in London after his father died. Hannah Wilberforce and her brother, John Thornton, were close friends of Newton and, when visiting in London from Olney, Newton became acquainted with young Wilberforce while in the Wilberforce home. With regard to Newton, Wilberforce said he remembered "reverencing him as a parent when I was a child."[68]

---

[66]Elizabeth Donnan, ed., *Documents Illustrative of the Slave Trade* (New York: Octagon, 1965) 2:555-57.

[67]Newton, *Works* 3:137-41.

[68]John Harford, *Recollections of William Wilberforce* (London: Longmans, 1864) 218.

As a young man, Wilberforce was brilliant and charming, in spite of his small and sickly physique. In 1780, after graduating from Cambridge, he took advantage of his family's prominence in Yorkshire, the largest county of England, to get elected as a Tory to the House of Commons. In London he joined a party crowd, and became known for talented singing and heavy drinking. Having inherited wealth, he became a high roller at gambling clubs. In 1781, Newton wrote Cowper: "Religious appearances . . . are to be regarded with caution. The strongest and most promising views of this sort I ever met with, were in the case of Mr. Wilberforce when he was a boy—but they seem now entirely worn off."[69]

In 1785, Wilberforce became interested in evangelical Christianity while reading the New Testament in Greek with Rev. Isaac Milner, the dean of Carlisle. Milner had championed evangelicalism after becoming a companion of Newton during his Olney years.[70] Wilberforce began accompanying his aunt when she attended the St. Mary Woolnoth Church.

The admiration for Newton that Wilberforce had had as a boy revived and he requested to meet with him in secret, perhaps to discuss becoming a minister. Even as Nicodemus wished to avoid being seen with Jesus who talked about radical rebirth, so the young man did not want to lose social standing with his comrades by speaking openly to someone who had Methodist sympathies. At the visit he was impressed when Newton told of remembering him as a boy and of praying for him over the years.[71] Wilberforce shared with Newton that he had been reading the Gospels and was struck by the verse, "If ye then, being evil, know how to give good gifts unto your children, how much more shall your heavenly Father give the Holy Spirit to them that ask him?"[72] That familial analogy of Jesus was the same one that Newton had pondered on the *Greyhound* when about the same age as Wilberforce. On leaving, Wilberforce wrote in his diary:

> Called upon Old Newton—was much affected in conversing with him—something very pleasing and unaffected in him. . . . On the whole he encouraged me. . . . When I came away I found my

---

[69]Martin, *John Newton*, 303.
[70]Newton, "Diary" 2:73.
[71]Bull, comp., *John Newton*, 282.
[72]Luke 11:13; Martin, *John Newton*, 304.

mind in a calm, tranquil state, more humbled, and looking more devoutly up to God.[73]

When Newton informed Cowper and Unwin that he had recently been conversing with Wilberforce, Cowper responded: "We were greatly pleased with your account of Mr. Wilberforce. May your new disciple's conduct ever do honor to his principles and to the instruction of the spiritual counselor whom he hath chosen."[74] Newton sent Cowper this further report on Wilberforce:

> His abilities are undoubtedly very considerable, and his situation and connections . . . are likely to afford him ample scope for usefulness in public life. I hope the Lord will make him a blessing, both as a Christian and as a statesman. How seldom do these characters coincide! But they are not incompatible.[75]

Wilberforce frequently returned to attend Newton's church and to receive guidance. On wondering if he should follow the tendency of many evangelicals and shun secular society, he learned that Newton associated saintliness with transforming the world, not with detachment from the world. He affirmed: "Christ has taken our nature into Heaven to represent us; and has left us on earth, with his nature, to represent him."[76]

Since Newton advised Wilberforce to combine his religious idealism with political leadership, the evangelical convert continued for the rest of his life to be the member of Parliament most steadfastly devoted to reform. He lived frugally, giving a quarter of his income to charities. Being a father figure to Wilberforce at a critical time for vocational determination, Newton helped effect not only an individual conversion but eventually the conversion of British culture on the pressing issue of slavery.

Wilberforce's strong connections in the House of Commons were due to his friendship with William Pitt, who had been at Cambridge with him and was also elected soon afterward to Parliament. Pitt's father had been a powerful prime minister, which helps to explain how his son was selected for the same post at the age of twenty-four. Since Pitt was a

---

[73]Robert Wilberforce and Samuel Wilberforce, *Life of Wilberforce* (Philadelphia: Perkins, 1839) 46.

[74]Southey, *The Life and Works of William Cowper* 3:258.

[75]Letter, 30 January 1786, Hanney Collection, Princeton University Library.

[76]Cecil, "Memoirs of John Newton" 1:62.

pragmatic politician with little social vision, Winston Churchill notes that "Wilberforce became the keeper of the young minister's conscience."[77]

Another important political and religious connection for Wilberforce was his first cousin Henry Thornton, a member of Parliament as well as a banker. A son of Newton's patron, John Thornton, he lived on the family estate at Chapham in a London suburb. Until he married in 1796, Wilberforce lived with Henry. As Hannah More had found out, the Chapham home was a popular meeting place for influential Anglican professionals who combined personal piety with public-spiritedness.

After Newton counseled Wilberforce to infuse religious values into his political vocation, criminal law was one of the first things he tackled. In Britain at that time, there were more than two hundred crimes punishable by death, and most were associated with stealing. Convinced that such laws were too severe, Newton asserted, "I would not make robbery a capital crime."[78] In discussing the commonplace use of gallows, he said: "If my pocket was full of stones, I have no right to throw one at the greatest backslider upon earth. I have either done as bad or worse than he; for I am made of just the same materials. If there be any difference, it is wholly of grace."[79] Newton was alluding to Jesus' story of the self-righteous men who were prepared to stone an adulteress, and he may have had in mind the familiar story of the early Calvinist who exclaimed on seeing criminals taken to be executed, "But for the grace of God there goes John Bradford."

Newton and Wilberforce were far ahead of church officials in attempting to make the criminal code more humane, for the archbishop of Canterbury and six bishops voted against a bill introduced in Parliament that would have eliminated the death penalty for stealing five shillings.[80] Property rights had become more sacred than personal rights, both for Britishers at home and on plantations abroad. Wilberforce also encouraged Jeremy Bentham in his prison reforms, for he was urging the novel idea that rehabilitation should be a main aim of the penal system. In another humane effort, Wilberforce sponsored a bill in 1786 that would have substituted hanging for burning as the penalty for a woman

---

[77]Winston Churchill, *A History of the English-Speaking Peoples*, 4 vols. (London: Cassell, 1956–1958) 3:219.

[78]Newton, *Letters*, 19.

[79]Newton, *Letters*, 51.

[80]Martin, *John Newton*, 344.

convicted of murdering her husband, but even that small change was
defeated in the House of Lords.[81]

Two years after Wilberforce began to consult with Newton, Wilberforce wrote in his journal, "God Almighty has set before me two great
objects, the suppression of the slave trade and the reformation of
manners."[82] When he tackled his principal sacred calling, he was about
the only member of Parliament who was vocally interested in either
restricting or abolishing the slave trade. In 1783, Prime Minister Lord
North had stated the settled opinion, held by king and commoners, that
it was an economic necessity. Most members of the House of Commons
regarded Wilberforce as an eloquent but impractical visionary.

At this time Newton was allied with Thomas Clarkson in attacking
the slave trade. Clarkson had given up plans to follow in his father's
profession as a Church of England clergyman in order to devote himself
to abolishing slavery. After reading what Benezet had collected about the
iniquitous trade, he felt called to the ministry of championing the human
rights of former Africans. Clarkson assiduously gathered firsthand reports
of the British slave trade, realizing that unsubstantiated accusations
would be hooted at by abolition opponents. After investigating the
business records of shipping companies in Liverpool and elsewhere,
sometimes at the risk of personal peril, Clarkson published in 1786 his
*Essay on the Slavery and Commerce of the Human Species.* Impressive docu-
mentation was provided to show that the human freight business violated
every principle of Christian humanity. Probably there had never been
before in history a gathering of so much authoritative evidence on any
social problem.

In 1787, Clarkson joined with Granville Clark and others to organize
the Society for the Abolition of the Slave Trade, to slay the Leviathan of
slavery's vested interests. Nine of the Society's dozen members were
Quakers, but they belonged to a small and unorthodox sect that had little
political power. The Society wisely made non-Quaker Granville Sharp
president, because of his notoriety in the Somerset case. Master potter
Josiah Wedgwood assisted by making ceramic copies of the Society's
logo, a chained African asking, "Am I not a man and a brother?" He
distributed large quantities of the china seal, some of which embellished
gentlemen's snuffboxes and ladies' jewelry.

---

[81]Leonard Cowie, *William Wilberforce 1759–1833* (New York: Greenwood, 1992)
7.

[82]Wilberforce, *Life,* 65.

Clarkson approached Wilberforce for political assistance and found that he was already concerned for the plight of slaves, mainly due to Newton's influence.[83] Pertaining to the slave trade, Wilberforce declared that "he never spent one half hour in his [Newton's] company without hearing some allusion to it."[84] Oliver Ransford, in his book on the slave trade, notes that Newton "conceived a hatred of the trade in the mind of William Wilberforce and then persuaded him to fight it, not from the pulpit as was the young man's immediate design, but in the Commons."[85]

Newton was "a key figure in the early stages of the abolition movement"[86] because he knew the slave-trade business inside out. There were then only a few in Britain who questioned the conventional wisdom that slave trading was morally acceptable. All sectors of the culture supported it—the king, Parliament, the established church, and public opinion in general. Holland Rose has found that "up to 1787 the bulk of the printed material about the subject was concerned with arguments as to the best means of promoting the slave trade, or eulogies on its importance, and little else."[87]

The British abolitionists were shrewd tacticians in opting for gradual amelioration rather than the immediate eradication of slavery. They realistically made ending slave *trade* their intermediate goal and did not aim at simultaneously freeing those already enslaved. Campaigning for a piecemeal approach, they presumed, would be less difficult because those who already had investments in slaves would not be alarmed at the loss of property they already possessed. It was also reasoned that if fresh slave imports were banned, the Caribbean plantation owners would have to depend on the natural increase of their laborers and brutality would lessen.

Without solicitation, Newton provided the Society for Abolition his invaluable firsthand knowledge of what was being opposed. The ship log he had kept several decades earlier refreshed his memory on details. At the beginning of that journal, he had written in Latin, "It will be pleasant to remember these things afterwards," but now it was painful to recollect and write down a full account of his experiences as slave ship captain.

---

[83]Newton, *Journal*, xiii.

[84]Robert Wilberforce and Samuel Wilberforce, *Correspondence of William Wilberforce* (London: Murray, 1838) 1:x.

[85]Ransford, *The Slave Trade*, 186.

[86]Jack Gratus, *The Great White Lie* (New York: Monthly Review, 1973) 62.

[87]Holland Rose, *The Cambridge History of the British Empire* (Cambridge: Cambridge University Press, 1929) 1:459.

Entitled *Thoughts upon the African Slave Trade* (1788), the frank testimony did much to rouse public support of the abolitionists' cause and to precipitate consternation among the opponents. On its title page, the Golden Rule is quoted and HOMO SUM is written boldly. That Latin slogan, meaning "I am a man," came from Terence, a Roman who lived before the Christian era.

Newton, like other abolitionists, appealed to the Golden Rule because he saw it as a basic part of folk morality regardless of religious orientation. Wesley had concluded his antislavery tract by quoting it. Similarly Thomas Paine had asked regarding the Africans: "If they could carry off and enslave some thousands of us, would we think it just? . . . To go to nations with whom there is no war, . . . purely to catch inoffensive people, like wild beasts, for slaves, is a height of outrage against humanity and justice."[88] As a slave captain, Newton had asked himself how he would like to be treated if he were in involuntary servitude. He responded by making sure the slaves on shipboard were not half-starved, not neglected when sick, or punished sadistically as he had been when at the mercy of slave traders in Africa.

When Newton began to rephrase his interpretation of the Golden Rule years later, he found it had a much deeper meaning. Now he projected himself imaginatively into the position of other free humans and asked, "If I were an African how would I want to be treated?" He realized that he would be infuriated if he were chained like a lion and made a lifelong captive, especially if he had done no crime to provoke such treatment. Newton joined the Hebrew prophets in declaring that acting justly is an essential standard for true religion.[89] To fulfill it requires, Newton discerned, a positive answer to this question, "Do you at all times, and in all respects, behave to every person as you would they should do unto you?"[90] Having been in effect a slave in Africa, it is surprising that decades passed before he gave a broader application to the principle of reciprocation.

Both information and contrition were effectively combined in Newton's *Thoughts*. In his opening sentence he used an adjective with theological overtones, in calling the slave trade the "*disgraceful* branch of commerce." He admitted, "I am bound in conscience to take shame to myself by a public confession, which, however sincere, comes too late to

---

[88]Thomas Paine, "African Slavery in America" (1775), in *Thomas Paine Reader*, ed. Michael Foot (New York: Penguin, 1987) 54.

[89]Micah 6:8; Hosea 14:9; Ezekiel 18:9.

[90]Newton, *Works* 2:201.

prevent or repair the misery and mischief to which I have, formerly, been accessory." He acknowledged that his "heart now shudders" to admit that for years he had, with calloused insensitivity, engaged in the slave business. Compounding that "wickedness" was his clear conscience and conviction then that he had been in "the line of life which divine providence had allotted."

Newton discerned that "men who once were no more destitute of the milk of human kindness" than average persons, tend to acquire "a spirit of ferociousness" when involved in slavery. He asserted that not even highway robbery so tends "to efface the moral sense" of participants as the environment of slave trading. It "gradually brings a numbness upon the heart and renders those who are engaged in it too indifferent to the sufferings of their fellow creatures."

The brutalizing effect of involvement in kidnapping humans was illustrated in this poignant manner, without identifying whether he was the culprit:

A mate of a ship, in a longboat, purchased a young woman, with a fine child, of about a year old, in her arms. In the night the child cried much, and disturbed his sleep. He rose up in great anger, and swore that if the child did not cease making such a noise, he would presently silence it. The child continued to cry. At length he rose up a second time, tore the child from the mother, and threw it into the sea. The child was soon silenced indeed, but it was not so easy to pacify the woman: she was too valuable to be thrown overboard, and he was obliged to bear the sound of her lamentations till he could put her on board his ship.

Newton pointed out ways that European traders rob Africans with impunity:

Every art is employed to deceive and wrong them. . . . Not an article that is capable of diminution or adulteration is delivered genuine, or entire. The spirits are lowered by water. False heads are put into the kegs that contain the gunpowder; so that, though the keg appears large, there is no more powder in it than in a much smaller. The linen and cotton cloths are opened, and two or three yards, according to the length of the piece, cut . . . out of the middle, where it is not so readily noticed. The natives are cheated in the number, weight, measure, or quality of what they purchase in every possible way.

Newton maintained that the unethical practices of Africans pale when compared to those of European slave traders. He recognized that Africans engage in the universal practice of bribery, but judged that "their laws, in the main, are wise and good." When he once accused an African of dishonesty, he received this disdainful reply, "What! Do you think I am a white man?" Newton also acknowledged the practice of slavery among Africans, but described it as "much milder than in our colonies" because physical abuse and excessive labor is not permitted. For them, slavery was usually punishment for unlawful behavior. A rich African who committed adultery with the wife of a poor man might be stripped of his entire wealth, or even be made a slave.

In Africa, Newton had observed governments controlled by tribal elders and their weak kings. He noticed that those leaders stimulated intertribal conflicts to obtain prisoners of war that they could use to barter for foreign items. The exchange operated in this manner:

> Supposing . . . they wish for European goods, may they not wish to purchase them from a ship just arrived? Of course, they must wish for slaves to go to market with; and if they have not slaves, and think themselves strong enough to invade their neighbours, they . . . make pretexts for breaking an inconvenient peace. . . . Though they do not bring legions into the field, their wars are bloody. I believe the captives reserved for sale are fewer than the slain.

Newton then explained how slaves were handled after being brought aboard ship, contrasting the English tight-packers with the Portuguese loose-packers. He gave this description of the berths:

> With our ships, the great object is to . . . take as many as possible. . . . The lodging rooms below the deck . . . are some-times more than five feet high, and sometimes less; and this height is divided towards the middle, for the slaves lie in two rows, one above the other, on each side of the ship, close to each other, like books upon a shelf. . . . [They are] kept down by the weather, to breathe a hot and corrupted air, sometimes for a week: this, added to the galling of their irons, and the despon-dency which seizes their spirits when thus confined, soon becomes fatal. . . . Upon an average . . . [the mortality rate from buying to selling is] one-fourth of the whole purchase.

The usual shipboard security system, according to Newton, was to fetter captives two by two, attaching irons on a hand and foot of each.

They remained in this condition day and night while aboard ship, sometimes for as long as ten months. When the slaves were brought on deck for exercise, their chains were locked down to ring bolts.

The painful incarceration made insurrection plotting rife, and those who informed their captors of potential uprisings were given favorable treatment. Newton pointed to the ironical transvaluation of values on slave ships. Freedom against tyranny, a high value in the British homeland, was treated as despicable when advocated by slaves. He noted:

> The traitor to the cause of liberty is caressed, rewarded, and deemed an honest fellow. The patriots, who formed and animated the plan, if they can be found out must be treated as villains, and punished, to intimidate the rest. . . . I have seen them sentenced to unmerciful whippings, continued till the poor creatures have not had power to groan under their misery, and hardly a sign of life has remained. I have seen them agonizing for hours, I believe for days together, under the torture of the thumbscrews; a dreadful engine, which, if the screw be turned by an unrelenting hand, can give intolerable anguish.

Although rarely acknowledged, Newton revealed that sexual violence was routine on slave ships:

> When the women and girls are taken on board a ship—naked, trembling, terrified, perhaps almost exhausted with cold, fatigue, and hunger, they are often exposed to the wanton rudeness of white savages. The poor creatures cannot understand the language they hear, but the looks and manners of the speakers are sufficiently intelligible. In imagination, the prey is divided upon the spot, and only reserved till opportunity offers. Where resistance or refusal would be utterly in vain, even the solicitation of consent is seldom thought of.

Some attempted to excuse slave rape, and other conduct condemned among civilized people, by claiming that the barbaric Africans are morally insensitive to such. To them Newton testified that he found standards of personal morality at least as high in Guinea as in London:

> I have lived long, and conversed much, amongst these supposed savages. I have often slept in their towns, in a house filled with goods for trade, with no person in the house but myself, and with no other door than a mat, in that security which no man in his senses would expect in this civilized nation, especially in this

metropolis without the precaution of having strong doors, strongly locked and bolted. And with regard to the women in Sherbro, where I was most acquainted, I have seen many instances of modesty, and even delicacy, which would not disgrace an English woman.

As terrible as the Atlantic passage was, Newton affirmed that slaves "would wish to spend the remainder of their days on shipboard, could they know, beforehand, the nature of the servitude which awaits them on shore." He referred to the "excessive toil, hunger, and the excruciating tortures of the cart whip, inflicted at the caprice of an unfeeling overseer." While admitting that some slaves in the West Indies were "comparatively happy" who serve "under the care and protection of humane masters," he judged that "their condition, in general, was wretched to the extreme." Also, family members who may have been together on a ship were sold separately and would probably never see one another again.

Another reason Newton thought the slave trade should be abolished pertained to the effects it was having on sailors. They could be obtained at little cost to the ship owner through the use of press gangs, so they were more expendable than slaves. Newton estimated that about one-fifth of them died annually, a rate far greater than was generally found in the English merchant marine. He attributed the high mortality to a combination of tropical diseases, drunkenness, sexual violence, and slave insurrections.

In his *Thoughts*, Newton stated that it was incumbent upon him as a minister of the gospel to relate slave trading to biblical principles. Even if it could be proved that "a principal branch of the public revenue depends upon the African trade," the government should shun it because the additional coins in British banks are like the pieces of silver which Judas returned to rulers of the Jerusalem temple. They said, "It is not lawful to put them into the treasury, because it is the price of blood" (Matthew 27:6). "God forbid," Newton warned, that his countrymen would continue to reap "any supposed profit . . . we can derive from the groans, and agonies, and blood, of the poor Africans."

After disclosing a number of things he had witnessed in his former career, Newton concluded his essay on a hopeful note. He did not think that many of his fellow countrymen had economic interests so dominant as to be willing to continue a trade that was "so iniquitous, so cruel, so oppressive, [and] so destructive."[91] He recalled the line, "The prisoner leaps to loose his chains" from "Jesus Shall Reign Where'er the Sun," by England's favorite hymnwriter, Isaac Watts. The stanza from which Newton quoted alludes to images from Psalm 72 affirming that God "shall break in pieces the oppressor" of the poor and needy. He was probably taught that most-famous missionary hymn by his mother, but only in later life did he see the conflict between what he had been singing and what he had been practicing.

The abolitionists recognized that Newton's testimony was the most powerful weapon they possessed because it appealed to both the mind and the heart. Also, Newton transcended political as well as religious parties, enabling him to communicate with a wide variety of citizens. He wrote, "I am neither Whig nor Tory, but a friend to both."[92] The Society for Abolition published and distributed several thousand copies of Newton's *Thoughts* in 1788.[93] Cowper commented that it contains "such evidence of conscientious candour" as to make it "the most satisfactory publication on the subject."[94]

Wanting to combine forces with Newton, the aged Wesley turned his attention again to what he called "a scandal not only to Christianity but to humanity."[95] He informed the Society for Abolition of what he had done with his 1772 tract on slavery: "I have printed a large edition of the *Thoughts upon Slavery* and dispersed them to every part of England. But there will be vehement opposition made, both by slave merchants and slaveholders; and they are mighty men. But our comfort is 'He that dwelleth on high is mightier.' "[96]

Prime Minister Pitt, whom Wilberforce had succeeded in getting interested in the abolitionist cause, appointed a privy council to make an extensive investigation of the slave trade. Daniel Mannix claims that Newton's *Thoughts* was a main reason for that parliamentary hearing

---

[91]Newton, "Thoughts upon the African Slave Trade," in *Works* 4:524-42.

[92]Newton, *Works* 4:576.

[93]Thomas Clarkson, *History of the Rise, Progress, and Accomplishment of the Abolition of the African Slave-Trade by the British Parliament* (Wilmington NC: Porter, 1816) 135.

[94]Southey, *The Life and Works of William Cowper* 3:434.

[95]Quoted in *A History of the Methodist Church*, ed. Rupert Davies and George Rupp (London: Epworth, 1965) 1:66.

[96]John Telford, ed., *The Letters of the Rev. John Wesley*, 8 vols. (London: Epworth, 1931) 8:23.

which dealt "a blow that eventually proved fatal" to the slave trade.[97] Clarkson traveled widely to find able witnesses but was disappointed to find only five, including Newton, who were willing to be publicly examined by the council.[98] Pitt introduced the revered Newton when he was invited before the privy council in 1788 as an expert witness. His witness carried more weight than the other humanitarians because he had more authoritative knowledge than anyone else. Also Newton had prominence because he had become widely known as the writer of a thrilling autobiography, a composer of popular hymns, and the pastor of an influential Church of England parish in the British capital.

The council was also given testimony of slaves singing "songs of lamentation for the loss of their country." One slave-ship captain, "more humane probably than the rest, threatened a woman with a flogging, because the mournfulness of her song was too painful for his feelings."[99] Clarkson was betrayed by Robert Norris, a slave-ship captain from Liverpool, who had pretended to be willing to champion the abolitionist cause before the council. However, he testified to "the humanity of the slave trade" because it rescued natives from the likelihood of becoming victims of the gruesome custom of human sacrifice by which the king of Dahomey killed many prisoners of war. Norris almost persuaded many to believe his account until, under cross-examination, it was shown to be a fabrication.[100] Norris also made the preposterous claim that the transatlantic voyage was a happy time for the slaves: "They have several meals a day . . . with the best sauces of African cookery. . . . Their apartments are perfumed with frankincense and lime juice. . . . The men play and sing."[101] Liverpool merchants expressed opposition to any change in slave trading, even to regulate it.[102] They claimed that there was only "a trifling" loss of life on slave ships, and that eliminating slavery would cut plantation revenues in half as well as result in the massacring of former masters.[103]

A pamphlet entitled *Slavery No Oppression*, written to address the parliamentary issue, contained these scurrilous lines:

---

[97]Daniel Mannix, *Black Cargoes* (New York: Viking, 1962) 89.

[98]Clarkson, *History of the Rise . . . of the African Slave-Trade*, 141.

[99]Clarkson, *History of the Rise . . . of the African Slave-Trade*, 198.

[100]Clarkson, *History of the Rise . . . of the African Slave-Trade*, 142, 145.

[101]*The Parliamentary History of England*, 36 vols., ed. William Cobbett et al. (London: T. C. Hansard; Longman, Hurst, Rees, Orme & Brown, 1806–1820) 28:46.

[102]Clarkson, *History of the Rise . . . of the African Slave-Trade*, 165.

[103]Clarkson, *History of the Rise . . . of the African Slave-Trade*, 189.

It is well known that the eastern and western coasts of Africa are inhabited by stupid and unenlightened hordes; immersed in the most gross and impenetrable gloom of barbarism, dark in mind as in body, prodigiously populous, impatient of all control, unteachably lazy, ferocious as their own congenial tigers, nor in any respect superior to these rapacious beasts in intellectual advancement but distinguished only by a rude and imperfect organ of speech, which is abusively employed in the utterance of dissonant and inarticulate jargon. Such a people must be often involved in predatory battles to obtain a cruel and precarious subsistence by the robbery and destruction of one another. The [slave] traffic has proved a fortunate event for these miserable captives.[104]

Another pamphlet written for the privy council was by Raymond Harris, pen name for Don Hormaza, a Jesuit who had been expelled from Spain and was living in Liverpool. Entitled *Scriptural Researches on the Licitness of the Slave Trade*, it received a huge award from the city of Liverpool. Using the Protestant argument that every verse of the Bible must be accepted as the inerrant Word of God, he contended that slavery had not only been sanctioned by God in the Old Testament era but that it was accepted by Jesus and his apostles. Harris warned that it was dangerous to apply the Golden Rule to social status because it would forbid any subordination of one human to another.[105]

John Matthews, a naval officer, testified that prisoners sold as slaves came from Muslims who, "following the means prescribed by their prophet, are perpetually at war with the surrounding nations who refuse to embrace their religious doctrine. . . . The prisoners made in these religious wars furnish a great part of the slaves which are sold to the Europeans; and would . . . be put to death if they had not the means of disposing of them."[106]

Newton strengthened Wilberforce's hands by encouraging others under his influence to use their talents to counter the slave trade advocates by protest writings while the privy council was receiving testimonies. Newton had earlier shared with Cowper graphic accounts of the

[104]Reginald Coupland, *Wilberforce* (Oxford: Clarendon, 1923) 115.
[105]Davis, *The Problem of Slavery in the Age of Revolution 1770–1823*, 542-45.
[106]Donnan, *Documents Illustrative of the Slave Trade* 2:570.

trade that he found appalling. Cowper's first criticism of slavery is found in a poem he published in 1784:

> I had much rather be myself the slave
> And wear the bonds than fasten them on him.
> We have no slaves at home: then why abroad?[107]

Cowper assisted in establishing a true understanding of black people by composing poetry in 1788 for distribution by the Society for Abolition. Thousands of copies of "The Negro's Complaint" were sent throughout England when Parliament was considering the elimination of the slave trade.[108] It became immensely popular and was sung as a ballad. Several poignant verses from the poem follow:

> Forced from home and all its pleasures,
> Afric's coast I left forlorn,
> To increase a stranger's treasures,
> O'er the raging billows borne;
> Men from England, bought and sold me,
> Paid my price in paltry gold;
> But, though theirs they have inrolled me,
> Minds are never to be sold.
>
> Still in thought as free as ever,
> What are England's rights, I ask,
> Me from my delights to sever,
> Me to torture, me to task?
> Fleecy locks, and black complexion
> Cannot forfeit nature's claim;
> Skins may differ, but affection
> Dwells in white and black the same.
>
> Why did all-creating Nature
> Make the plant for which we toil?
> Sighs must fan it, tears must water,
> Sweat of ours must dress the soil.
> Think, ye masters, iron-hearted,
> Lolling at your jovial boards,
> Think, how many blacks have smarted
> For the sweets your cane affords.
>
> Is there, as you sometimes tell us,

---

[107]Southey, *The Life and Works of William Cowper* 6:28.
[108]Clarkson, *History of the Rise . . . of the African Slave-Trade*, 249.

Is there one, who rules on high?
Has he bid you buy and sell us,
Speaking from his throne, the sky?
Ask him if your knotted scourges,
Fetters, blood-extorting screws,
Are the means that duty urges!
Agents of his will to use?[109]

Cowper's satirical poems also aroused compassion for the slaves. A verse from "Sweet Meat Has Sour Sauce," echoed what he had heard about slave-ship captains who grow "rich in cargoes of despair":

Here's padlocks and bolts, and screws for the thumbs,
That squeeze them so lovingly till the blood comes;
They sweeten the temper like comfits or plumbs,
Which nobody can deny.[110]

Aother Cowper poem, "Pity the Poor Africans," expressed British insensitivity toward luxuries being produced by slave labor. He treated with sarcasm the rationalizations for continuing the slave trade:

I own I am shocked at the purchase of slaves,
And fear those who buy them and sell them are knaves;
What I hear of their hardships, their tortures, and groans,
Is almost enough to draw pity from stones.

I pity them greatly, but I must be mum,
For how could we do without sugar and rum?
Especially sugar, so needful we see;
What, give up our desserts, our coffee, and tea!

Besides, if we do, the French, Dutch, and Danes,
Will heartily thank us, no doubt, for our pains:
If we do not buy the poor creatures, they will,
And tortures and groans will be multiplied still.[111]

Cowper's affirmation that souls have no "discriminating hue," and his judgment that slavery was the "foulest blot" on humanity, carried much weight. He had become recognized as the most outstanding English poet of his generation. (An indication of his influence can be found in Bartlett's *Familiar Quotations*, an American publication, where

---

[109]Southey, *The Life and Works of William Cowper* 6:234.
[110]Southey, *The Life and Works of William Cowper* 6:239.
[111]Southey, *The Life and Works of William Cowper* 6:236.

there are four columns from Cowper but two from George Washington, his close contemporary.)

Newton also motivated Hannah More to become involved in the abolitionist movement. Distorted reports on the slave trade were being circulated by its apologists, so he sent her a copy of his *Thoughts*, noting that his account "has the merit of being true."[112] He further commented to More on what he had written:

> I am not afraid of being solidly contradicted by any or by all who are retained by interest to plead on the other side. Some of my friends wish I had said more, but I think I have said enough. They who are not convinced by what I have offered, would hardly be persuaded by a folio filled with particular details of misery and oppression. . . . [If Parliament decides against abolition] I should tremble for the consequences; for whatever politicians may think, I assuredly know there is a righteous Judge who governs the earth. He calls upon us to redress the injured, and should we perversely refuse, I cannot doubt but he will plead his cause himself.[113]

More responded by commending Newton for his "sensible, judicious, well-timed, and well-tempered pamphlet." She informed him that she had heard that Wesley praised it highly when he preached on the slave trade.[114] *Thoughts* inspired her to contribute a poem entitled "The Slave Trade" that was widely distributed in 1788 by the Society for Abolition. She contrasted the savage slaveholders to the kindly slaves, and appealed to British political ideals:

> They have heads to think, and hearts to feel,
> And souls to act, with firm, though erring zeal;
> For they have keen affections, kind desires,
> Love strong as death, and active patriot fires. . . .
>
> Shall Britain, where the soul of freedom reigns,
> Forge chains for others she herself disdains?
> Forbid it, Heaven! O let the nations know
> The liberty she loves, she will bestow.[115]

---

[112]M. G. Jones, *Hannah More* (New York: Greenwood, 1968) 82, 88.
[113]Roberts, *Memoirs of the Life and Correspondence of Mrs. Hannah More* 1:274.
[114]Bull, comp., *John Newton*, 289.
[115]Hannah More, *The Works of Hannah More, with a Sketch of Her Life*, 2 vols.

More, Cowper, and Wilberforce were the three most outstanding lay Christians of the late eighteenth century. Newton introduced them to each other and they shared him as guru. Belonging to the cultured class, they gained adherents among many ladies and gentlemen in literary and political circles. They did more than any others to give evangelicalism and abolitionism respect among national leaders.

When Wilberforce reported the findings of the privy council to the House of Commons in 1789, he said of Africa:

> The persons in power there were naturally fond of our commodities; and to obtain them, which could be done by the sale of their countrymen, they waged war on one another, or even ravaged their own country, when they could find no pretence for quarreling with their neighbours: in their courts of law, many poor wretches, who were innocent, were condemned; and, to obtain these commodities in greater abundance, thousands were kidnapped, torn from their families, and sent into slavery.[116]

Wilberforce also relayed testimony from the council showing that approximately one-eighth of the slaves died during the middle passage and one-third of those who arrived safely died while being broken in at plantations. He concluded, "Out of every lot of one hundred shipped from Africa, seventeen died in about nine weeks, and not more than fifty lived to become effective laborers in our islands."[117] Although Pitt thought the evidence was overwhelming, pressures on the members of Parliament resulted in a decision to postpone action pending still further investigation.

Before a 1790 committee of the House of Commons, Newton emphasized the human qualities of Africans who have not been affected by social contagion from the outside. He testified:

> With equal advantages they would be equal to ourselves in point of capacity. . . . I do not think they are naturally indolent. . . . They learn our customs, they wear our apparel, they get our furniture; but they are generally worse in their conduct in proportion to their acquaintance with us. The most humane and

---

(Philadelphia: J. J. Woodward, 1830) 1:28-31.

[116]Margaret Cropper, *Sparks among the Rubble* (London: Longmans, 1955) 194.

[117]Clarkson, *History of the Rise . . . of the African Slave-Trade*, 199.

moral people I ever met with in Africa . . . were the people who had the least intercourse with Europe.[118]

Newton had come to realize that most of the Africans who were kidnappers and fraudulent had become so as the result of the degradation that accompanied having contact with Caucasians who were slave pirates. It would be perverse, therefore, to use the disintegrated African cultures in slaving areas as typical, and as justification for slavery.

When Newton was asked by the House of Commons about the profitability of voyages, he responded that they were "a sort of lottery" with many losses, but every ship owner hoped to make big profits.[119] To a question about the fettering of slaves, Newton replied: "I never put them out of irons till we saw the land in the West Indies. . . . It was the universal custom at that time."[120] When asked about the effect of the slave trade on seamen, he said: "I suppose there is no trade in which seamen are treated with so little humanity. . . . I have myself seen them when sick beaten for being lazy till they have died under the blows."[121]

The mortality rate of seamen was higher on a slave-ship voyage than among the slaves. This was because they were on board for many more months than the slaves and they were more expendable. If they died from punishment, disease, or malnutrition there would probably be no loss of revenue to the captain, but there was a certain loss if healthy slaves were not delivered for sale. In 1787, on the eighty-eight slave ships from Liverpool, twenty per cent (642 out of 3,170) of the sailors died. Extrapolating on those statistics, Wilberforce stated, "More sailors die in one year in the slave trade than die in two years in all our other trades put together."[122]

Wilberforce presented facts to Parliament that the opposition could not refute. He read a letter written in 1788 from Governor Perry of Barbados on "the ill treatment which the British sailors endured at the hands of their savage captains." Sailors who were able to survive the rigors of Africa were mostly dispensable on arriving in the West Indies and were often abandoned by their captain. With no slaves to guard on the return trip, fewer sailors were needed; frivolous reasons were given

---

[118]Newton, *Journal*, xiii.
[119]Newton, *Journal*, 81.
[120]Newton, *Journal*, 25.
[121]Newton, *Journal*, xiv.
[122]*Parliamentary History*, 28:56.

for discharging sailors to avoid payment of wages at the end of the voyage.

Wilberforce perceived that the trade had a natural tendency to harden hearts of all participants.[123] Wilberforce told further of an incident involving six English ships anchored off the African coast near Calabar. When the captains learned that the native traders were demanding payment for slaves higher than the current market price, they bombarded the town with sixty-six guns. After twenty Africans were killed and many injured, the natives were forced to accept the price offered.[124] Wilberforce also dealt with the issue under debate by appealing to early English history. He reminded his countrymen of the time when Britons were carried off into slavery by Romans who viewed them as barbarians fit only for servitude.

The efforts of Newton, Wilberforce, Clarkson, and other abolitionists drew increasing fire from those who argued that slaves were privately owned and that property rights were more inviolable and sacred than human rights. Before the vote was taken in 1791 on a motion in the House of Commons to abolish slave trade, a member claimed that "the property of the West Indies was at stake; and though men might be generous with their own property, they should not be so with the property of others."[125]

Domestic as well as colonial economic considerations were of primary concern to most members of Parliament. Impressive arguments and statistics were marshaled to prove that abolition would ruin British plantations, shipbuilders and shipowners, exporters of many goods to Africa and importers of plantation produce. By 1790, Britain was transporting more than half of the 74,000 annual shipment of slaves to the Americas and most of these were packed in ships operating out of Liverpool. Seymour Drescher, in an essay entitled "The Slavery Capital of the World," describes Liverpool at that time as the preeminent slave port because it "played by the eighteenth-century capitalist rule."[126] Profits from the slave-based enterprises were helping to finance industries associated with the rising Industrial Revolution in several cities. Owners of Liverpool shipyards, Manchester cotton mills, and Birmingham

---

[123]Clarkson, *History of the Rise . . . of the African Slave-Trade*, 204.

[124]Coupland, *Wilberforce*, 163.

[125]Clarkson, *History of the Rise . . . of the African Slave-Trade*, 289.

[126]Patrick Manning, ed., *Slave Trades, 1500–1800* (Aldershot, Hampshire: Variorum, 1996) 129.

foundries pleaded that abolition would cause vast unemployment and ruin their cities.

There were other opposing arguments to ending the slave trade. Farmers in the Bristol area were concerned about sales of horse beans, the staple diet of slaves on shipboard. A London alderman offered this convoluted testimony:

> The abolition of the trade would ruin the West Indies, destroy our Newfoundland fishery, which the slaves in the West Indies supported, by consuming that part of the fish which was fit for no other consumption, and consequently, by cutting off the great source of seamen, annihilate our marine.[127]

Wilberforce admitted that the elimination of the slave trade would result in economic adjustments and losses, at least in the immediate future, but even so it must be done out of fidelity to the standards of European law and biblical principles. He concluded his famous advocacy speech with this inquiry: "When we think of eternity and of the future consequences of all human conduct, what is there in this life that should make any man contradict the dictates of his conscience, the principles of justice, and the laws of God?"[128]

During the 1791 House of Commons debate, Prime Minister Pitt also gave an impassioned speech against the slave trade, noting that "this most complicated scene of robbery and murder which mankind had ever witnessed had been honored by the name of trade."[129] Of Africans, he pointed out that "it was ridiculous to say that we bettered their condition when we dragged them from everything dear in life to the most abject state of slavery.[130] Pitt urged the British to accept the religious teaching that "in the sight of their Maker, all mankind were equal."[131]

In spite of the efforts of Wilberforce and the Prime Minister, the motion to eliminate slave trade was resoundingly defeated in the House of Commons by a two-to-one margin. The basic reason was economic: Pitt had admitted that West Indies trade accounted for eighty percent of British income from overseas. Newton, having little respect for the moral character of the majority who voted against the abolition bill, wrote, "If the seats in the House of Commons could be determined by a lottery,

---

[127]*Parliamentary History*, 29:343.
[128]Coupland, *Wilberforce*, 129.
[129]Clarkson, *History of the Rise . . . of the African Slave-Trade*, 284.
[130]Clarkson, *History of the Rise . . . of the African Slave-Trade*, 286.
[131]Clarkson, *History of the Rise . . . of the African Slave-Trade*, 287.

abundance of mischief and wickedness might be prevented, and perhaps the nation might be represented to as much advantage by this as by any other method."[132]

The differing sentiments toward abolition expressed in the House of Commons mirrored the viewpoints of leading British citizens. For example, James Boswell was as strong an antiabolitionist as Samuel Johnson was the opposite. Regarding the representative from Hull, Boswell vituperated:

> Go Wilberforce, with narrow skull,
> Go home, and preach away at Hull,
> No longer to the Senate cackle,
> In strains which suit the Tabernacle.[133]

As an aside about the slave trade in his 1791 biography of Johnson, Boswell protested against "the wild and dangerous attempt" of "zealots" who were agitating in Parliament "to abolish so very important and necessary a branch of commercial interest." He believed that Wilberforce was leading an unwarranted attack on property rights. To his economic declaration, Boswell added a humanitarian rationalization:

> To abolish a status which in all ages God has sanctioned, and man has continued, would not only be robbery to an innumerable class of our fellow subjects; but it would be extreme cruelty to the African savages, a portion of whom it saves from massacre or intolerable bondage in their own country, and introduces into a much happier state of life; especially now when their passage to the West Indies and their treatment there is humanely regulated. To abolish that trade would be to shut the gates of mercy on mankind.[134]

Bernard Martin satirizes the theological dimension of Boswell's argument:

> Negroes were heathen, and would therefore go to Hell. As slaves they might be converted to Christianity; either by God's grace, or from the example of the sailors who chained them below decks and the overseers who whipped them to work every day. The propaganda did not express the point in just such words; but it

---

[132]Newton, *Works* 4:572.
[133]James Boswell, *No Abolition of Slavery* (London: Faulder, 1791).
[134]G. B. Hill, ed., *Boswell's Life of Johnson* (Oxford: Clarendon, 1934) 3:203-204.

persuaded many simpletons that slavery had a civilizing influence on the barbarous Blacks.[135]

Meanwhile, an autobiography by Olaudah Equiano came to the attenion of octogenarian Wesley. Equiano was a former slave from Guinea who was now an evangelical living in London. He had survived in 1756 the "middle passage" on the *African*, probably the same ship Newton had commanded a few years earlier. As one of the first black Africans to write about his slave experiences, the account was published by the Society for Abolition and widely circulated. Working with that Society, Equiano must have known Newton personally. After Wesley read Equiano's testimony, he was stimulated to write Wilberforce what would be, appropriately, his final letter:

> Reading this morning a tract written by a poor African, I was particularly struck by that circumstance, that a man who has a black skin, being wronged or outraged by a white man, can have no redress; it being a *law* in our colonies that the *oath* of a black against a white, goes for nothing. What villainy is this![136]

Due to pressures from outside and inside Parliament, the bill to make slave trade illegal was debated and defeated eleven times. But the guilty social conscience that resulted from testimonies gathered by investigative government committees was eventually to end not only the slave trade, but slavery itself. This gradual enlightenment was due in substantial part to the persistence of Wilberforce who exposed the festering sore to Parliament year after year.

Petitions supporting abolition were gathered from many British political districts, eventually containing hundreds of thousands of signatures, and were annually presented to Parliament. Never had a government received so many petitions, and they were disproportionately from evangelical Christians. Accumulated were five hundred petitions for abolition, as compared to five against.

Wilberforce carried on his Christian humanitarianism with rhetoric such as this in addressing Parliament:

> Never, never will we desist, till we have wiped away this scandal from the Christian name; till we have released ourselves from the load of guilt under which we at present labour; and till we have

---

[135]Martin, *John Newton*, 309.
[136]Telford, *The Letters of the Rev. John Wesley* 8:265.

extinguished every trace of this bloody traffic, which our posterity, looking back to the history of these enlightened times, will scarcely believe to have been suffered to exist so long, a disgrace and dishonour to our country.[137]

In 1792, the House of Commons passed a resolution for the gradual abolition of the slave trade.[138] The debate then went to the House of Lords, where the Earl of Abingdon compared any tampering with the slave system to the opening of Pandora's box, unleashing democratic forces that would destroy both monarchy and rank.[139] Agitated by the philosophy of that Jean Jacques Rousseau had advocated in France, the Earl asked:

> What does the abolition of the slave trade mean more or less in effect, than liberty and equality? What more or less than the rights of man? And what is liberty and equality, and what the rights of man, but the foolish fundamental principles of this new philosophy.[140]

In 1793, the House of Lords rejected abolition even if postponed for a future beginning, fearful that egalitarian measures would overthrow aristocracy and royalty. Some influential members of that legislative body were absentee landlords of West Indies plantations, and this caused many years of further delay. Historian Basil Davidson describes the situation at that time: "The abolitionists were denounced, pilloried, and vilified by the slaving lobby, still powerful in Parliament and high places. Many respectable people found it utterly incomprehensible that honesty should drive other men to radical opinions."[141] Newton was dismayed over the inability of most politicians to rise above narrow self-interest and rectify wrong, even if some economic sacrifice was necessary. In 1793, he snorted, "If I were to add another article to our litany, it might run thus: 'From poison and politics, good Lord deliver me.' "[142] Newton was becoming painfully aware that it might take as long for the scales of custom-sanctioned blindness to be removed from the eyes of his countrymen as it had for him.

---

[137]Mannix, *Black Cargoes*, 171.
[138]Clarkson, *History of the Rise . . . of the African Slave-Trade*, 312.
[139]Davis, *The Problem of Slavery in the Age of Revolution 1770–1823*, 345.
[140]*Parliamentary History*, 30:654.
[141]Basil Davidson, *Black Mother* (Boston: Little, Brown, 1961) 71.
[142]Newton, *Letters*, 11.

When Newton was a slave-ship commander, he thought of himself as a transformed person and wrote in his diary, "One thing I know, that whereas I was blind, I now see in some measure, enlightened by the Sun of Righteousness."[143] But forty years later, Newton was baffled by how his Christian profession could have been so firm while he was so blind. While editing letters he had written while a captain, with eyes at last wide open, he pondered in amazement:

> The reader may perhaps wonder, as I now myself, that knowing the state of the vile traffic to be as I have here described, and abounding with enormities which I have not mentioned, I did not at the time start with horror at my own employment as an agent in promoting it. Custom, example, and [commercial] interest had blinded my eyes.[144]

The Society for Abolition organized an economic boycott of slave-produced sugar, to emphasize that purchasers of what was then considered a luxury were causing human repression. After some years there were several hundred thousand who abstained from sugar.[145] In 1794, Newton cautiously expressed to Wilberforce willingness to place his prestige behind the protest:

> Religion is not confined to devotional exercises, but rather consists in doing all we are called and qualified to do, with a single eye to His glory and will, from a grateful sense of His love and mercy to us. This is the alchemy which turns every thing into gold, and stamps a value upon common actions. . . . I shall be glad of your judgment respecting the associations rapidly forming to stop the consumption of West Indian produce. If you and your friends, who have exerted yourselves so nobly for the abolition of the slave trade and are likewise known friends to government, were to recommend such a measure, I should readily adopt it. At present, and especially as a minister, I do not enforce it; I think it premature, and rather beginning, as we say, at the wrong end. In these noisy times I would be cautious of taking any steps which might even remotely seem to imply dis-

---

[143]Newton, "Diary" 1:37.
[144]Newton, *Works* 4:72.
[145]Clarkson, *History of the Rise . . . of the African Slave-Trade*, 295.

satisfaction with government. . . . But I wish, if you please, to have the sanction of your own name."[146]

The French Revolution, beginning with the storming of the Bastille in 1789, was the "noisy times" to which Newton referred. That year the French National Assembly declared, "Men are born free with equal rights; free and equal they remain." Abolitionism was seen as an obvious implication of that first article, and of the *liberté, égalité, fraternité* motto of the Revolution. The accompanying reign of terror and the guillotining of Louis XVI caused British royalists to become wary of all human-rights defenders who might destabilize the government. Even though Wilberforce and Pitt were staunch supporters of the crown, some viewed their championing of rights for the dispossessed as subversive. Wilberforce was especially suspect after the French Parliament bestowed honorary citizenship on him, along with Thomas Paine. The latter's *Rights of Man*, published in 1791, caused a retreat by earlier abolitionist sympathizers.[147] The French declaration of war on Britain in 1793 strengthened those who wanted no social or political changes in Britain. With loss of sympathy in his nation for the French revolution, Wilberforce was swimming against the tide of public opinion, and abolition was set back at least a decade.

The 1791 mulatto-led insurrection and massacres in St. Domingue (now Haiti) was pointed to as the dangerous result of talk by political idealists.[148] That had been the wealthiest Caribbean colony until the French Revolution inspired 30,000 slaves to revolt. In 1794, the French government made slavery illegal for colonies, as it earlier had for mainland France. The precipitous decline in production after 1791 by what had been the largest sugar-exporting colony in the West Indies caused the British to fear that the antislavery movement would also stimulate anarchy in their colonies located nearby and ruin their lucrative trade.

Finding his London parishioners disturbed over the mobocracy that followed the French Revolution, Newton preached a sermon in 1794 in which he compared the five years of brutality in France, for which the British were not to blame, with the greater butchery resulting from African slave trading, in which the British were heavily implicated. He

---

[146]Wilberforce, *Correspondence* 1:116-17.
[147]Davis, *The Problem of Slavery in the Age of Revolution 1770–1823*, 94.
[148]Clarkson, *History of the Rise . . . of the African Slave-Trade*, 254.

was disturbed by the many deaths of Africans that were resulting from delaying the passage of antislave-trade legislation. Newton asserted that

> Petty and partial interests prevail against the voice of justice, humanity, and truth. . . . If you are justly shocked by what you hear of the cruelties practiced in France, you would, perhaps, be shocked much more, if you could fully conceive of the evils and miseries inseparable from this [slave] traffic, which I apprehend, not from hearsay, but from my own observation, are equal in atrocity, and, perhaps superior in number, in the course of a single year, to any or all the worst actions which have been known in France since the commencement of their revolution. There is a cry of blood against us; a cry accumulated by the accession of fresh victims, of thousands, of scores of thousands . . . from year to year.[149]

In light of the unpopularity of democracy in Britain after the French Revolution, Pitt's unequivocal support of abolition subsided. He capitulated to the strong political and commercial pressure groups that opposed it. West Indian economy was so vibrant that the English slave trade more than doubled during the years he was prime minister. Pitt supported free trade, having been deeply influenced by what Adam Smith wrote in *The Wealth of Nations*. Thus he did not want to alienate the slave merchants who advocated laissez-faire economics. The abolitionists thought it necessary for the government to intervene to eliminate the slave business and also to enforce any law curtailing or abrogating slavery. Abolition had to wait until after Pitt died in 1806 and his Whig opponent, Charles Fox, became prime minister.

---

[149]Newton, *Works* 3:606.

# 6

# As Long as Life Endures

### Conversion Considerations

In the second stanza of "Amazing Grace," Newton testifies:

'Twas grace that taught my heart to fear,
And grace my fears relieved;
How precious did that grace appear,
The hour I first believed!

When, for Newton, was the "hour I first believed?" As he sang this hymn and reflected on the beginning of his religious faith, did he focus on the time when he ejaculated prayer words while confronting a perilous storm at sea? For the rest of his life he did give significance to the date of that storm. On March 21, 1775, close to the time of the hymn composition, he inserted into his diary, "The anniversary of the day when the Lord stretched out his mighty arm and saved me from sinking into the ocean and into hell and made the first impression upon my heart towards recovering me from my dreadful apostasy."[1] Two decades later, he reflected on how little change in conduct accompanied that traumautic experience:

The anniversary of my great deliverance at sea when in the *Greyhound* in 1748. . . . I then expected . . . that every time the vessel descended in the sea, she would rise no more. . . . Thou didst cause the storm to subside. . . . Then for a season I thought myself thankful. . . . But, alas, in a few months I nearly relapsed into my former state. Oh! What a wretch! . . . The greater part of my life has been a series of repeated backslidings.[2]

On that anniversary in 1805, Newton recorded in large bold script his last diary entry: "Not well able to write, but I endeavour to observe the return of this day with humiliation, prayer, and praise."[3]

---

[1]Newton, "Diary" 2:72.
[2]Newton, "Diary" 2:314.
[3]Newton, "Diary" 2:331.

Many interpreters of Newton have claimed for him a one-time radical change that totally transformed his life. In a recent book focusing on Christian conversion and entitled *Amazing Grace*, the noted writer Kathleen Norris has this to say about Newton: "A slave trader, he had grown attracted to Christianity, and one day, when he was in his ship's cabin reading a sermon of John Wesley, he suddenly saw the evil of what he was doing. He ordered the ship to turn around in mid-ocean, and returning to Africa, he set his human cargo free."[4] Except for Newton having been a slave-ship captain, Norris's comments are a ludicrous fabrication.

Ian Bradley asserts that on the day before the momentous 1748 tempest, Newton "was converted to Christianity reading Thomas à Kempis's *Imitation of Christ* while on his ship in the mid-Atlantic."[5] Those establishing the Newton Centenary Fund, after telling of his position as slave ship captain, describe his dramatic "conversion" this way: "It was in the midst of that slavery business, mid storm and tempest within and without, that once again the 'Spirit of God moved upon the face of the waters.' "[6] The impression is given that Newton abandoned slave-ship work after that experience. Yet Newton continued to buy and sell slaves long *after* he was "converted."

With the recent rise in popularity of *Amazing Grace*, several authors have assumed Newton was involved in the slave-ship business when he wrote hymns. In his book, *What's So Amazing about Grace?* Philip Yancy states that a "cruel slave trader" composed "Amazing Grace" and that Newton also "wrote the song 'How Sweet the Name of Jesus Sounds' while waiting in an African harbor for a shipment of slaves."[7] Actually, he wrote the hymns long after his years as a ship captain.

Mary Rourke and Emily Gwathmey assume Newton was not only aboard a slave ship at the time of this crisis conversion but soon afterward wrote "Amazing Grace" to commemorate that occasion and his leaving such inhumane employment. In their recent biographical sketch, they state that "Newton was a slave trader, a libertine, and a self-professed philanderer. But that all changed one terrifying night at sea

[4]Kathleen Norris, *Amazing Grace. A Vocabulary of Faith* (New York: Riverhead Books/Penguin Putnam, 1998) 97.
[5]Jack Ernest Shalom Hayward, ed., *Out of Slavery: Abolition and After* (London/Totowa NJ: F. Cass, 1985) 72.
[6]John Callis et al., ed. *John Newton: Sailor, Preacher, Pastor, and Poet: Centenary Memorials* (London: S. W. Partridge, 1908) 113.
[7]Philip Yancey, *What's So Amazing about Grace?* (Grand Rapids: Zondervan, 1997) 281.

when a winter storm nearly sank his ship." They claim that "a massive infusion of grace struck John Newton on that stormy night" and, as a consequence of this, he subsequently "treated captives as human beings."[8] But Newton was not on a slave ship during the life threatening North Atlantic storm, and the historical record does not show that his behavior toward slaves shifted after the shipwreck.

Newton's crisis religious experience aboard the *Greyhound* did effect a change from verbal impiety to piety. Subsequently he avoided profane speech and engaged in personal devotions. When he later became the captain of a slave ship, he led divine services for his crew. At the end of the eighteenth century, Newton wrote: "The terrors of that storm first touched my heart and gave me some sense of my need of mercy, though the eyes of my mind were not opened till long afterwards. . . . I began to pray, I ceased to blaspheme. Yet my heart was not changed."[9] Again he wrote, in 1802, about his deliverance from that storm: "I seemed humbled and thankful. But I was still blind to the gospel."[10]

"The hour I first believed" may well have had reference not only nor primarily to his *Greyhound* experience, but to other pivotal ones as well. A case can be made from Newton's own writings that several of his life experiences can be construed as the time when he began to live as a Christian. In his autobiography he tells of first learning to trust the promises of God as a child, and that the faith transmitted on his mother's knee oscillated between dormancy and activity as he grew to adulthood. In his eighth decade of life, he prayed:

> My whole life has been a signal display of Thy goodness and care. I was cast upon Thee from the womb; Thou wast my hope when I hung upon the breast. . . . I thank Thee for a pious mother, who endeavored to store my mind, when very young, with religious principles and to teach me to love and reverence Thy holy word. I have been told that from my birth she devoted me to Thy service in the ministry.[11]

Thus Calvinism, which stressed perceiving divine providence in the happenings of one's life, was maternally transmitted to Newton. But his faith journey included times of questioning these religious values and

---

[8]Mary Rourke and Emily Gwathmey, *Amazing Grace in America* (Santa Monica CA: Angel City, 1996) 38, 66, 70.
[9]Newton, "Diary" 2:325.
[10]Newton, "Diary" 2:327.
[11]Newton, "Diary" 2:327.

time of embracing other values. Some experiences advanced his religious maturation and others retarded it.

David Cecil maintains that Newton's real conversion was at the time he made his last delivery of slaves as ship captain:

> One evening in 1754 when his ship was at anchor in the port of St. Christopher he came across a Captain Clunie, who told him about Evangelicalism. Before the evening was out Newton had given himself up to this new creed as he had to his love for Miss Catlett. Here was the religion he wanted—a creed that spoke to the heart, that commanded the undivided allegiance of the whole personality, that fired the imagination and gave scope to the desire for action. It was the turning point of his life. He had found what he had been looking for ever since he was ten years old. For the remaining forty years of his life every thought, feeling and action was dedicated, without a faltering, to the faith of his choice.[12]

Hindmarsh, in his scholarly study of Newton, dates his conversion nine years after his last command of a slave ship. Newton wrote his brief autobiography at that time, and in its conclusion he began to express qualms over his former employment:

During the time I was engaged in the slave trade, I never had the least scruple as to its lawfulness. I was, upon the whole, satisfied with it, as the appointment Providence had marked out for me. . . . It is indeed accounted a genteel employment, and is usually very profitable, though to me it did not prove so, the Lord seeing that a large increase of wealth would not be good for me. However, I considered myself as a sort of jailer or turnkey; and I was sometimes shocked with an employment that was perpetually conversant with chains, bolts, and shackles. In this view I had often petitioned in my prayers, that the Lord, in his own time, would be pleased to fix me in a more humane calling; and . . . place me where I might have more frequent converse with his people and ordinances, and be freed from those long separations from home which very often were hard to bear.[13]

Hindmarsh describes the spiritual course of Newton's life as "more U-shaped than V-shaped"[14] and argues that the events of 1763 caused his

---

[12]Lord David Cecil, *The Stricken Deer* (London: Constable, 1944) 117-18.

[13]Newton, *Works* 1:65-66.

[14]Bruce Hindmarsh, *John Newton and the English Evangelical Tradition* (New York: Oxford University Press, 1996) 29.

life to turn from private reflection to public commitment.[15] During that year he shifted his career from work associated with the port of Liverpool to work as an Anglican pastor that would consume the second half of his life. In 1795, Newton gave significance to that time by following his usual remembrance of March 21, 1748 with this prayer: "29 April 1764 likewise an important memorial day for then Thou didst by Thy providence admit me into the ministry."[16]

When Newton wrote "Amazing Grace" in Olney, the slave trade was repugnant to him, but only after he came to London as pastor did it give him a sense of moral outrage. Even as Bunyan's allegory described Christian's gradual and difficult movement from evil situations to the heavenly community, so Newton's life documents a pilgrim's progress from accepting a vicious form of white racism with no guilty conscience on the one hand to confessing its inhumanity and working toward its elimination. A strong case can be made that Newton recognized that his complete conversion, or full spiritual enlightenment, came when he turned from actively or passively accepting the economic status quo to becoming part of the forces determined to eliminate the slave trade.

Newton repeatedly noted that spiritual life increases incrementally: "We are as yet but entered upon the A. B. C. of Christianity; we are mere hornbook believers, and, like young scholars, we think we know a great deal, because we are ignorant of what remains to be learnt."[17] He cautioned that change to a Christlike person is not completed on this side of death:

> The Christian's growth is not instantaneous, but by degrees, as the early dawn increases in brightness till the perfect day, and as the corn comes forward surely though unperceived. In this manner your views of gospel truth shall increase in clarity, evidence, and influence till you are removed from this land of shadows to the regions of perfect light to behold the truth as it shines in the person of Jesus without a veil and without a cloud forever.[18]

The hymn "Amazing Grace" has usually been associated with a sudden individual change that enables "lost sheep" to be "found" and then enter or reenter the congregational fold. This has been due in part to evangelists telling about alleged right-about-face transformations in

---

[15]Hindmarsh, *John Newton and the English Evangelical Tradition* 47.
[16]Newton, "Diary" 2:318.
[17]Martin, *John Newton*, 364.
[18]Newton, *Works* 2:87.

revival meetings. However, Newton intended the hymn to refer to a complex conversion that might begin early in life and continue to grow sporadically for the remainder of life. As conveyed by two chapter titles of this study, the hymn's opening stanza can be thought of as alluding to conversion stages. When blind persons are lost they may use their other senses to find out about their situation and thereby become somewhat oriented. But if their sight is restored they can then use their most important sense to see amazing vistas and to set forth on daring adventures.

Newton's outlook was in line with the three tenses by which the apostle Paul rendered the verb "to save."[19] Newton could assert that he *was* saved one stormy night at sea, and go on to say that he *was being* saved by means of daily deliverance from wrongful thought and actions, but that he *will be* saved in the life after death when he will see love (*agape*) "face to face" (1 Corinthians 13:12). Christian salvation can be viewed as a past event, a present experience, and a future hope.

Newton perceived that religious maturity comes about in a slow but sturdy manner: "A Christian is not of hasty growth, like a mushroom, but rather like the oak, the progress of which is hardly perceptible, but in time becomes a great deep-rooted tree."[20] He described to Hannah More the process of natural and spiritual development:

> The full-grown oak, that overtops the wood, spreads its branches wide, and has struck its roots to a proportionable depth and extent into the soil, springs from a little acorn: its daily growth, had it been watched from its appearance above ground, would have been imperceptible, yet it was always upon the increase; it has known a variety of seasons, it has sustained many a storm, but in time it attained to maturity, and now is likely to stand for ages. The beginnings of spiritual life are small likewise in the true Christian . . . but he advances, though silently and slowly, yet surely, and will stand forever.[21]

---

[19]Romans 5:10; 8:24; 1 Corinthians 1:18.
[20]Newton, *Works* 1:422.
[21]William Roberts, *Memoirs of the Life and Correspondence of Mrs. Hannah More,* 2 vols. (New York: Harper & Brothers, 1835) 1:278.

## The Londoner's Wider Impact

In London, Newton wrote, "My sphere of service is extremely enlarged, . . . and not being under any attachment to systems and parties I am so far suited to my situation."[22] He set aside rigid custom by stating that Congregationists would be "heartily welcome" if they wished to share in the sacrament at St. Mary Woolnoth.[23] In a 1782 letter, Newton told of those attending his church: "Churchmen and dissenters, Calvinists and Arminians, Methodists and Moravians, now and then I believe, Papists and Quakers, sit quietly to hear me."[24] Pleased that members of "almost all denominations" were occasional visitors, he said:

> My congregation is made up from various and discordant parties, who in the midst of differences can agree in one point, to hear patiently a man who is of no party. I say little to my hearers of the things wherein they differ, but aim to lead them all to a growing and more experimental knowledge of the Son of God, and a life of faith in him.[25]

Newton counseled a fellow minister to adopt Jesus' approach when confronted with people of differing religious convictions.[26] His disciples were disturbed on seeing someone outside their band engaging in religious activity. Jesus advised them to let him alone because "he that is not against us is for us" (Luke 9:50). Newton quoted that saying and remarked about a contemporary person who was attempting to be helpful: "He is doing good, according to his views. Let us pray for him, and by no means weaken his hands. Who knows but God may one day put him far above our heads both in knowledge and usefulness!"[27] Newton asked those disturbed over the conduct of others to recognize

---

[22]Josiah Bull, compiler, *John Newton of Olney and St. Mary Woolnoth: An Autobiography and Narrative*, compiled chiefly from his diary and other unpublished documents by the Rev. Josiah Bull (London: Religious Tract Society, 1868) 259.

[23]Martin, *John Newton*, 301.

[24]Newton, *Works* 4:351.

[25]William Barlass, *Sermons and Correspondence* (New York: Eastburn, 1818) 575.

[26]Newton, *Works* 4:330.

[27]Richard Cecil, "Memoirs of John Newton," in *The Works of the Rev. John Newton*, 2 vols., ed. Richard Cecil (Philadelphia: Uriah Hunt, 1831) 1:75.

that "another Christian may be doing God's work, though his mode of doing it may not meet your taste, any more than your taste meets his."[28]

Newton also looked to Paul for authority, lamenting "that shameful contention of denomination, parties, and favourite preachers, for which the apostle reproved the Corinthians."[29] The apostle wrote: "Every one of you saith, I am of Paul; and I of Apollos; and I of Cephas; and I of Christ. Is Christ divided? was Paul crucified for you?" (1 Corinthians 1:12-13). "I believe all denominations," Newton confessed, "abound with bigotry in favour of their own side."[30] While discussing who should compose the church, Newton alluded to the ecumenical outlook stated in Ephesians 6:24: "I hardly expect to see prejudice give way everywhere, and Christians of all parties all loving each other fervently; but I hope there are a few individuals of every party who will enter into the views of their Lord, and cheerfully express their love to all who love him in sincerity."[31]

Considering the times in which Newton lived, his acceptance of a wide range of religious diversity was especially remarkable. London writer Henry Fielding typified the prevailing attitude with his character, the Rev. Mr. Thwackum. In the novel *Tom Jones*, Thwackum responds to an opinion that true religion might be found in a number of the world's faiths by declaring: "When I mention religion, I mean the Christian religion; and not only the Christian religion, but the Protestant religion; and not only the Protestant religion, but the Church of England."[32]

Annually, Newton spent a vacation month in the summer with Walter Taylor, an affluent dissenter in Southampton. No Anglican church there opened its pulpit to someone with Methodist leanings, so he preached to hundreds from neighboring villages who gathered in Taylor's home.[33] Newton was puzzled by those who used "Methodist" reproachfully because he was unable to obtain from them what they meant by the term. "Till I do," he said, "I am at a loss whether to confess or deny that I am a Methodist. If it be supposed to include anything, whether in principle or conduct, unsuitable to the character of a regular minister of the

---

[28]Martin, *John Newton*, 302.

[29]Newton, *Works* 4:407.

[30]Barlass, *Sermons and Correspondence*, 555.

[31]Barlass, *Sermons and Correspondence*, 559.

[32]Henry Fielding, *The History of Tom Jones: A Foundling*, 4 vols. (London: A. Millar, 1749) 3:3.

[33]George Redford, ed., *The Autobiography of the Rev. William Jay* (New York: Carter, 1855) 310.

Church of England, I may, and I do disown it."[34] Newton, like Wesley, did not think one needed to choose between being a Methodist minister and an Anglican priest, for one was an evangelical expression of the other.

Wesley had discerned at the beginning of Newton's ministry what would be one of his major contributions to religious history. In a 1765 letter, Wesley wrote: "You appear to be designed by Divine Providence for an healer of breaches, a reconciler of honest but prejudiced men, and an uniter of the children of God that are needlessly divided from each other."[35] As a priest in the Church of England, Newton said to clergy of other denominations:

> We preach no other gospel than you do; we love and respect many of your ministers for their knowledge, piety, and exemplary conversation. . . . They who love and preach the Lord Jesus Christ in sincerity whatever name they bear among men, and whatever body of people they are united to, are engaged in one common cause. . . . How desirable then is it, that, while we live here, we should be at peace amongst ourselves, and live in the spirit of that love which seeketh not its own, is not easily provoked, thinketh no evil, but beareth, hopeth, and believeth all things![36]

Like Wesley, Newton admired the simple dependence on Jesus of a group who first called themselves Unity of Brethren. They were refugees from persecution in the central European province of Moravia. Their desire to spread the gospel internationally was intense and in the English colonies they worked among the native Americans and the slaves from Africa. Newton said of those who came to be known as Moravians, "Very few of those societies which are ready to censure them can exceed them in the real fruits of the Spirit."[37] He gave them this high commendation, "I do not know more excellent, spiritual, evangelical people in the land."[38] Coupled with that is this accolade:

---

[34]Newton, *Works* 4:561.

[35]John Telford, ed., *The Letters of the Rev. John Wesley*, 8 vols. (London: Epworth, 1931) 4:293.

[36]Newton, *Works* 3:433, 436.

[37]Newton, *Works* 4:342.

[38]Barlass, *Sermons and Correspondence*, 583.

They are a people little known, and therefore despised and undervalued by many, but not by me. I judge that true Christian discipline is better observed by them than by any other body of people that profess the gospel. . . . I consider them as the most exemplary, peaceful, and spiritual society of all that bear the Christian name. . . . They have done more in promoting the knowledge of the true gospel, in about fifty years than has been done by all Christendom in fifteen hundred years before them.[39]

In 1737, Moravian Georg Schmidt became the first Protestant missionary to Africa and some Moravians went to West Africa in the mid-eighteenth century, but none survived more than a few years.[40]

Newton also appreciated the rich devotional tradition of the Moravians, which included hymns such as "Fairest Lord Jesus." In writing a Moravian family one December, he indicated that he shared with them the awareness that the first day of every week was a mystical commemoration of Easter:

The Lord is risen indeed. This is his day, when we are called to meet in his house, and to rejoice at his table. . . . If I am not mistaken, I have met you this morning already. Were you not at Gethsemane; have you not been at Golgotha? did I not see you at the tomb? . . . O thou Saviour and sun of the soul, shine forth this morning, and cheer and gladden all our hearts![41]

John Campbell, a young Scottish minister, sent Newton "The Dialogue between the Devil and a Socinian," which ridiculed Unitarians. They were not protected by the English Toleration Act because they were not trinitarians, but Newton had no contempt for them. He responded, "I think it more becoming a Christian to be unwilling to give any one up" to the Devil.[42] He had come to view all fellow humans as potential, if not actual, reflections of God's glory. The Christian, he said, "rejoices in the image of God wherever he sees it, and in the work of God, wherever it is carried on."[43] Newton also maintained, "If a man's conduct is right it is but of small consequence by what name he is called or

---

[39]Newton, *Letters*, 84, 99-100.
[40]Diedrich Westermann, *Africa and Christianity* (London: Oxford University Press, 1937) 136-37.
[41]Newton, *Works* 4:409.
[42]Newton, *Letters*, 6.
[43]Newton, *Works* 1:331.

whether the place he chooses to worship God in has a steeple, or tower, or cupola, or none of the three."[44] His tolerance extended even beyond accepting Unitarians:

> I wish to exercise all moderation and benevolence: Protestants or Papists, Socinians or Deists, Jews, Samaritans or Mahomedans, all are my neighbours; they have all a claim upon me for the common offices of humanity. As to religion, they cannot all be right; nor may I compliment them by allowing the differences between us are but trivial when I believe and know they are important; but I am not to expect them to see with my eyes.[45]

Pertaining to his London congregation, Newton wrote: "If my hearers had not other means of information, I think they would not know from me that there are such creatures as Arminians or Calvinists in the world. But we talk a good deal about Christ."[46] He instructed Campbell that Christianity is not so much a doctrinal system as a new life:

> If a man be not born again, it signifies little whether he be called Calvinist or Arminian, whether he belongs to Church or Kirk, Relief, Circus, or Tabernacle. He may have a name to live amongst his part, but he is dead, and incapable, as to spirituals, as the stone in the street. . . . Calvinists should be the meekest and most patient of all men, if consistent with their own principle, "that a man can receive nothing, unless (and until) it is given him from above."[47] . . . There is not a person in Britain more unlikely or unfit for His service than I once was: but grace has long and strong arms, and His mercy is boundless![48]

Newton was amused by those who were determined to pin on him a doctrinal label. He told a friend, "I find I am considered as an Arminian among the high Calvinists, and as a Calvinist among the strenuous Arminians."[49] When a person who disliked Calvinists accused Newton of being one, he said: "If you mean by a rigid Calvinist, one who is fierce, dogmatical, and censorious, and ready to deal out anathemas against all

---

[44]Martin, *John Newton*, 196.
[45]Newton, *Works* 1:439.
[46]Martin, *John Newton*, 275.
[47]John 3:27.
[48]Newton, *Letters*, 149-51.
[49]Cecil, "Memoirs of John Newton" 1:57.

who differ from him, I hope I am not more such a one than I am a rigid Papist."[50]

Because of Newton's theological breadth as well as depth of scholarship, he was asked to propose a curriculum for a dissenters' seminary at Newport. In his "Plan of Academical Preparation for the Ministry," Newton recommended readings in pagan literature, in addition to standard Christian texts, so that students could sharpen their wits by disputing such matters as "whether Caesar or Pompey was the better man."[51] Newton thought young ministers might model their literary style on Joseph Addison, Samuel Johnson, and Isaac Watts.[52] The school, which was financed by John Thornton and headed by Newton's friend William Bull, continued for many years.[53]

In a letter to Thornton, Newton summed up his views on freedom of expression:

> I wish every person the same liberty in religious matters, which I desire for myself. And I think human authority has not much right to interfere with pains and penalties, to force the consciences of those who are peaceable subjects. The truth is strong, and as able to maintain itself now, as in the early days of Christianity, when it had no protection from civil government, but was oppressed with violence in every place. Constraint can only make hypocrites.[54]

Newton's liberality extended even to the intolerant:

> It is necessary, all things taken together, to have connection more or less with narrow-minded people. If they are, notwithstanding their prejudices, civil to us, they have a right to some civility from us. We may love them, though we cannot admire them, and pick something good from them, notwithstanding we see much to blame. It is, perhaps, the highest triumph we can obtain over bigotry, when we are able to bear with bigots themselves.[55]

Newton wrote an *Apologia* to a minister of an independent church in order to defend why he, as an evangelical, had remained in the estab-

---

[50]Newton, *Works* 3:465.
[51]Newton, *Works* 3:489.
[52]Martin, *John Newton*, 300.
[53]Bull, comp., *John Newton*, 259.
[54]Hindmarsh, *John Newton and the English Evangelical Tradition*, 320.
[55]Newton, *Works* 1:597.

lished church. It was not, as some nonconformists charged, that he was a dissenter by conviction who had remained in the Church of England in hopes of receiving a larger salary. The dissenters included mainly Congregationalists in England and Presbyterians in Scotland who in earlier generations would have been called Calvinistic Puritans. In the eighteenth century the Methodist movement, first within the established church and later as a separate denomination, provided another option for those who wanted to put Newton in a denominational pigeonhole. He commented:

> I think my sentiments and experience are as orthodox and Calvinistic as need be; and yet I am a sort of speckled bird among my Calvinistic brethren. . . . The dissenters think me defective . . . for staying where I am. Well! there is a middle party, called Methodists, but neither do my dimensions exactly fit with them. I am somehow disqualified for claiming a full brotherhood with any party. But there are a few among all parties who bear with me and love me, and with this I must be content at present. But so far as they love the Lord Jesus, I desire, and by his grace I determine to love them all.[56]

Newton claimed that the gospel, rather than the polity of particular denominations, should be the principal binding force for Christians. National churches have an appropriate secondary purpose of meeting needs that might otherwise be neglected in their regions. Newton acknowledged that the Lord Jesus, and not an earthly monarch, should be the ultimate sovereign of the body of all Christians. Moreover, none of the ecclesiastical denominations, whether they be Roman Catholic, Greek Orthodox, Anglican, Baptist, Presbyterian, and the like, can rightly claim to possess exclusively the true form of church governance. Newton was critical of schismatic dissenters as well as high church Anglicans who identified the Lord's people with their organization. The distinction that interested Newton was between nominal members of any religious order and regenerated Christians who lived by the gospel.[57]

Hindmarsh finds the "religious pluralism" contained in the *Apologia* remarkable. Rejecting "a monopolistic national church" that promoted uniformity, Newton viewed the status of the Church of England as a "society which people would choose to join, or not, as a matter of private judgement." His "understanding of evangelicalism was rooted in a

---

[56]Newton, *Works* 1:597.
[57]Newton, *Works* 3:401-36.

religious landscape of acceptable diversity." Hindmarsh associates Newton's "transdenominationalism" with Whitefield, who said, "If the Pope himself would lend me his pulpit, I would gladly proclaim the righteousness of Jesus Christ therein." An inclusive "low church ecclesiology" was the price Newton "was willing to pay to maintain a maximum evangelical solidarity."[58]

The evangelical revival was powered by the theological acumen of Jonathan Edwards, the preaching gift of George Whitefield, and the organizational ability of John Wesley. Newton's equally strong leadership in the movement was based on his great capacity for reconciling different approaches to faith. In 1795, he reviewed the course of evangelicalism in the Church of England over his lifetime:

> Many of our great towns, which were once sitting in darkness, have now the true light. Some of those places were as a wilderness in my remembrance, and now they are as gardens of the Lord. And every year the gospel is planted in new places— ministers are still raising up—the work is still spreading. I am not sure that in the year 1740 there was a single parochial minister who was publicly known as a gospel preacher, in the whole kingdom; now we have, I know not how many, but I think not fewer than four hundred.[59]

Binns writes of the increasing notoriety of the Londoner who had returned to finish his life in his native city:

> Newton's power and influence were almost unbounded in the Evangelical world, and by many his ministry was valued beyond that of even the greatest of his contemporaries. . . . His wide experience of life, and the depths into which he had plunged, gave him a clear insight into the failings of others, and yet did not rob them of his sympathy. As a kind of Evangelical "confessor" he had no rival.[60]

Newton achieved both national and international influence in one of the world's largest cities. In London, as James Stalker puts it, he "exercised, without the name of bishop, a more than episcopal sway over

[58]Hindmarsh, *John Newton and the English Evangelical Tradition*, 320-22.
[59]Newton, *Letters*, 76.
[60]Leonard Binns, *The Evangelical Movement and the English Church* (London: Methuen, 1928) 18.

those within the State Church who were coming under the influence of the revival."[61] Newton was recognized as the most prominent clergyman among those who favored a Wesleyan-type revival in the Church of England. This movement stressed personal conversion, simple worship, emotional enthusiasm, and social justice. Those who had read in his *Authentic Narrative* about how wild he was in Africa were curious to see what kind of creature he had later become. He quipped about this notoriety to Cowper: "I live a strange life. . . . My time is divided between running about to look on other people, and sitting at home like a tame elephant or a monkey for other people to come and look at me."[62]

Newton's books were being translated into other European languages and were widely circulated in the United States.[63] Eight American reissuings of his autobiography, in addition to the ten in Britain evidenced his increasing international fame. He stated that his writings were known "by people with different languages, from India and New Holland to Labrador."[64] Newton's publications and friendships resulted in his being honored by the College of New Jersey, now Princeton University. He admired Presbyterian minister John Witherspoon, the president of the Calvinist institution. In turn, Witherspoon requested his trustees to honor Newton with a Doctor of Divinity degree. In 1791, the College conferred the degree on Newton at the same time that Alexander Hamilton and Thomas Jefferson became Doctors of Law.[65] Newton told a friend about the recognition:

> If any letters come to me, addressed to Dr. Newton, I shall be obliged to send them back unopened. I know of no such person. . . . I have been informed that a college in America, I think in New Jersey, has given me the honourary degree of Doctor. So far as this mark of their favor indicates a regard to the gospel truths which I profess, I am much pleased with it. But as to the title itself, I renounce it heartily; nor would I willingly be known by it, if all the universities in Europe conferred it upon me. My youthful years were spent in Africa, and I ought to take my

---

[61]James Stalker, "Evangelicalism," in *Encyclopaedia of Religion and Ethics*, ed. James Hastings (New York: Scribner's, 1912) 5:603.

[62]Martin, *John Newton*, 276.

[63]Bull, comp., *John Newton*, 273, 297.

[64]Newton, "Diary" 2:315.

[65]*Princeton University Library Chronicle* (Fall 1962): 6.

degrees (if I take any) from thence. Shall such a compound of misery and mischief as I then was, be called *Doctor*? Surely not.[66]

This self-deprecating comment helps to explain Newton's grace-filled life. He lived by the admonition expressed in 1 Peter 5:5: "Be subject one to another, and be clothed with humility; for God resisteth the proud, and giveth grace to the humble."

William Jay, a young clergyman, told of the pleasure he had in frequently coming to Newton's home for breakfast:

> On these occasions one met with ministers and Christians of all denominations. . . . In the family worship, after reading a chapter, he would add a few remarks on some verse or sentence, very brief, but weighty and striking. . . . The prayer was never long, but remarkably suitable and simple. After the service and the breakfast, he withdrew to his study with any of his male friends who could remain for awhile, and there, with his pipe, he would converse in a manner the most easy, and free, and varied, and delightful, and edifying.[67]

Jay admired the way in which Newton dealt with his life experiences:

> He always seemed to have a present and lively feeling of his obligation to Divine grace in saving him from his former state. . . . Though, at his first awakening, . . . he was not struck with the evil of the accursed slave trade—yet, when led to just reflection upon that subject, no one could think worse of its enormity, or bewail himself more for the share he had had in it.[68]

Even as Martin Luther's disciples kept a record of their master's "table talk," Jay took down Newton's pithy sayings and eventually published them. He reported that one morning Newton read from the New Testament, "The Lord . . . is long-suffering to us-ward, not willing that any should perish, but that all should come to repentance" (2 Peter 3:9). He began his exposition by admitting that these words "are a hard bone for a Calvinist to pick." Someone then asked Newton if he was really a Calvinist. He replied: "I use my Calvinism in my writing and my preaching as I use this sugar"; then stirring a lump into his teacup, he

---

[66]Newton, *Letters*, 5-6.
[67]Redford, *The Autobiography of the Rev. William Jay*, 305.
[68]Redford, *The Autobiography of the Rev. William Jay*, 315.

added, "not whole but mixed and diluted."[69] On another occasion he said, "Calvinism should be diffused through our ministry as sugar is in tea; it should be tasted everywhere though prominent nowhere."[70]

Jay, who became an eminent dissenter preacher and author, called Newton an exemplary Calvinist, and deemed him "the most perfect instance of the spirit and temper of Christianity" he had ever known.[71] He offered this description of Newton's character:

> There was nothing dull, or gloomy, or puritanical, according to the common meaning of the term. As he had much good nature, so he had much pleasantry, and frequently emitted sparks of lively wit, or rather humor. . . . Sometimes he had the strangest fetches of drollery. Thus one day . . . when I asked him how he slept, he instantly replied, "I'm like a beef-steak—once turned and I'm done." . . . [Newton told of a fellow] who said to his minister, "You often speak of our FORE-fathers; now, I know only of three—Abraham, Isaac, and Jacob. Pray, sir, who is the fourth?"[72]

Some who gathered in Newton's home decided to form the Eclectic Society "for mutual intercourse and the investigation of spiritual truth." The name reveals that the group was made up of evangelicals who were interested in examining several streams of Christian thought. There were four charter members, Newton being the oldest, but the Society was soon composed of a dozen or so noted professionals, including clergy of several denominations, artists, and businessmen.[73] They met in the vestry of St. John's Chapel to discuss issues pertaining to the practice of evangelical religion. Hindmarsh states that for Newton "it was the perfect institutional embodiment of his ideals—a nonpartisan group of evangelical believers, gathered in a spirit of friendship for improving spiritual conversation."[74] Marcus Loane writes: "It soon became the great London centre for the noblest clergy and all the most influential laymen in the closing years of the century. . . . Some of the greatest movements in the later

[69]Redford, *The Autobiography of the Rev. William Jay*, 307-308.
[70]John Pratt, ed., *The Thought of the Evangelical Leaders* (London: Nisbet, 1856) 281.
[71]Redford, *The Autobiography of the Rev. William Jay*, 190, 322.
[72]Redford, *The Autobiography of the Rev. William Jay*, 306.
[73]Bull, comp., *John Newton*, 262-63.
[74]Hindmarsh, *John Newton and the English Evangelical Tradition*, 313.

story of the whole Church rose out of the debates of this little Society."[75] The influential *Christian Observer* journal was established by the Society.

Preferring voluntary associations, Newton stated that he had little interest in formal "assemblies, consistories, synods, councils, benches, or boards."[76] He described the Society as functioning in this way:

> We hear what each person has to say. . . [and] sometimes differ in opinion. . . . Perhaps it might be a good rule, where spiritual matters are decided by vote, that the minority should determine the point; for in most places the *few* are more likely to be right than the *many*.[77]

A sampling will be given of contributions Newton made to the discussions during the two decades he participated in the Society. On the question, "How far is gravity binding upon the ministerial character?" Thomas Scott asserted, "Christ sighed and wept, but never laughed." Newton rejoined, "Jesus smiled, perhaps. . . . His example, therefore is no proof of there being sin in levity."[78] Scott had left Olney to become chaplain at the Chapel of Lock Hospital, which specialized in treating women with venereal disease. A scholarly evangelical, he became well known in both Britain and America for his *Family Bible with Notes*.

At one session, the discussion was on administering censure. Newton said, "Reproof in secret, in season, and in love—this is the right thing."[79] A query was raised, "What is the best preparation for the pulpit?" Newton contributed: "Consider, I may be preaching my last sermon. This leads to setting forth Christ as 'the Way, the Truth, and the Life.' "[80] In a discussion of how to distinguish between true and counterfeit Christian experience, Newton remarked, "True experience leads a man to a reverence of God, meekness toward others, and humbleness in himself."[81] When asked what instruction can be found in the Book of Job, Newton responded, "I have learned from this book the unprofitableness of controversy. If God had not interposed, and Job and his friends had lived

---

[75]Marcus Loane, *Oxford and the Evangelical Succession* (London: Lutterworth, 1950) 128, 216.

[76]Newton, *Letters*, 64.

[77]Newton, *Letters*, 65.

[78]Pratt, ed., *The Thought of the Evangelical Leaders*, 114.

[79]Pratt, ed., *The Thought of the Evangelical Leaders*, 104.

[80]Pratt, ed., *The Thought of the Evangelical Leaders*, 116.

[81]Pratt, ed., *The Thought of the Evangelical Leaders*, 172.

to this day, they would have disputed till now."[82] To the question, "What is the proper province of reason in the reception of Christianity?" Newton asserted, "What the gospel proposes is highly reasonable, and will appear so to the man who is taught of God."[83] After hearing a tiresome debate over whether faith or repentance was more important, Newton exclaimed: "Are not the heart and lungs of a man both equally necessary to the life of the man! This resembles the point you have been discussing!"[84]

Newton continued his advocacy for Africans during the last twenty years of his life. He was interested not only in halting slave-trade atrocities but in doing something positive to make amends for its evils. A problem confronting the British was what should be done to help the ex-slave refugees from America. In 1775, Lord Dunmore, the colonial governor of Virginia, had offered emancipation to all slaves who deserted rebel colonists to fight for the British. In 1783, after the Revolutionary War, hundreds who had served in the King's army and navy were taken to Nova Scotia. The refugees disliked the reception they received there and the unfavorable climate. The Sierra Leone Company was formed to assist destitute former slaves who wished to return to Africa. Newton was made one of its directors because of his knowledge of the region and his influence in encouraging philanthropy.[85] In 1791, a fleet of ships carried more than one thousand ex-slaves from Nova Scotia to the West African coast. At a former slave trading site, they named their settlement Freetown and attempted to develop agriculture in the region. The settlers hoped to exchange African produce for British manufactured goods.

Physical and political perils threatened the fledgling Sierra Leone community, but eventually it became noted for peace and order. Clarkson noted that "schools, places of worship, agriculture, and the habits of civilized life, were established."[86] The settlers challenged the indigenous tribes in the region that had been involved with slave trading. Wilberforce received word that they showed "a practical proficiency in Christianity, such as might put Europeans to the blush."[87] A mixture of African

---

[82]Pratt, ed., *The Thought of the Evangelical Leaders*, 209.

[83]Pratt, ed., *The Thought of the Evangelical Leaders*, 232.

[84]Edward Bickersteth, *Memoirs of the Rev. John Newton* (New York: Episcopal Society, 1858) 294.

[85]Martin, *John Newton*, 324.

[86]Thomas Clarkson, *History of the Rise, Progress, and Accomplishment of the Abolition of the African Slave-Trade by the British Parliament* (Wilmington NC: Porter, 1816) 293.

[87]William Wilberforce, *An Appeal to the Religion, Justice, and Humanity of the*

pastors and British missionaries led the development of evangelical Protestantism there and established a school named the African Academy. Those missionaries did not follow a strategy used in earlier centuries of going into tribal areas and focusing on converting the chief, assuming others would follow. Rather, they worked with the common people to develop a community expressing justice and mercy for all, which became the pattern for subsequent missionary activity throughout Africa. When the Sierra Leone Company relinquished its control in 1808, Parliament established a crown colony there and used Freetown as a base from which illegally operating slave ships could be intercepted. The population of Sierra Leone grew rapidly from freed Africans who arrived on ships captured by the British navy. Missiologist Andrew Walls states: "Sierra Leone was the first success story of the modern missionary movement. The years from 1787 to 1830 saw . . . a mass movement towards the Christian faith."[88]

At a meeting of the Eclectic Society in 1799, the Society for Missions to Africa and the East was born, with Newton as one of its founders.[89] Scott became the first secretary of the Society and oversaw sending its first missionary to Sierra Leone in 1804. In 1813, this Society became known as the Church Missionary Society, and eventually became one of the largest mission organizations in the world. It was sponsored by the Church of England that had previously engaged in virtually no foreign missions. Newton also assisted Thomas Haweis, a founder of the nondenominational London Missionary Society that later sponsored missionary pathfinder David Livingstone. Cecil no doubt expressed Newton's outlook in thinking of the Christian mission enterprise as a compensation for the reproach that slavery had brought to Christianity.[90]

### The Last Years

Betsy Catlett, the daughter of Mary's brother, added much delight to the Newtons' home in London, as earlier she had in Olney. For two years Eliza Cuningham, another orphaned niece, also lived with the Newtons

---

*Inhabitants of the British Empire, in Behalf of the Negro Slaves in the West Indies* (London: Hatchard, 1823) 48.

[88]Andrew Walls, *The Missionary Movement in Christian History* (Maryknoll NY: Orbis, 1996) 102.

[89]Eugene Stock, *The History of the Church Missionary Society* (London: Church Missionary Society, 1899) 1:69.

[90]Loane, *Oxford and the Evangelical Succession*, 217.

in London. Newton wrote her dying mother about Eliza's having "taken possession of a large room" in his heart. "Her affectionate, obliging, gentle behaviour," he added, "has endeared her very much to me." Eliza's health was poor and the Newtons were greatly grieved when she died at the age of fifteen.[91] Newton enshrined her life by publishing a lengthy memorial tribute, in which he indicated that the "union of hearts" she brought was second only to that of his marriage.[92]

Newton estimated that Mary was ill for a quarter of the forty years of their marriage, and after coming to live in London she was often incapacitated by "nervous complaints."[93] He informed More that "Mrs. Newton, though seldom visited with severe illness, is seldom well."[94] This situation explains the little mention of Mary participating with her partner in activities outside home both in Olney and in London. In 1785, Newton displayed his lifelong love affair with Mary in the last letter he wrote her, after a brief separation:

> I think of our hoped-for meeting on Tuesday next with much the same anticipation of pleasure as when I have formerly been on the return to you from an African voyage. What difference there is, I compare to the difference between the blossom and the fruit. The blessing of the Lord upon our connection has, in the course of thirty-five years, ripened the passion of love into a solid, inexpressible tender friendship, which, I trust, in its most valuable properties, will subsist forever. I shall never find words fully to tell you how much I owe you, how truly I love you, nor the one half of what my heart means when I subscribe myself, your most affectionate and obliged husband.[95]

Newton contrasted the plight of marriages that are not bonded by religion with the connubiality of helpmates who are:

> The marriage state, when entered into without a regard to God . . . is seldom productive of an abiding union of hearts; and if this be wanting, the case of either party may be compared to that of a dislocated limb, which is indeed still united to the body, but, not being in its proper place and connection, is useless and

---

[91]Bull, comp., *John Newton*, 264, 279.
[92]Newton, *Works* 3:504.
[93]Newton, *Works* 4:407.
[94]Roberts, *Memoirs of the Life and Correspondence of Mrs. Hannah More* 1:296.
[95]Newton, *Works* 4:203.

painful itself, and the cause of pain and uneasiness to the whole body. . . . [God-dependent couples] have one faith, one aim, one hope. Their mutual affection, intimacy, and perfect confidence, greatly enhance the value and relish of the comforts in which they participate, and alleviate the weight of their burdens and trials. Love sweetens labour, and blunts the sting of sorrow. The vicissitudes of life give energy to prayer; and repeated supports and deliverances, in answer to prayer, afford new motives and causes for praise and thanksgiving.[96]

For a year before Mary's death, she was bedridden from inoperable breast cancer. Facing her terminal illness, Newton wrote: "There is a comfort in the strength of love. It makes a thing endurable, which else would break the heart, and overset the brain."[97] When Mary died in December 1790, a month after the death of his best male friend, John Thornton, Newton's prayer of resignation was, "What Thou wilt, when Thou wilt, how Thou wilt."[98] Cecil aptly compared his response to that of David after the loss of his infant son. Both men surprised their friends by arising soon after the loss and going to worship in a sanctuary.[99] On the Sunday after Mary's death, Newton broke with custom by preaching her funeral sermon.[100]

For many years Newton had thought that his greatest tribulation would be to have Mary predecease him. Finding verses from the Hebrew Bible on joy in spite of deprivation, he decided at the beginning of his ministry that he would not preach on them unless he should survive her.[101] Accordingly, after her body was interred in the vault under their London church, the text for Newton's sermon was from these concluding verses of Habakkuk:

Although the fig tree shall not blossom, neither shall fruit be in the vines; the labour of the olive shall fail, and the fields shall yield no meat; the flock shall be cut off from the fold, and there shall be no herd in the stalls: Yet I will rejoice in the Lord, I will joy in the God of my salvation. (Habakkuk 3:17-18)

---

[96]Newton, *Works* 4:500.
[97]Margaret Cropper, *Sparks among the Rubble* (London: Longmans, 1955) 138.
[98]Hindmarsh, *John Newton and the English Evangelical Tradition*, 233.
[99]2 Samuel 12:19-21.
[100]Cecil, "Memoirs of John Newton" 1:49.
[101]Bull, comp., *John Newton*, 304.

The memorial service included a hymn he composed for the occasion that supplements the prophet's sentiments:

The earth with rich abundance stored,
To answer all our wants,
Invites our hearts to praise the Lord
For what His bounty grants.

Flocks, herds, and corn, and grateful fruit,
His gracious hand supplies;
And while our various tastes they suit,
Their prospect cheers our eyes.

To these He adds each tender tie
Of sweet domestic life;
Endearing joys the names imply,
Of parent—husband—wife![102]

After Mary's death, Newton inserted in his family Bible this tribute to her, "The partner of my joys, sorrows, and cares; the hinge upon which all the principal events of my life turned."[103] At that time, he wrote More:

Creature-love is a passion. . . . The high affection of some people may be compared to a summer's brook after a hasty rain, which is full and noisy for a little time, but soon becomes dry. But true divine love is like a river which always runs, though not always with equal depth and flow, and never ceases till it finds the ocean.[104]

While in acute grief, Newton confided to Betsy: "Your dear Mamma's image follows and meets me in every place." In a letter to a friend, he lamented: "What is the world to me now? All the treasures of the Bank of England could not repair my loss." Some months after Mary's death, Newton thought of himself as the stricken deer in Cowper's poem: "I carry the arrow with me wherever I go. I cannot forget her;—no! not for five minutes."[105] Yet, as indicated by a letter he wrote a few months after

---

[102]Bickersteth, *Memoirs of the Rev. John Newton*, 231.

[103]Donald Demaray, *The Innovation of John Newton* (Lewiston NY: Edwin Mellen, 1988) 35.

[104]Roberts, *Memoirs of the Life and Correspondence of Mrs. Hannah More* 1:360.

[105]Martin, *John Newton*, 333-34.

Mary's death, Newton had resiliency that was assisted by congregational support: "My health and spirits are good. . . . In the time of my trial, and since, there has been an additional blessing going forth. . . . The church is more thronged than formerly, and there seems an attention and earnestness in the hearers which is very encouraging."[106] His response shows that he was able to put into practice an insight he expressed to Mary shortly after marriage:

> I believe there may be persons who can keep themselves in tolerable good humour, by the strength of their own minds, in a course of prosperity; but when crosses and disappointments take place, or when they are constrained to part from what they hold most dear, if they cannot call in religion to their aid, they usually sink and despond.[107]

For five years Newton commemorated the day of Mary's death by writing poetic tributes he published as "Anniversaries." The first poem expressed his keenly felt loss, as this sample from the thirty-eight verses illustrates:

> The parting struggle all was mine;
> " 'Tis the survivor dies";
> For she was freed, and gone to join
> The triumph of the skies.[108]

On Mary's memorial day five years later Newton said, "I think of her, not only once a year but every day in the year, and every hour in the day. . . . She is as present to my mind as when she first left me."[109] Yet, the last of his "anniversaries" reveals that his bereavement wound was healing:

> Then let me change my sighs to praise,
> For all that He has done,
> And yield my few remaining days
> To Him, and Him alone.[110]

---

[106]Bull, comp., *John Newton*, 308.
[107]Newton, *Works* 4:15.
[108]Newton, *Works* 4:216.
[109]Newton, "Diary" 2:319.
[110]Bull, comp., *John Newton*, 330.

In 1793, Newton published *Letters to a Wife* "as a monument of respect and gratitude" to the memory of one he called "my pleasing companion, my most affectionate friend, my judicious counsellor."[111] His purpose in publishing excerpts from his letters to Mary was to give "some testimony in favour of the happiness of wedded life, some intimation of the snares and abatements which attend it."[112] To those who "think lightly of marriage, . . . preferring the wealth, and pomp, and glare of the world to a union of hearts," Newton testified that "the marriage state, when properly formed and prudently conducted, affords the nearest approach to happiness that can be attained in this uncertain world."[113] His letter to Mary after two years of marriage shows that his till-death-do-us-part vow did not connote finality for him:

> My regard for you often leads my views beyond the grave, and alleviates the thought, that we must sooner or later be separated here, with the prospect of being joined hereafter, upon much preferable terms; where our love will be refined and ennobled, and the consciousness of our being mutually and for ever happy will fill us with a joy of which we have no present conception; and yet, perhaps, this joy will be among the least in that happy state.[114]

In 1791 a Scotsman named Claudius Buchanan left Glasgow University to wander with his violin, ending up in London dissipated and destitute. After hearing Newton preach, reading his autobiography, and talking with him about his disappointments, he decided to become an evangelical Anglican clergyman. Buchanan then wrote his mother about Newton: "If he had been my father, he could not have expressed more solicitude for my welfare. Mr. Newton encouraged me much . . . and gave me a general invitation to breakfast with him when and as often as I could." Newton recommended Buchanan to Henry Thornton, who funded the young man's study at Cambridge.[115]

While Buchanan was completing theological and mathemathical studies, he and Newton frequently corresponded. Newton suggested that

[111]Newton, *Works* 4:13.
[112]Newton, *Works* 4:10.
[113]Newton, *Works* 4:11.
[114]Newton, *Works* 4:70.
[115]Hugh Pearson, *Memoirs of Claudius Buchanan* (Philadelphia: Byington, 1837) 15, 22.

his protege consider service in India and, after working as a curate at St. Mary Woolnoth for a year, he became an Anglican educational missionary in 1796.[116] On his voyage to India, Buchanan sadly acknowledged that he would probably not see his old mentor again. "I fear you will have learnt many a song in heaven before I come," wrote his "affectionate son."[117] After several years in India he was attracted to an English woman, in part because she was an avid reader of Newton's publications, and married her. Buchanan informed Britons of the Indian culture and of the importance of teaching Indians the best of European literature and science.[118]

While supportive of efforts to promote Christianity overseas, Newton also was concerned that missionaries might introduce undesirable aspects of Western civilization. Recalling no doubt British arrogance in Africa, Newton was especially insistent that missionaries should not attempt to emulate European oppressors. He was chagrined to admit, "Asia knows little of Christianity, unless they have learnt it in the eastern parts from the cruelty and tyranny of men who bear the name of Christians."[119] Pertaining to the colonization in India, he wrote:

> I hardly know how to wish that Government should attempt to form a settlement among so simple, untainted, and kind a people. . . . Alas! what a ruined people they will be, if we make a settlement upon their shores, to communicate to them wants and vices and diseases, to which they are at present happily strangers.[120]

William Carey, who focused on communication through translation, engaged in the type of mission work Newton favored. That Baptist's evangelicalism had been nourished by Scott, and Carey often walked over from his home near Olney to hear him preach and to sing selections from the *Olney Hymns*.[121] Before leaving for India in 1793, Carey visited Newton in London for counsel. Newton "advised him with the fidelity and tenderness of a father and encouraged him to persevere in his purpose, despite all opposition."[122] Newton kept in contact with that first,

---

[116]Pearson, *Memoirs of Claudius Buchanan*, 54, 69.

[117]Pearson, *Memoirs of Claudius Buchanan*, 75.

[118]Pearson, *Memoirs of Claudius Buchanan*, 107-109, 370-80.

[119]Newton, *Works* 3:294.

[120]Martin, *John Newton*, 324.

[121]Timothy George, *Faithful Witness* (Birmingham AL: New Hope, 1991) 17, 128.

[122]Eustace Carey, *Memoirs of William Carey* (Hartford CT: Caufield, 1837) 84.

and one of the foremost, Protestant missionaries in India. When writing Buchanan in 1802, Newton commented, "I do not look for miracles; but if God were to work one in our day, I should not wonder if it were in favour of Dr. Carey."[123] Again he said, "Carey is more to me than bishop or archbishop: he is an apostle."[124]

As Newton approached the scriptural limit for the normal life span, he wrote with satisfaction: "I have health, peace, plenty, friends, acceptance; I can still preach, and have reason to hope I am useful. . . . But I am drawing near 70, and cannot be far from Jordan."[125] Two years later he reported:

My church is full and crowded; . . . there are many eminent Christians among them . . . and we have particularly a fine show of young people springing up, and increasing in numbers and graces, like willows by the watercourses. In a word, the blind receive their sight, the lame walk, the lepers are cleansed, the deaf hear, the hungry are fed, the burdened are set at liberty.[126]

In spite of Newton's abiding interest in preaching, he believed he was most useful to religion through the letters he wrote. Loane agrees, saying, "He was the letter writer *par excellence* of the evangelical revival; this was his distinctive contribution to that great movement."[127] During his lifetime, about five hundred of his letters were published. Like Paul, he communicated much of his message through epistles, not only to the individual recipients but also to the many others who read them.

Newton was frustrated that he could not keep up with responding to all the letters he received. In a 1794 letter, he said: "I have about sixty unanswered letters, and while I am writing one I usually receive two; so that I am likely to die much in debt."[128] Two years later he explained why he was far behind in his correspondence: "I have so many visitants that I can seldom call an hour my own when I am at home. . . . There was a time when I did not know that I had a friend in the world, excepting my dear Mary's family; but the Lord has given me so many since, that I can not express a proper regard to them all."[129]

---

[123]Bull, comp., *John Newton*, 352.
[124]Pearce Carey, *William Carey* (New York: Doran, 1923) 134.
[125]Newton, *Letters*, 49.
[126]Bull, comp., *John Newton*, 333.
[127]Loane, *Oxford and the Evangelical Succession*, 117.
[128]Bull, comp., *John Newton*, 323.
[129]Bickersteth, *Memoirs of the Rev. John Newton*, 258-59.

Domestic servants, who in European culture were expected to stay in strict subordination, were treated with dignity by Newton. Amid letters to distinguished persons in *Cardiphonia*, there is also one to his housemaid. More than a hundred of his letters to servants are extant, and their problems are mentioned in his diary. He remarked, "I get more warmth and light sometimes by a letter from a plain person who loves the Lord Jesus, though perhaps a servant maid, than from some whole volumes put forth by learned doctors."[130] About the faithful women who had long been in his "family," he reported:

> Phoebe is drooping, and I think will not hold out long; Crabb is very asthmatic; Sally but so-so. Perhaps one young, healthy servant could do as much as all our three; but then we live in love and peace, and bear each other's burdens as much as we can. . . . I shall always think myself more obliged to them than they can be to me, and I hope nothing but death shall part us.[131]

After one servant died, Newton noted: "Phoebe's place is well supplied by a niece of Crabb; we took her up at the age of ten years, a helpless orphan, liable to fall into bad hands. She is now a good servant, of about twenty-one years of age, and *she likewise* thinks she has reason to love us." Newton remembered the household servants in his will and provided them retirement residences so that they might "live like ladies."

In 1799, Cowper wrote his last poem before losing his lucidity for the last time. Entitled "The Castaway," it describes being washed overboard by roaring waves and soon drowning in the abyss. Newton estimated that during the several decades of their friendship, Cowper had ten good years. In a letter to More in 1800, Newton told of conducting Cowper's funeral. He acknowledged that he was still puzzled over why Cowper "who both by talents and disposition seemed qualified . . . to reform the age in which he lived [was] harassed by distresses and despair."[132]

Betsy became the constant companion and secretary of the elderly Newton; he called her "the staff and comfort of my old age." She went with him on his trips and read to him when his eyes failed. Ten years after Mary's death, Newton made this diary note, "In her attention and affection, I find the best substitute in the removal of my dear wife, that the nature of the case can possibly admit."[133] But soon afterwards Betsy

---

[130]Hindmarsh, *John Newton and the English Evangelical Tradition*, 75.
[131]Bull, comp., *John Newton*, 341-42.
[132]Bickersteth, *Memoirs of the Rev. John Newton*, 274.
[133]Newton, "Diary" 2:324.

was seized with a mental disorder. In spite of various treatments, her depression became worse; consequently she was taken to the Bethlehem (the proper name for which was contracted into "Bedlam") Hospital. Newton, nearly blind, was led each day to the fence near her room and waited until being told that she waved a handkerchief from her window. He wrote in 1801, "My dear child is still deranged, but she is relieved from the dreadful horrors which once and long overwhelmed her." After a year in Bedlam she improved, returned home, and subsequently married. She and her husband took care of Newton for the remainder of his life.[134]

During Newton's old age, many laypersons and clergy cherished his example of evangelical spirituality. As Loane describes him, he was "revered as a kind of patriarch and was treated as a sort of oracle by the men of a new generation. A sound scholar and diligent pastor, a clear thinker and dignified author, he stood for those ideals of doctrine and practice which the whole Revival had embodied for England."[135]

Newton continued his pastoral relationship with Wilberforce as he battled steadfastly against the formidable forces that opposed abolition. Ten years after Wilberforce first proposed antislavery legislation, Newton sent him this word of encouragement: "You are not only a representative for Yorkshire, you have the far greater honor of being a representative for the Lord, in a place where many know him not, and an opportunity of showing them what are the genuine fruits of that religion which you are known to profess."[136] Newton went on to remind Wilberforce that the biblical Daniel had enemies who could not prevail against him when he served in government.

Wilberforce wrote a book in 1797 that aimed at communicating with the upper ranks of society. The title gives the theme: *A Practical View of the Prevailing Religious System of Professed Christians, in the Higher and Middle Classes in This Country, Contrasted with Real Christianity*. After it was published, Newton noted: "I can scarcely talk or write without introducing Mr. Wilberforce's book. . . . His situation is such that his book *must* and *will* be read by many in the higher circles, to whom we little folks can get no access."[137] It went through forty reprintings and several translations. Newton joined Wilberforce in believing that the

---

[134]Bull, comp., *John Newton*, 346-56.
[135]Loane, *Oxford and the Evangelical Succession*, 128.
[136]Robert Wilberforce and Samuel Wilberforce, *Correspondence of William Wilberforce* (London: Murray, 1838) 1:132.
[137]Bull, comp., *John Newton*, 335.

status quo was iniquitous and in hoping that the outcome of evangelical Christianity would be a moral regeneration of British society.

On a date set aside in 1797 to commemorate Britain's naval victories, many preachers probably quoted Thomson's popular poem:

> When Britain first, at Heaven's command,
> Arose from out the azure main,
> This was the charter of the land,
> And guardian angels sung this strain:
> Rule, Britannia, rule the waves;
> Britons never will be slaves.[138]

Rather than speak with pride of the accomplishments of his country, Newton pointed out that foreign wars had brought little hardship at home and that there had been apostasy in spite of the growth of a global empire. He used the occasion as another opportunity for raising British consciousness over the immorality of the slave trade:

> The sins of Great Britain are of a deeper dye than those of any nation in Europe; because they are committed against greater advantages and privileges than any other people have enjoyed. . . . From Wycliff's time, we have been favoured with a succession of preachers of the gospel. . . . Nor is there any Protestant country where religious liberty is so universally enjoyed and with so little restraint as in the dominions of Great Britain. . . . I have more than once confessed with shame in this pulpit, the concern I too long had in the African slave trade. This trade . . . is still carried on, and under the sanction of the legislature. . . . When I was engaged in it, we generally supposed, for an accurate calculation was not practicable, that there were not less than a hundred thousand persons, men, women, and children, brought off the coast, by the European vessels of all nations; and that an equal number lost their lives annually, by the wars and other calamities occasioned by the traffic, either on shore without reaching the ship, or on shipboard before they reached the places

---

[138]James Thomson, Alfred. *A Masque. Represented before Their Royal Highnesses the Prince and Princess of Wales, at Clieffden, on the First of August, 1740* (London: A. Millar, 1740) 2.5. In *Morning Post* (May 1801) the last line was parodied: "Blacken your sugar isles with slaves."

of sale. It was also supposed that more than one-half, perhaps three-fifths of the trade, was in the hands of the English."[139]

At this time Newton may have inspired Samuel Taylor Coleridge to become an abolitionist and to create a long poem about an "Ancient Mariner" who bears some resemblance to Newton.[140] Even as the mariner was cursed by the albatross he had slain, so Newton was burdened by the unethical practices of his seafaring years. With glittering eye and agonizing heart old Newton made Britons wiser by his ghastly tales of slaving. A verse of Coleridge expresses how Newton had now acquired a divine breadth of compassion:

He prayeth best, who loveth best
All things both great and small;
For the dear God who loveth us,
He made and loveth all.[141]

In 1804, Newton attended his last meeting of the Eclectic Society. As a war with Napoleon was raging, the topic of discussion was "By what arguments shall we plead with God to deliver us from the French?" One clergyman said, "There is more true religon in this nation than any other"; another one said, "If France prevails, everything great and good will be extinguished." In contrast to those chauvinist responses, Newton offered this ethnodeprecating comment: "Considering our advantages, we are worse than any nation under the sun."[142] No doubt Newton was thinking of Britian's slave trade dominance.

Because of the change in life expectancy, a man in his seventies in 1800 was roughly equivalent to a man in his nineties in 2000. During his last decade of life, Newton increasingly thought of his mortality and said: "I am like a labourer in harvest, who does not wish to leave the field till he has finished his day's work, yet who looks now and then at the sun, and is glad to see the approach of evening, that he may go to rest."[143] He reflected:

---

[139]Newton, *Works* 2:244-51.

[140]Patrick Keane, *Coleridge's Submerged Politics* (Columbia: University of Missouri Press, 1994) 157.

[141]Samuel Taylor Coleridge, *The Rime of the Ancient Mariner* (London: Sampson Low, Marston, Low and Searle, 1798) 7.23.

[142]Pratt, *The Thought of the Evangelical Leaders*, 329-30.

[143]Martin, *John Newton*, 346.

Healthy as I am, I labour under a growing disorder, for which there is no cure—I mean old age. I am not sorry it is a mortal disease from which no one recovers; for who would live always in such a world as this, who has a scriptural hope of an inheritance in the world of light? I am now in my seventy-second year, and seem to have lived long enough for myself; I have known something of the evil of life, and have had a large share of the good. I know what the world can do, and what it cannot do: it can neither give nor take away that peace of God which passeth all understanding.[144]

In 1801, Newton wrote More: "The old man of seventy-six is still favored with perfect health, and can still preach as loud, as long, and as often, as formerly."[145] Even so, he wrote her on another occasion:

What is death to a believer in Jesus! It is simply a ceasing to breathe. If we personify it, we may welcome it as a messenger sent to tell us that the days of our mourning are ended, and to open to us the gate into everlasting life. The harbingers of death, sickness, pain, and conflict, are frequently formidable to the flesh, but death itself is nothing else than a deliverance from them all.[146]

In 1804 Wilberforce was finally able to get a majority in the House of Commons interested in outlawing the slave trade. The Irish and British legislatures had united and most of the one hundred added Irish members were abolitionists. On learning that the House of Commons had voted overwhelmingly to abolish slave trade forever from British domains, Newton wrote Wilberforce in 1804:

Though I can scarcely see the paper before me, I must attempt to express my thankfulness to the Lord and to offer my congratulations to you for the success which he has so far been pleased to give to your unwearied endeavours for the abolition of the slave trade, which I have considered as a millstone, sufficient, of itself sufficient, to sink such an enlightened and highly favoured nation as ours to the bottom of the sea. My thoughts upon the subject have long been gloomy, for I was afraid the

---

[144]Cecil, "Memoirs of John Newton" 1:51.
[145]Bickersteth, *Memoirs of the Rev. John Newton*, 285.
[146]Bickersteth, *Memoirs of the Rev. John Newton*, 268.

mistaken perspective of the West India planters would prove an insuperable obstacle, but I have a new proof now of what I always professed to believe, that to prayer, faith, and patient perseverance all things are possible. Whether I, who am within two months of entering my eightieth year, shall live to see the accomplishment of the work, is only known to Him in whose hands are all our times and ways, but the hopeful prospect of its accomplishment will, I trust, give me daily satisfaction so long as my declining faculties are preserved."[147]

Wilberforce responded that the other house of Parliament would have to ratify the legislation before he could join his mentor "in the shout of victory."[148] It took another three years before the House of Lords gave their approval.

Had it not been for Wilberforce's conviction that he had a divine vocation, it is unlikely he would have been able to endure attacks for so many years. Coupland explains that his determination "was mainly due to the substance and the strength of his Christian faith." As a result, the biographer states, he did "more than any other man to save the liberty of the black races of mankind from the despotism of the white."[149] Wilberforce, like Newton, was a person of intense personal piety and they became two of the most effective political reformers in British history.

In one of his last diary entries in 1804, Newton noted that he was facing death like a grateful guest who had completed a satisfying full-course meal.[150] When he conducted a wedding that year he had to ask William Bull, his assistant, in the midst of the ceremony, "What do I here?" Apologizing for his memory loss, he quipped, "I never experienced before what it was to be seventy-nine." Afterward, he wrote Bull: "There is one interview yet to come, better than them all together. I trust, through grace—rich, free, all-sufficient grace—we shall, ere long, meet to part no more—*forever*."[151] At that time, Newton commented on metamorphosis in Christians life after death, "No man looking at the grubworm in the garden would ever suspect that it would become a butterfly; so neither doth it appear what believers shall be."[152]

---

[147]Wilberforce, *Correspondence* 1:302-303.
[148]Martin, *John Newton*, 356.
[149]Hugh Martin, ed., *Christian Social Reformers* (London: SCM, 1933) 50, 76.
[150]Newton, "Diary" 2:330.
[151]Bull, comp., *John Newton*, 354.
[152]Newton, *Letters*, 174.

As Newton became feeble, forgetful, and unable to read, Cecil kindly suggested that he retire from his pulpit ministry. That prompted this cry: "What! Shall the old African blasphemer stop while he can speak?"[153] Once he asked to be reminded about his activities that day and was amazed to hear that he had just returned from preaching at St. Mary Woolnoth. The octogenarian gave his last sermon in 1806 at a benefit for the widows and orphans of those who had died a year earlier in the Trafalgar naval battle.

The Act for Abolition of the Slave Trade was at last passed in 1807 by both houses of Parliament and assented to by George III. Newton's mood then must have been like that of the aged Simeon who, on seeing the fulfillment of his hopes in the coming of Christ, prayed, "Lord, now lettest thou thy servant depart in peace" (Luke 2:29). Newton lived for several months after learning that the nation most involved in the slave trade had declared that business to be immoral and illegal, providing fulfillment to his main social concern during the last two decades of his life.

Several weeks before he died, Newton said to Jay, "My memory is nearly gone; but I remember two things: that I am a great sinner, and that Christ is a great Saviour."[154] In his sermons, hymns, letters, and person-to-person discussions, Newton always made the person and teaching of Jesus the focus of his considerations. Also among Newton's last recorded words were, "More light, more love, more liberty."[155] While a ship captain, Newton had stated that liberty and love were meaningful concepts for Britishers but not for Africans; now he recognized that all humans had those qualities but not in sufficient quantity. He had over his lifetime grown into the full grace that integrated gospel teachings about light, love, and liberty with human rights struggles. Physically blind in old age but spiritually clearsighted, Newton had led his fellow Britishers to sing "Amazing Grace" with deepest meaning.

To the end, Newton put in practice what he had preached, that the gospel "enables the believer to meet death with composure, dignity, and hope."[156] Shortly before he died at the age of eighty-two, Betsy commented: "It is a pleasing and a painful service to attend on him, pleasing to see such sweetness and composure of mind that everything is right that

---

[153]Bull, comp., *John Newton*, 357.
[154]Redford, *The Autobiography of the Rev. William Jay*, 316.
[155]Bull, comp., *John Newton*, 359.
[156]Newton, *Works* 4:12.

is done for him."[157] To a friend, he said, "I am packed and sealed and waiting for the post."[158] The postman arrived at Christmastide 1807.

Newton had given some attention to his own final rites in his will. "It is my desire," he asserted, "that my funeral may be performed with as little expense as possible, consistent with decency."[159] His mortal remains were placed beside those of his wife in a tomb under the church. In 1893, to make way for a subway station in London, their remains were moved to the graveyard beside the church he served in Olney. Newton's executors were also charged that if any epitaph tablet were erected, the permitted text should be only this:

JOHN NEWTON, CLERK
ONCE AN INFIDEL AND LIBERTINE,
A SERVANT OF SLAVES IN AFRICA,
WAS, BY THE RICH MERCY OF OUR LORD AND SAVIOUR
JESUS CHRIST,
PRESERVED, RESTORED, PARDONED,
AND APPOINTED TO PREACH THE FAITH
HE HAD LONG LABORED TO DESTROY.

This inscription in marble can still be seen by the St. Mary Woolnoth pulpit. Newton's reference to his African plight was in accord with his persistent reflection throughout his adult years. He had written More: "My case is almost as singular as Jonah's. He was the only one delivered after having been entombed in the belly of a fish; and I, perhaps, the only one ever brought from bondage and misery in Africa to preach 'Jesus Christ and him crucified.' "[160] In 1803, while a servant was putting shoes on feeble Newton, he mused: "I had not this trouble in Africa, for I had no shoes! When I rose in the morning and shook myself like a dog, I was dressed."[161] The epitaph appropriately concludes with an allusion to his preeminent apostolic role model. Paul had also confessed that he "now preacheth the faith which once he destroyed" (Galatians 1:23).

At Newton's request, Cecil conducted his funeral. He reported that "Mr. Newton gradually sunk as the setting sun, shedding to the last those declining rays, which gilded and gladdened the dark valley."[162]

[157]Martin, *John Newton*, 357.
[158]Bull, comp., *John Newton*, 358.
[159]Cecil, "Memoirs of John Newton" 1:55.
[160]Bickersteth, *Memoirs of the Rev. John Newton*, 275.
[161]Bickersteth, *Memoirs of the Rev. John Newton*, 291.
[162]Josiah Prat, ed., *The Works of the Rev. Richard Cecil* (New York: Haven, 1825)

Cecil offered this praise, "There was a gentleness, a candour, and a forbearance in him that I do not recollect to have seen in an equal degree among his brethren; and which had so conciliating an effect that even the enemies of truth often spoke loudly in praise of his character."[163] Among those attending Newton's funeral, Cecil recognized many for whom he had been a "father in Christ."[164]

Cecil's veneration for Newton resulted in his becoming his mentor's first biographer. Loane writes:

> He spent many an hour with him as his intimate companion in those years of momentous influence, and watched over him with the most tender care and solicitude when life and health began to fail. Then he prepared the narrative of his life for the press and brought out a complete edition of his works; it was his last tribute to one who had helped to bring heaven down to earth for him.[165]

As Newton's Boswell, Cecil edited the notes he had made after following him about, and published them in 1808. Selections from his potpourri follow:

> My principal method for defeating heresy is by establishing truth. One proposes to fill a bushel with tares; now if I can fill it first with wheat, I shall defy his attempts. . . .
>
> When some people talk of religion, they mean they have heard so many sermons and performed so many devotions, and thus mistake the means for the end. . . .
>
> Many have puzzled themselves about the origin of evil; I observe there is evil, and that there is a way to escape it, and with this I begin and end. . . .
>
> I can conceive a living man without an arm or a leg, but not without a head or a heart; so there are some truths essential to vital religion. . . .
>
> I endeavour to walk through the world as a physician goes through Bedlam: the patients make a noise, pester him with impertinence, and hinder him in his business; but he does the best he can, and so gets through. . . .

---

93.

[163]Cecil, "Memoirs of John Newton" 1:74.
[164]Hindmarsh, *John Newton and the English Evangelical Tradition*, 240.
[165]Loane, *Oxford and the Evangelical Succession*, 214.

Love and fear are like the sun and moon, seldom seen together. . . .

I dreamt one night that I saw Matthew Henry lay open at this text, "Let your women keep silence in the churches," and thought I read the following note at bottom: "We see the reason why women are forbid to preach the gospel, for they would persuade without argument, and reprove without giving offence." . . .

I measure ministers by square measure. I have no idea of the size of a table if you only tell me how long it is; but if you also say how broad, I can tell its dimensions. So when you tell what a man is in the pulpit, you must also tell me what he is out of it, or I shall not know his size. . . .

Tell me not how a man died, but how he lived.[166]

Josiah Bull, son of William Bull, wrote a more complete biography of Newton in 1868, containing many previously unpublished sources. He concluded with a tribute that appropriately lifts Pauline phrases about the marks of a Christian: "He was peculiarly distinguished for his tenderness and compassion. He literally wept with those that wept, and rejoiced with them that rejoiced. The law of love was in his heart, and the language of it on his lips."[167] Newton's wide appeal, in Bull's judgment, was due in large part to the catholicity of his spirit:

Of narrowness, sectarianism, bigotry, he seemed utterly incapable, and he beautifully showed how a man may love the particular denomination to which he is by conviction attached, and yet possess a charity that can embrace all who without its pale are agreed in the great fundamentals of Christianity.[168]

In evaluating Newton, Loane states, "He stood as high above most men in his knowledge both of the human heart and of the gospel life as did Sir Isaac Newton in the field of science and of philosophy."[169] Alexander Pope, the most outstanding poet of the English eighteenth-century Enlightenment, composed a famous couplet to Isaac Newton.[170]

---

[166]Cecil, "Memoirs of John Newton" 1:60-65.

[167]Bull, comp., *John Newton*, 366.

[168]Bull, comp., *John Newton*, 367.

[169]Loane, *Oxford and the Evangelical Succession*, 126.

[170]Alexander Pope, "Epitaph: Intended for Sir Isaac Newton" (ca. 1730): "Nature and Nature's laws lay hid in night: / God said, *Let Newton be!* and all

A paraphrase of that hyperbolic epitaph is an appropriate tribute for another amazing Newton who lived a century later:

> Slave trade brutality lay hid in night;
> God said, "Let Newton be!" and all was light.

---

was light."

# *Afterword*

# *Marxian Economics versus Newtonian Christianity*

Karl Marx was arguably the most troublesome debunker of all religions during the past millennium. According to that nineteenth-century intellectual, "the religious world is but a reflex of the real world,"[1] namely, metaphysical materialism. In his model of society, the ideological "superstructure" that includes religion and politics is no more than a decorative front; the essential thing is the economic "foundation" upon which it is built. Only as there is change in the raw materials, the production machinery, and the social relationships between capitalists and laborers who compose the base can there be modification of religious and political consciousness.

Marx endorsed the dictum of Ludwig Feuerbach, the most influential critic of religion in modern times, that religious ideology is never a force for social change but is always a reinforcing agent for the established social order. Marx accepted that position after rebelling against the Lutheran pietism to which he was exposed. As a school boy, he composed essays full of saccharin sentimentality in which he advocated that all admit their wickedness and be uplifted by their Redeemer. However, as a young adult, he could not discern any impact that sermonizing such as this had on social relationships in European history. He became convinced that there was a tacit conspiracy operating to drug the common people into adopting uncritically the established economy of the culture.[2]

The life and times of Newton provide an example to show that Marx's philosophy is not supported by historical facts. It was not changes

---

[1]Karl Marx, *Capital. Manifesto of the Communist Party*, ed. Friedrich Engels, trans. Samuel Moore and Edward Aveling, rev. by Marie Sachey and Herbert Lamm, Great Books of the Western World 50, ed. Robert Hutchins (Chicago: Encyclopaedia Britannica, 1952) 35.

[2]David McLellan, *The Thought of Karl Marx: An Introduction* (London: Macmillan; New York: Harper & Row, 1971) 3-22.

in the material mode of production that brought about the abolition of the slave traffic. With the invention of the cotton gin in 1794, there was more demand than ever for slave labor to supply bales of raw cotton to the Lancashire textile industry. At that time virtually no one seriously thought that machines of the industrial revolution could replace slave labor needed for the production of sugar and cotton cash crops, or that a laboring force of free wage earners could provide greater profit to plantation owners than the slave system.

Marx knew well the details of the slave trade and its strategic importance to British capitalism, having studied economic history intensively for many years in the great library of the British Museum. In his major work, *Capital*, Marx noted that British slave-based wealth rapidly increased during the eighteenth century. As evidence he cited that "Liverpool employed in the slave trade, in 1730, 15 ships; in 1751, 53; in 1760, 74; in 1770, 96; and in 1792, 132."[3] In 1798, Prime Minister Pitt calculated that West Indian plantations provided Britain with an annual income of four million pounds sterling, compared with one million from all other areas of its global empire. It was estimated that the probable loss from the abolition of the slave trade at Liverpool would be seven and one-half million pounds, equivalent now to approximately a billion dollars.[4]

Sugar was king of the cash crops and it was widely acknowledged that the slave trade was intrinsic to that labor-intensive operation. As planter John Pinney put it, "Negroes are the sinews of a plantation, and it is as impossible for a man to make sugar without the assistance of the negroes as to make bricks without straw."[5] The blood and sweat of blacks was the principal reason for the enormous rise in sugar production—from 30,000 tons in 1700 to 220,000 in 1800—that made many merchants fabulously wealthy.

In Marx's day, cotton had surpassed sugar in importance to the British economy. In an 1846 letter, Marx succinctly stated:

> Without slavery, you have no cotton, without cotton you have no modern industry. It is slavery that has given value to the colonies; it was the colonies that created world trade; it is world

---

[3]Marx, *Capital*, 377.

[4]Eric Williams, *Capitalism and Slavery* (Chapel Hill: University of North Carolina Press, 1994) 53, 63.

[5]Quoted in Patrick Richardson, *Empire and Slavery*, Seminar Studies in History (London: Longmans; New York: Harper & Row, 1968) 9.

trade that is the necessary condition for large-scale machine industry. Also, before the slave trade in Negroes, the colonies supplied the Old World with but very few products and did not visibly change the face of the earth. Slavery is thus an economic category of the highest importance.[6]

Marx might well have used Newton's career as ship captain to illustrate his contention that religion functions like an "opiate," making a person insensitive to rapacious activity that maximizes profits for the upper class. The first two decades of Newton's adult life show that Christianity caused some alteration in his vocabulary and devotional behavior, but brought with it no awareness of the inhumaneness of his daily employment.

When Newton was a slave-ship captain, profanity seems to have headed his list of the seven deadly sins, the others being Sabbath breaking, gambling, wenching, boozing, dancing, and theatergoing.[7] The wall between private morality and economic activity in his compartmentalized religion was epitomized in the Sunday services he conducted on shipboard. Neither he nor his crew seemed to have had any pangs of social conscience while they were going through the forms of Anglican worship, even as their innocent captives suffered torment below deck in the stinking confines where they were stuffed.

During those years, Newton was high on Jesus and the thought of going to be with him in heaven, but there is no evidence to suggest that his conduct of business was markedly different from what it would have been if he had remained an infidel. His religion tended to be little more than a private comfort device, assuring him that deity was on the side of professing Christians who were engaged in employment that had long been approved in his culture. By neatly segregating his life into sacred and secular isolation wards, he was able to fantasize that God sanctioned white racism and British imperialism. Will and Ariel Durant, who display an awesome comprehension of world history in their many volumes on the subject, have referred to the eighteenth-century slave trade as "probably the most criminal action in history."[8] Yet Captain Newton

---

[6]Karl Marx, *The Letters of Karl Marx*, ed. Saul K. Padover (Englewood Cliffs NJ: Prentice-Hall, 1979) 50.

[7]Newton, *Works* 1:37-38; 4:82.

[8]Will Durant and Ariel Durant, *The Age of Napoleon: A History of Civilization from 1789 to 1815*, part 11 of *The Story of Civilization* (New York: Simon and Schuster, 1975) 368.

thought of his work as his Christian calling and would have been shocked if slave trading were called a crime at all.

Marx told of Rev. Joseph Townsend, a contemporary of Newton, who provided a religious justification for schemes that deprived the poor of basic human needs. Townsend argued that the total human happiness was increased when an underclass is used for the most sordid and servile work. By this scheme, he said, "the more delicate are not only relieved from drudgery . . . but are left at liberty, without interruption, to pursue those callings which are suited to their various dispositions." For Parliament to interfere in the situation and offer relief would "destroy the harmony and beauty, the symmetry and order of that system, which God and nature have established in the world."[9] "In a thoroughly brutal way," Marx retorted, "the Church of England parson, Townsend, glorified misery as a necessary condition of wealth."[10] Townsend was a well-respected writer who had earlier published *Every True Christian a New Creature* (1769).

Townsend was not thinking of plantation workers but of laborers he saw about him in England. The situation of workers in grimy factory towns after the rise of the Industrial Revolution was probably not greatly different from that of the Caribbean slave.[11] Both means of labor were viewed as acceptable ways of producing goods as cheaply as possible. For both, the environs were squalid, the average workweek was about seventy hours, and the average life expectancy was less than forty years. Wilberforce tried in vain to get the Apprentice's Act passed that would have limited the working hours in cotton mills to twelve hours a day.[12] The monied class trampled on human rights in both domestic and overseas enterprises. Many in England feared sedition might result from teaching literacy to the poor, even as many planters thought the same with regard to slaves.

The examples of Captain Newton and Parson Townsend show that there is at least some truth in Marx's philosophy of religion. If he had

---

[9]Joseph Townsend, *A Dissertation on the Poor Laws* (rept.: Berkeley/London: University of California Press, 1971; orig. 1786) 35-36.

[10]Marx, *Capital*, 320.

[11]A report to Parliament contended that working conditions for children in Yorkshire cotton mills were at least as miserable as for slaves in the West Indies. David Charles Douglas, ed., *English Historical Documents* (12 vols., 1968), vol. 11, *1783–1832* (London: Eyre & Spottiswoode, 1959) 740-42.

[12]Leonard Cowie, *William Wilberforce 1759–1833* (New York: Greenwood, 1992) 11.

said that *some* religion is an opiate, he would have been echoing a theme from ancient prophets in his own Jewish tradition. Amos, for instance, thundered against fellow Israelites who participated in the rituals prescribed by priests, while turning their eyes away from the downtrodden. He declared that God was angered by those who were involved in massive slavetrading and who sold innocent people into slavery (Amos 1:6, 9; 2:6). In no uncertain terms, Amos asserted that God despises ceremonies that do not lead to equitable relations with other people (Amos 5:21-24). Likewise, as a divine spokesman, Isaiah exposed sham religion: "Though you offer many prayers, I [God] will not hear: your hands are full of blood. . . . Seek justice! Relieve the oppressed!" (Isaiah 1:15, 17).

Rabbi Jesus continued and fulfilled the prophetic message of freedom that began with Moses. In his Nazareth synagogue manifesto, Jesus taught the liberation theme as gospel truth. Quoting lines from Isaiah, he declared that God had anointed him "to preach deliverance to the captives, and . . . to set at liberty them that are bruised" (Luke 4:18). It was no otherworldly figure who made that emancipation proclamation at the beginning of his ministry and who subsequently gave it specific application.

Jesus was at least as aware as the Hebrew prophets before him, or Marx after him, that piety can be a cosmetic to cover injustices. The religious establishment in every century focuses more on orthodoxy (right doctrine) than on orthopraxis (right practice). To counter that chronic tendency, Jesus told a shocking parable about the way in which the righteous "sheep" will be separated from the unrighteous "goats." The basis for making the division was not who had professed Jesus as Savior or who had regularly attended a house of worship, but who had cared for the needy in a way that improved their situation (Matthew 25:32-36).

The founder of Christianity was an acknowledged do-gooder (he "went about doing good," said Peter) as well as a praying and scripture-quoting person who wanted to conserve the devotional qualities of his Jewish religion. Had these two foci on faith and works been kept paramount as Christianity developed over the centuries, the slave trade would not have flourished in some areas of Christendom in the seventeenth and eighteenth centuries, and Marxism would not have had a resounding impact in the nineteenth and twentieth centuries. However, those involved in slavery generally accepted Christian theology but rejected much of its social duties, whereas the Marxists often accepted much of New Testament social practices but rejected its theology. Marx's slogan, "From each according to his ability, to each according to his needs,"[13] paraphrases a practice of the earliest Christians; they placed their possessions in a common fund and "distribution was made to each as any had need."[14] Townsend, like most church people, attempted to explain away that communistic scheme. He claimed that God did not approve of the "mistaken zeal" that resulted in Jesus' disciples sharing all things in common.[15]

Even though there are similarities between the judgments of Marx, who looked at religion as an outside heckler, and of the biblical prophets, who looked at religion as inside participants, Marx's dogma that all religion functions merely as a tranquilizing drug goes far beyond the evidence. Indeed, there are significant historical situations where religion has been more like dynamite than like dope. In spite of the wealthy Goliaths—Liverpool shipowners, Manchester manufacturers, and West Indian planters—the humanitarian Davids stimulated core changes in the social relations of economic production. Marx cunningly selected Townsend to buttress his theory while overlooking the much-more-noted and influential parson Newton and his fellow abolitionists, who were publicly condemning slave trading at the same time Townsend published his denunciation of those who would subject the economic structure to government reform. Contrary to the doctrine of economic determinism, middle-class Newton, William Cowper, and Hannah More, as well as upper-class William Wilberforce and William Pitt, were advocates for servile workers. Courageous abolitionists, beginning with individuals from the Quaker sect and augmented by some evangelicals in the established Church of England, aroused the populace to the injustice of continuing an economically successful enterprise. Perhaps realizing that the effect of such religiously motivated abolitionists undermined his basic economic theory, Marx gave them the silent treatment.

When Newton moved away from perverted religion and became gradually converted to authentic Christianity, he became convinced of the heinous sin of slavery. Without overlooking those individual personal behaviors he formerly called sins, he also became aware that "total depravity" includes the evil social actions of exploitation and racism. He came to see that "wretches" needed to be saved from treating black people as the means for increasing WASP wealth. As a mature Christian, Newton was not so preoccupied with saving individuals to the next world that he neglected his social responsibility in this world. Whenever

---

[13]McLellan, *The Thought of Karl Marx*, 224.
[14]Acts 4:35.
[15]Townsend, *A Dissertation on the Poor Laws*, 58.

the opportunity arose during the last quarter of his life, he gave personal testimony and influenced political and cultural leaders regarding the immorality of the slave trade. He agonized over the thousands of slaves that perished during the twenty years it took to pass the antislave trade bill.

Newton came to recognize that the quintessential freedom theme of the Bible pertained to release from physical as well as spiritual bondage. Israelite history began with redemption from Egyptian slavery. Newton, like Moses, realized from his experience with slavery that "redemption" had a this-worldly dimension. In his journal, he stated that he "redeemed" a French captain from his African captors,[16] obtaining his freedom by making a payment. In his early ministry Newton focused on the theological meaning of being "redeemed," but he later stressed that it pertained to more than individuals being rescued from perdition to a life with the saved. In time he identified with the enslaved Africans who groaned under the whip of taskmasters and longed to be redeemed. The amazing thing is not that it took decades after the hour he first believed before his scales of blindness fell away, but that Newton preceded most of his contemporaries in envisioning the evil of slavery. After his thoroughgoing conversion, he worked zealously to reverse what he and others had done to Africans.

At a time when it was greatly to England's economic advantage to develop slavery, Newton and his colleagues were motivated by religious ideology to place human value higher than monetary gain. The activities of Newton's grace-filled life as an Anglican priest helped to shatter the slave institution. He became convinced that those who had been blind but now can see are those who sing gospel hymns as they lobby for civil rights legislation and participate in appropriate economic sanctions. As a latter-day Christian, Newton integrated his earlier devotional orientation into a liberation theology. It dawned on him that he and his church could not be faithful to their Judeo-Christian commitments unless their prayer and praise led to an advocacy of better lives for the oppressed. In his hymn "How Sweet the Name of Jesus Sounds," he included "prophet" as one of Jesus' roles, and he knew that the biblical prophets' judgment on sin was directed toward people's violent conduct toward their fellow humans. Prophetic religion was not a narcotic for desensitizing social responsibilities but a stimulant for exposing those who trample upon the poor.

---

[16]Newton, *Journal*, 40.

Newton became committed to the New Testament concept of authentic religion. The term "religion" is found in Newton's English Bible only in the Epistle of James. There it pertains not to doctrine but to social ethics and personal morality (James 1:27). According to James, monotheists who fail to provide their laborers equitable wages deceive themselves if they think of themselves as religious (James 5:4). In his sermon entitled "A Dead Faith," Newton shows that James ridicules those whose religion is limited to professing belief in God. Even the devil acknowledges that God exists, James chides, so belief without practice of the gospel has no religious merit (James 2:19). Newton exclaimed, "How little does it signify what you believe, or what you say, unless your acknowledged principles have an effect upon your conduct!"[17] In his notes on *Pilgrim's Progress*, Newton reinforced this point:

> Mr. Bunyan lays down practical godliness as the most undoubted evidence of a real church. "By their fruits ye shall know them," says our Lord. We cannot judge of the goodness of a tree by its luxuriant growth of leaves, or by its being covered with a fair and beautiful bloom; but by the fruit, which it afterwards produces. Thus it is no proof that we are Christ's disciples by our making an outward profession, or by telling a fine story of our experiences, but by doing the things which he has commanded us.[18]

Newton would probably have found some truth in the saying of Marx that was inscribed on Marx's gravestone in a London cemetery, "The philosophers have only *interpreted* the world in various ways; the point, however, is to *change* it."[19] Neither Marx nor Newton admired ivory-tower intellectuals who isolated themselves from the harsh predicaments confronting most people. Marx, as well as Newton, was incensed at the plantation economy, and wrote:

> It is accordingly a maxim of slave management, in slave-importing countries, that the most effective economy is that which takes out of the human chattel in the shortest space of time the utmost amount of exertion it is capable of putting forth. It is in tropical culture, where annual profits often equal the whole capital of

---

[17]Newton, *Works* 2:212.

[18]John Bunyan, *Pilgrim's Progress* (Exeter NH: Williams, 1819) 78.

[19]Karl Marx, *Theses on Feuerbach* (1845) (New York: International Publishers, 1963) no. 11.

plantations, that negro life is most recklessly sacrificed. It is the agriculture of the West Indies, which has been for centuries prolific of fabulous wealth, that has engulfed millions of the African race.[20]

Anglo-American philosophers in the so-called Age of Enlightenment had little direct effect on crushing slavery. David Hume is often ranked as the most outstanding English-speaking philosopher, but he declared in 1771, "There never was a civilized nation of any other complexion than white, nor even any individual eminent either in action or speculation—no ingenious manufactures amongst them, no arts, no sciences." Although Hume claimed to rely on experience to discover truth, he compared the intelligence of blacks, whom he had probably never observed, with that of parrots who can be taught to speak a few words that they do not understand.[21]

Slave owner Thomas Jefferson happened to publish his views on slaves at the time parliamentary debate was beginning in Britain on abolishing the slave trade. Although he is admired as America's best representative of the Enlightenment and as the author of the most outstanding declaration pertaining to human freedom in United States history, he viewed blacks as less than human. He wrote about them in his only book:

> Love seems with them to be more an eager desire than a tender delicate mixture of sentiment and sensation. Their griefs are transient. . . . In memory they are equal to the whites; in reason much inferior; . . . in imagination they are dull, tasteless, and anomalous. . . . Blacks . . . are inferior to the whites in the endowments both of body and mind. . . . The unfortunate difference of colour, and perhaps of faculty, is a powerful obstacle to the emancipation of these people.[22]

In spite of his slogan that criticized philosophers, Marx spent most of his life collecting, organizing, and publishing ideas. It was as a philosopher devoted to reinterpreting history, and not as a proletarian labor organizer, that he made his impact on the world. Marx's fresh ideas contributed to social change even though this contradicted his doctrine

---

[20]Marx, *Capital*, 50:129.

[21]David Hume, *Essays* (London: Longmans, 1875) 1:252.

[22]Thomas Jefferson, *Notes on the State of Virginia*, 2nd English ed. (London: J. Stockdale, 1787) query 14.

that ideology is not a cause of social revolutions that bring more justice and liberty.

Newton, as well as Marx, believed that fundamental change in social institutions was needed before liberty and justice for all could become a reality. Yet he had an altogether different outlook on ultimate reality than Marx, an outspoken atheist and materialist. Newton's mature faith in the God of liberty enabled him to see more objectively the malaise of his own culture. That theology provided him with the will power and the emotional stimulus needed for denouncing the slave traffic.

In the twentieth century, the argument over the role of economics in effecting social change has continued. In *Capitalism and Slavery*, Eric Williams has defended Marx's theory that history is not shaped by individual personalities. "The decisive forces . . . are the developing economic forces," Williams concludes.[23] Consequently, holding abolitionists in esteem is little more than sentimental twaddle. Countering Williams's thesis, historian Roger Anstey's more-recent and more-thorough study shows that Quakers and Evangelicals "produced a new, foursquare, theologically based condemnation of slavery and a dynamic of faith and action which largely created and sustained the abolition campaign."[24] In spite of the vested interests of British manufacturers and West Indies planters, the religious idealism expressed by Newton and his spiritual advisees was a mighty factor. Anstey documents that they were carrying out their effective reform when slave-trade profits were greatest.[25] Economist Seymour Drescher also provides data to show that the British slave system produced more sugar in the West Indies from 1783–1807 than could have been obtained by free labor.[26]

Historian G. R. Balleine should also be included in the chorus of those who have carefully examined the way in which slavery was eliminated in the British commonwealth:

> Not a single historian expresses a doubt as to where the credit is due. Quakers and Methodists played their part; towards the end all that was best in the country was united on this subject; but the men who bore the brunt of the fight, who

---

[23]Williams, *Capitalism and Slavery*, 210.

[24]Roger Anstey, *The Atlantic Slave Trade and British Abolition 1760–1810* (London: Macmillan, 1975) 96.

[25]Anstey, *The Atlantic Slave Trade and British Abolition 1760–1810*, 57.

[26]Seymour Drescher, *Econocide* (Pittsburgh: University of Pittsburgh Press, 1977) 184.

supplied the leaders, who supplied the organization, who supplied the enthusiasm, who supplied the funds, were the Evangelicals in the Church of England.[27]

The abolitionists introduced tactics for mobilizing public opinion that have become standard operating procedures. Widely circulated pamphlets by prominent national figures that defended the rights of the oppressed were accompanied by intensive lobbying and governmental investigation. Slogans were prominently displayed in public, speeches were made wherever an audience could be found, hundreds of petitions were sent to the government by various groups, and a boycott of consumer goods was encouraged. Anstey commends the slave-trade protestors in this way:

> Their organization was masterly and their doggedness surpassing. Behind the political activity of the religiously inspired men who constituted the core of the abolition lobby was a theology of a profoundly dynamic kind, and one which, especially through the particular way in which the concept of redemption was worked out and applied, had profound significance for the theology of antislavery, and for future social reform.[28]

For the past two centuries the story of Newton's change from lost prodigal to saved captain has rivaled only his hymns in popularity. But his crucial involvement in economic and political affairs has been largely overlooked. Most writers about Newton have given scant attention to his years as social activist. Richard Cecil did not mention his mentor's abolitionist role either in the eulogy he gave at his funeral or in the biography he published the year the British slave trade officially ended. There is only a passing reference to the matter in the next significant biography, written in 1868 by Josiah Bull.[29] Newton's association with the antislavery movement is overlooked in articles about him in editions of the *Encyclopaedia Britannica*. The *Dictionary of Hymnology* not only fails to mention the mature Newton's antislavery convictions, but states with no hint of irony, "The six . . . years during which he commanded a slave ship matured his Christian beliefs."[30] The *Dictionary of National Biography*

---

[27]G. R. Balleine, *A History of the Evangelical Party in the Church of England* (London: Church Press, 1951) 119.

[28]Anstey, *The Atlantic Slave Trade and British Abolition 1760–1810*, 409.

[29]Bull, comp., *John Newton*, 61.

[30]John Julian, ed., *Dictionary of Hymnology* (New York: Scribner's, 1892) 803.

has published an extensive article on Newton, but dismisses his work as an abolitionist in one sentence.

The most recent of such distorted treatments is a biography of Newton by John Pollock—who has also written the life stories of Dwight L. Moody and Billy Graham. According to Pollock, Newton's Christian conversion was displayed in his resolve never again to swear like a sailor.[31] Ten times more attention is given to describing Newton's pietism on ship and shore than to his championing the abolition cause. Pollock concentrates on individual emotional experiences but gives little attention to the believer's subsequent actions on behalf of others. Evangelicals of the past century, many of whom have been called fundamentalists, have sometimes placed inordinate emphasis on "saving souls," but have neglected responsibility for saving their culture. Many seated in comfortable pews prefer that their preachers condone the economic system that has given them prosperity, ignoring human rights abuses.

All educated persons today are aware of the inhumane slaughter of Jews by the Nazis, but how many know the circumstances out of which the debilitating social disease of racism began? The vividness and repulsiveness of the European holocaust among Caucasians may be due not only to there being people still alive who remember and tell about it, but also because it was persons of their own race who were liquidated. Many more people died from the African slave trade than from the Nazi persecution. For the ten million Africans who worked as slaves in the New World, there were at least that many who died in battles stimulated by the slave trade or on their way to the slave ships. Another million died aboard ship and three million did not survive the initial "seasoning" when being broken in for plantation work. Today there are many who are still not aware of the extent of the atrocities that were carried out by white men in the slave trade. In order to avoid incriminating the white race, Euro-American history texts have tended to deal cursorily with the slave trade. Christopher Hill, a leading British historian, finds remarkable "the coy silence of many orthodox economic historians on the subject."[32]

Few know anything about the civilizations that flourished in West Africa before the arrival of the slave ships. Kingdoms there had qualities that matched those found in Europe at the same period. Slave traders did not want knowledge of those cultures to be known, for it would have

[31]John Charles Pollock, *Amazing Grace: John Newton's Story* (London: Hodder & Stoughton; San Francisco: Harper & Row, 1981) 81.
[32]Christopher Hill, *Some Intellectual Consequences of the English Revolution* (Madison: University of Wisconsin Press, 1980) 36.

exposed their false propaganda that fierce, licentious savages were being rescued for a better life in America. Justifications for the slave trade have not altogether ceased. Charles McKinney, speaking at a Washington convention of the National Association of Evangelicals in 1981, asserted, "The greatest thing God ever did for blacks in this country was to send some white men in ships to Africa and bring us back to this country so that we could know Jesus Christ." It is reported that this minister's statement "drew thunderous applause and a standing ovation from the largely white audience."[33] It may be impossible to obtain black/white reconciliation in our time until Euro-Americans probe into the ugliest chapter of their ethnic heritage and face honestly, as Newton did, their gross transgressions against Africans.

Dietrich Bonhoeffer confronted a culture in Germany similar to what Newton encountered. Both men were brought up in a tradition of Protestant pietism in which it was considered improper for clergymen to speak out on political and economic issues. Both came to realize that it was imperative for Christians to become involved in overcoming the social evils of their times. Bonhoeffer perceived that he and his fellow middle-class churchgoers all too often sought "cheap grace." They sang contentedly that Jesus had forgiven their sins while being oblivious to the sins of their society. The German Lutheran outlook, Bonhoeffer proclaimed, was a desecration of the concept of grace that early Christians held because it produced no change "in the life of bourgeois respectability." By contrast, genuine "costly grace" moves beyond awareness of personal salvation to pursue with steadfast determination justice for all.[34] Bonhoeffer was one of the first German clergymen to publicly protest Nazi restrictions on the rights of "non-Aryans," and he joined the underground resistance movement against Hitler's racism, militarism, and totalitarianism.

What made grace in the life of Newton "amazing" was that it moved from the cheap to the costly type. In defiance of those economic policies that were considered essential for Britain's national prosperity and international imperialism, Newton joined with others to end the "slave coast" and "middle passage" holocaust. Without forsaking his concern for revivalist "soul winning," he incorporated into the evangelical movement some approaches of the liberal Quakers. He was a vital combination of

---

[33]*The Christian Century* (8 April 1981): 373.
[34]Dietrich Bonhoeffer, *The Cost of Discipleship* (New York: Macmillan, 1959) 35-47.

pietism and practicality, of tender gospel preaching and tough political pressure, of single-minded fervor and rational judgment.

Battles led by warriors carrying the cross have long been associated with iniquitous medieval attacks on Muslims in the eastern Mediterranean. Newton is a more fitting person to be associated with an authentically Christian "crusade." Historian Frank Klingberg appropriately credits him as "one of the chief leaders in the crusade" against the slave trade.[35] A small but resolute group of humanitarians fought for monumental social changes even at the expense of economic productivity. Stimulated by the Anglo-American Quakers, evangelical clergy such as Wesley and Newton inspired Wilberforce and others to attack the slave trade. That small but resolute group fought against those who were primarily committed to raising the gross national product. Gerald Cragg, after telling about Newton and other evangelicals in the Church of England, writes:

> The crusade against the slave trade represents perhaps the greatest victory of the awakened Christian conscience over a strongly entrenched evil. . . . It had been an axiom of British policy that the prosperity of the country—the expansion of its manufacturing, shipping, and colonial trade—required active participation in this traffic. The trade in slaves had been sanctioned by three seventeenth-century charters. . . . During the century before 1786, the British alone transported at least 2,000,000 negroes to the new world.[36]

The noted English historian William Lecky ranked Newton and the abolitionists high, probably because of the connection between the two. He described Newton as one who changed from a "profligate slave dealer" to "one of the most devoted and single-hearted of Christian ministers."[37] Of the abolitionists, Lecky comments: "The unwearied, unostentatious, and inglorious crusade of England against slavery may probably be regarded as among the three or four perfectly virtuous acts recorded in the history of nations."[38]

---

[35]Frank Klingberg, *The Anti-Slavery Movement in England* (New Haven CT: Yale University Press, 1926) 70.

[36]Gerald Robertson Cragg, *The Church and the Age of Reason 1648–1789*, Pelican History of the Church 4 (London: Hodder & Stoughton, 1962) 154-55.

[37]William Edward Hartpole Lecky, *A History of England in the Eighteenth Century*, 8 vols. (New York: D. Appleton, 1882–1890) 2:653, 682.

[38]William Edward Hartpole Lecky, *History of European Morals from Augustus to Charlemange*, 2 vols., 3rd ed. rev. (New York: D. Appleton, 1879) 1:161.

The lives of Newton and those he counseled regarding the slavery issue underwent a profound reorientation, but there was also a much larger impact. George Trevelyan, the dean of British historians, has said, "It was a turning point in the history of the world when William Wilberforce and his friends succeeded in arousing the conscience of the British people to stop the slave trade in 1807, and to abolish slavery in the Empire in 1833."[39] Wilberforce died a month before the Emancipation Bill was passed in 1833 that would free nearly a million slaves. Like Moses, he was only able to see at some distance the freedom realm for those he had persevered to deliver for almost half a century.

Thanks to the impact of Newton and his followers, Britons during the past two centuries have been less a part of the problem of racial injustice and more a part of its solution. After inflicting for two centuries more suffering through the slave business than any other European nation, Great Britain has done more than any other nation to enforce its prohibition. Evangelical David Livingstone called the Arab slave trade the "open sore" of civilization and exposed its ugliness to the world. In contemporary society, Anglican Bishop Desmond Tutu of South Africa has been the most distinguished evangelical who has worked for liberation. While the pressure of economic interest continues to oppress a large underclass of people globally, Newtonian Christians are receiving amazing grace so as to combine personal faith in liberator Jesus with effective public witness.

---

[39]George Macaulay Trevelyan, *History of England*, new and enl. ed. (London/New York: Longmans, Green and Co., 1937) 599.

# A Bibliography

Anstey, Roger. *The Atlantic Slave Trade and British Abolition 1760–1810.* London: Macmillan, 1975.

Bailey, Albert. *The Gospel in Hymns.* New York: Scribner's, 1950.

Balleine, G. R. *A History of the Evangelical Party in the Church of England.* London: Church Press, 1951.

Barlass, William. *Sermons and Correspondence.* New York: Eastburn, 1818.

Bede, the Venerable. *The Ecclesiastical History of the English Nation from the Coming of Julius Caesar into this Island, in the Sixtieth Year before the Incarnation of Christ, till the Year of Our Lord 731.* London: J. Batley and Meighan, 1723).

Belden, Albert. *George Whitefield.* New York: Macmillan, 1953.

Benet, Stephen Vincent. *John Brown's Body.* New York: Doubleday, 1929.

Benezet, Anthony, et al. *Some Historical Account of Guinea, Its Situation, Produce, and the General Disposition of Its Inhabitants. With an Inquiry into the Rise and Progress of the Slave Trade, Its Nature and Lamentable Effects. Also a Republication of the Sentiments of Several Authors of Note, on This Interesting Subject; Particularly an Extract of a Treatise, by Granville Sharp.* Philadelphia: Joseph Crukshank, 1771.

Bennet, Benjamin. *Christian Oratory.* Norristown PA: Winnard, 1819.

Benson, Louis. *Studies of Familiar Hymns.* Philadelphia: Westminster, 1926.

Berkeley, George. *Works.* London: Dove, 1820.

Betjeman, John. *The City of London Churches.* London: Pitkin, 1974.

Bickersteth, Edward. *Memoirs of the Rev. John Newton.* New York: Episcopal Society, 1858.

Binns, Leonard. *The Early Evangelicals.* Greenwich CT: Seabury, 1953.

_____. *The Evangelical Movement and the English Church.* London: Methuen, 1928.

Blackburn, Robin. *The Making of New World Slavery.* London: Verso, 1997.

Bonhoeffer, Dietrich. *The Cost of Discipleship.* New York: Macmillan, 1959.

Boswell, James. *No Abolition of Slavery.* London: Faulder, 1791.

Brady, Terence, and Evan Jones. *The Fight against Slavery.* London: British Broadcasting Corporation, 1975.

Bull, Josiah, compiler. *John Newton of Olney and St. Mary Woolnoth: An Autobiography and Narrative, Compiled Chiefly from His Diary and Oher Upublished Documents by the Rev. Josiah Bull.* London: Religious Tract Society, 1868.

Bunyan, John. *Pilgrim's Progress.* Exeter NH: Williams, 1819.

Buxton, Thomas. *The African Slave Trade and Its Remedy.* London: Cass, 1967.

Cairns, William. *The Religion of Dr. Johnson and Other Essays.* London: Oxford University Press, 1946.

Callis, John, et al., editors. *John Newton: Sailor, Preacher, Pastor, and Poet: Centenary Memorials*. London: S. W. Partridge, 1908.

"Calvinism." In *Dictionary of Philosophy*. Edited by Dabobert D. Runes. New Students Outline Series 119. Repr.: Ames IA: Littlefield, Adams, 1958 (1955).

Carey, Eustace. *Memoirs of William Carey*. Hartford CT: Caufield, 1837.

Carey, Pearce. *William Carey*. New York: Doran, 1923.

Cecil, Lord David. *The Stricken Deer*. London: Constable, 1944.

Cecil, Richard. "Memoirs of John Newton." In *The Works of the Rev. John Newton Containing an Authentic Narrative, etc., Letters on Religious Subjects, Cardiphonia, Discourses Intended for the Pulpit, Sermons Preached in the Parish Church of Olney, a Review of Ecclesiastical History, Olney Hymns, Poems, Messiah, Occasional Sermons, and Tracts, to Which Are Prefixed Memoirs of His Life, &c. by the Rev. Richard Cecil*. Two volumes. Edited by Richard Cecil. Philadelphia: Uriah Hunt, 1831. *See also below*, John Newton and Thomas Haweis.

_____. *Memoirs of the Rev. John Newton, Late Rector of the United Parishes of St. Mary Woolnoth, and St. Mary Woolchurch Haw, Lombard Street, with General Remarks on His Life, Connexions, and Character*. London: printed for J. Hatchard, Piccadilly, 1808; New York: Thomas A. Ronalds, 1809. New edition: London: printed for L. B. Seeley, J. Seeley, 1820.

Churchill, Winston. *A History of the English-Speaking Peoples*. Four volumes. London: Cassell, 1956–1958.

Clarkson, Thomas. *History of the Rise, Progress, and Accomplishment of the Abolition of the African Slave-Trade by the British Parliament*. Wilmington NC: Porter, 1816.

_____. *An Essay on the Slavery and Commerce of the Human Species, Particularly the African, Translated from a Latin Dissertation, Which Was Honored with the First Prize in the University of Cambridge, for the Year 1785, with Additions*. London: J. Phillips, 1786. Repr.: Philadelphia: Joseph Crukshank, 1786.

_____. *A Summary View of the Slave Trade and of the Probable Consequences of Its Abolition*. London: J. Phillips, 1787. Pp. 16. Extracts and summary of above, *An Essay on the Slavery. . . .*

Cobbett, William, et al., editors. *The Parliamentary History of England*. Thirty-six volumes. London: T. C. Hansard for Longman, Hurst, Rees, Orme & Brown, 1806–1820.

Coleridge, Samuel Taylor. *The Rime of the Ancient Mariner*. London: Sampson Low, Marston, Low and Searle, 1798.

Cooper, Anthony Ashley, Third Earl of Shaftesbury. *Characteristics of Men, Manners, Opinions, Times*. Three volumes. Edited by J. M. Robertson. New York: Bobbs-Merrill, 1964; orig. 1711. New edition: Foreword by Douglas Den Uyl. Indianapolis: Liberty Fund, 2001.

Copleston, Frederick. *A History of Philosophy*. Westminster MD: Newman, 1959.

Coupland, Reginald. *Wilberforce*. Oxford: Clarendon, 1923.

Cowie, Leonard. *William Wilberforce 1759–1833*. New York: Greenwood, 1992.

Cowper, William. *The Letter and Prose Writings of William Cowper*. Edited by James King. Oxford: Clarendon, 1979.

_____. *See also below*, John Newton and William Cowper.

Cragg, Gerald Robertson. *The Church and the Age of Reason 1648–1789*. Pelican History of the Church 4. London: Hodder & Stoughton, 1962.

Cropper, Margaret. *Sparks among the Rubble*. London: Longmans, 1955.

Cunningham, Peter, editor. *The Works of Oliver Goldsmith*. New York: Putnam, 1908.

Curnock, Nehemiah, and John Telford, editors. *The Journal of the Rev. John Wesley, Enlarged from Original Mss., with Notes from Unpublished Diaries, Annotations, Maps, and Illustrations*. London: Epworth, 1938.

Dallimore, Arnold. *George Whitefield*. London: Billing, 1970.

Davidson, Basil. *Black Mother*. Boston: Little, Brown, 1961.

Davies, Rupert, and George Rupp, editors. *A History of the Methodist Church*. London: Epworth Press, 1965.

Davis, David. *The Problem of Slavery in the Age of Revolution 1770–1823*. Ithaca NY: Cornell University Press, 1975.

_____. *The Problem of Slavery in Western Culture*. Ithaca NY: Cornell University Press, 1966.

Demaray, Donald. *The Innovation of John Newton*. Lewiston NY: Edwin Mellen, 1988.

Doddridge, Philip. *Hymns Founded on Various Texts in the Holy Scriptures. By the Late Reverend Philip Doddridge, D.D. Published from the Author's Manuscript by Job Orton*. Edited by Job Orton. Salop [Shropshire], England: J. Eddowes and J. Cotton, with J. Waugh and W. Fenner; London: J. Buckland, 1755.

_____. *Sermons to Young Persons, on the Following Subjects, viz. I. The Importance of the Rising Generation. II. Christ Formed in the Soul the Foundation of Hope. III. A Dissuasive from Keeping Wicked Company. IV. The Young Christian Invited to an Early Attendance on the Lord's Table. V. The Orphan's Hope. VI. The Reflections of a Pious Parent on the Death of a Wicked Child. VII. Youth Reminded of Approaching Judgment*. Third edition. London: printed for M. Fenner, 1743.

Donnan, Elizabeth, editor. *Documents Illustrative of the Slave Trade*. New York: Octagon, 1965.

Douglas, David Charles, editor. *English Historical Documents* (12 vols., 1968). Volume 11, *1783–1832*. London: Eyre & Spottiswoode, 1959.

Drescher, Seymour. *Econocide*. Pittsburgh: University of Pittsburgh Press, 1977.

Durant, Will, and Ariel Durant. *The Age of Napoleon: A History of Civilization from 1789 to 1815*. Part 11 of *The Story of Civilization*. New Simon and Schuster, 1975.

Edwards, Paul, editor. *Equiano's Travels*. New York: Praeger, 1967.

Faber, Frederick. *Jesus and Mary: or, Catholic Hymns*. London: Burns, 1849.

Fielding, Henry. *The History of Tom Jones: A Foundling*. Four volumes. London: printed for A. Millar, 1749.

Forman, Kristen. *The New Century Hymnal Companion*. Cleveland OH: Pilgrim Press, 1998.

Fryer, Peter. *Staying Power: The History of Black People in Britain*. London, 1984.

Furneaux, Robin. *William Wilberforce*. London: Hamilton, 1974.

Gariepy, Henry. *Songs in the Night*. Grand Rapids MI: Eerdmans, 1996.
George, Timothy. *Faithful Witness*. Birmingham AL: New Hope, 1991.
Granfield, Linda. *Amazing Grace: The Story of the Hymn*. Illustrated by Janet Wilson. Toronto: Tundra; Plattsburg NY: Tundra Books of Northern New York, 1997.
Gratus, Jack. *The Great White Lie: Slavery, Emancipation, and Changing Racial Attitudes*. New York: Monthly Review Press, 1973.
Graves, Robert, and Raphael Patai. *Hebrew Myths: The Book of Genesis*. Garden City NY: Doubleday, 1964.
Green, Thomas (with Heinrich Rimius). *A Dissertation on Enthusiasm, Shewing the Danger of Its Late Increase, and the Great Mischiefs It Has Occasioned, Both in Ancient and Modern Times . . . to Which Is Added, by Way of Appendix, an Extract (with Some Additional Remarks) from Mr. Rimius's Late Account of the Moravians, and Their Doctrines*. London: J. Oliver and T. Payne, 1755.

Harford, John. *Recollections of William Wilberforce*. London: Longmans, 1864.
Haweis, Thomas. *See* John Newton and Thomas Haweis.
Hayward, Jack Ernest Shalom, editor. *Out of Slavery: Abolition and After*. London/Totowa NJ: F. Cass, 1985.
Hill, Christopher. *Some Intellectual Consequences of the English Revolution*. Madison: University of Wisconsin Press, 1980.
Hill, G. B., editor. *Boswell's Life of Johnson*. Oxford: Clarendon, 1934.
Hindmarsh, Bruce. *John Newton and the English Evangelical Tradition*. New York: Oxford University Press, 1996.
Hochschild, Adam. *King Leopold's Ghost*. Boston: Houghton Mifflin, 1998.
*Humble Advice of the Assembly of Divines, The, Now by Authority of Parliament Sitting at Westminster, concerning a Confession of Faith, with the Quotations and Texts of Scripture Annexed*. London/Edinburgh: Evan Tyler, Printer to the King's Most Excellent Majestie, 1647. Includes the "Westminster Confession of Faith."
Hume, David. *Essays*. London: Longmans, 1875.

Jefferson, Thomas. *Notes on the State of Virginia*. Second English edition. London: J. Stockdale, 1787.
Jeffrey, David, editor. *A Burning and a Shining Light*. Grand Rapids MI: Eerdmans, 1987.
Johansen, John. *The Olney Hymns*. Springfield OH: Hymn Society of America, 1956.
Jones, M. G. *Hannah More*. New York: Greenwood, 1968.
Julian, John, editor. *Dictionary of Hymnology*. New York: Scribner's, 1892.

Keane, Patrick. *Coleridge's Submerged Politics*. Columbia: University of Missouri Press, 1994.
King, James. *William Cowper*. Durham NC: Duke University Press, 1986.

_____. *See also* William Cowper.

Klingberg, Frank. *The Anti-Slavery Movement in England.* New Haven CT: Yale University Press, 1926.

Latourette, Kenneth Scott. *Three Centuries of Advance, A.D. 1500–A.D. 1800.* Volume 3 of *A History of the Expansion of Christianity.* New York: Harper, 1939.

Lecky, William Edward Hartpole. *A History of England in the Eighteenth Century.* Eight volumes. New York: D. Appleton, 1882–1890.

_____. *History of European Morals from Augustus to Charlemange.* Two volumes. Third edition revised. New York: D. Appleton, 1879.

Loane, Marcus. *Oxford and the Evangelical Succession.* London: Lutterworth, 1950.

Long, Edward. *History of Jamaica.* London: Lowndes, 1774.

Manning, Patrick, editor. *Slave Trades, 1500–1800.* Aldershot, Hampshire: Variorum, 1996.

Mannix, Daniel. *Black Cargoes.* New York: Viking, 1962.

Marshall, Madeleine, and Janet Todd. *English Congregational Hymns in the Eighteenth Century.* Lexington: University Press of Kentucky, 1982.

Martin, Bernard. *John Newton: A Biography.* London: Heinemann, 1950.

Martin, Hugh, editor. *Christian Social Reformers.* London: SCM Press, 1933.

Marx, Karl. *Capital. Manifesto of the Communist Party.* Edited by Friedrich Engel. Translated by Samuel Moore and Edward Aveling. Revised by Marie Sachey and Herbert Lamm. Great Books of the Western World 50. Chicago: Encyclopaedia Britannica, 1952.

_____. *The Letters of Karl Marx.* Edited by Saul K. Padover. Englewood Cliffs NJ: Prentice-Hall, 1979.

_____. *Theses on Feuerbach.* New York: International Publishers, 1963; orig. 1845.

Mathews, Donald. *Slavery and Methodism.* Princeton NJ: Princeton University Press, 1965.

Maxwell, John. *Slavery and the Catholic Church.* London: Rose, 1975.

Mbiti, John. *African Religions and Philosophy.* Garden City NY: Anchor, 1970.

McClure, David, and Elijah Parish, editors. *Memoirs of the Rev. Eleazer Wheelock.* Newbury: Norris, 1811.

McKim, Lindo Jo. *The Presbyterian Hymnal Companion.* Louisville: Westminster/John Knox, 1993.

McLellan, David. *The Thought of Karl Marx: An Introduction.* London: Macmillan; New York: Harper & Row, 1971.

Montesquieu, Charles de Secondat, baron de. *The Spirit of Laws.* Two volumes. Translated by Thomas Nugent. London: printed for J. Jourse and P. Vaillant, 1750. Repr.: Great Books of the Western World 38. Chicago: Encyclopaedia Britannica, 1980.

Montgomery, James. *Olney Hymns.* Glasgow: Collins, 1829.

More, Hannah. *An Estimate of the Religion of the Fashionable World.* London: printed for T. Cadell, 1791.

_____. *Practical Piety; or, The Influence of the Religion of the Heart on the Conduct of the Life.* Two volumes. New York: D. Appelton & Co., 1800.

_____. *Sacred Dramas: Chiefly Intended for Young Persons: the Subjects Taken from the Bible. To Which Is Added, Sensibility, a Poem.* London: T. Cadell, 1782.

_____. *Strictures on the Modern System of Female Education: with a View of the Principles and Conduct Prevalent among Women of Rank and Fortune.* Two volumes. London: printed for T. Cadell, jun. and W. Davies, 1799.

_____. *Thoughts on the Importance of the Manners of the Great to General Society.* London: printed for T. Cadell, 1788.

_____. *The Works of Hannah More, with a Sketch of Her Life.* Two volumes. Philadelphia: J. J. Woodward, 1830.

Morel, Edmund. *The Black Man's Burden.* New York: Modern Reader, 1969.


Newton, John. *Cardiphonia; or, The Utterance of the Heart, in the Course of a Real Correspondence.* London: printed for Hamilton & Adams, 1780. Pp. iv+476.

_____. "Diary of John Newton," unpublished. Princeton University Library.

_____. *The Journal of a Slave Trader.* Edited by Bernard Martin and Mark Spurrell. London: Epworth Press, 1962.

_____. *Letters and Conversational Remarks by the Late Rev. John Newton.* Edited by John Campbell. New York: S. Whiting & Co., Paul & Thomas, 1811.

_____. *Letters and Sermons: Including Cardiphonia and the Messiah: A Review of Ecclesiastical History, Hymns, and Miscellaneous Pieces.* London: for J. Johnson, 1798.

_____. *Letters to a Wife (by the Author of Cardiphonia).* London: printed for J. Johnson, 1793.

_____. *The Life of the Rev. John Newton, Rector of St. Mary Woolnoth, London.* "An Authentic Narrative," Written by Himself: To Which Some Further Particulars Are Added.* London: Religious Tract Society, 1800; New York: American Tract Society, 1830. *See also below,* John Newton and Thomas Haweis.

_____. *A Review of Ecclesiastical History, So Far as It Concerns the Progress, Declensions, and Revivals of Evangelical Doctrine and Practice: With a Brief Account of the Spirit and Methods by Which Vital and Experimental Religion Have Been Opposed in All Ages of the Church.* London: printed for Edward and Charles Dilly, 1770.

_____. *Thoughts upon the African Slave Trade.* London: printed for J. Buckland, in Pater-Noster Row; and J. Johnson, in St. Paul's Churchyard, 1788. Pp. 41.

_____. *Twenty-Five Letters of the Rev. John Newton.* Edinburgh: Johnstone, 1840.

_____. *Twenty-Six Letters on Religious Subjects: To Which Are Added Hymns, and an Appendix Containing Fourteen Letters etc. Formerly Published Separately under the Signature of Vigil.* London: printed and sold by T. Wilkins, J. Buckland, J. Johnson, ?1750; 1785.

_____. *The Works of the Rev. John Newton Containing an Authentic Narrative, etc., Letters on Religious Subjects, Cardiphonia, Discourses Intended for the Pulpit, Sermons Preached in the Parish Church of Olney, a Review of Ecclesiastical History,*

*Olney Hymns, Poems, Messiah, Occasional Sermons, and Tracts, to Which Are Prefixed Memoirs of His Life, &c. by the Rev. Richard Cecil.* Two volumes. Edited by Richard Cecil. Philadelphia: Uriah Hunt, 1831.

_____. *The Works of the Rev. John Newton . . . from the Last London Edition.* Four volumes. New Haven: Nathan Whiting, 1828.

_____, and Richard Cecil. *The Life of the Rev. John Newton, Rector of St. Mary Woolnoth, London / Written by Himself to A.D. 1763, and Continued to His Death in 1807 by Richard Cecil.* New York: American Tract Society, 1850.

Newton, John, and William Cowper. *Olney Hymns in Three Books. Book I. On Select Texts of Scripture. Book II. On Occasional Subjects. Book III. On the Progress and Changes of the Spiritual Life.* London: W. Oliver, 1779.

Newton, John, and Thomas Haweis. *An Authentic Narrative of Some Remarkable and Interesting Particulars in the Life of \*\*\*\*\*: Communicated in a Series of Letters to the Rev. Mr. Haweis, Rector of Aldwinckle, Northamptonshire, and by Him (at the Request of Friends) Now Made Public.* London: printed by R. Hett for J. Johnson, 1764. The later American edition removed the anonymity with Newton's name in the title: New York: printed by W. A. Davis for C. Davis, 1796.

Norris, Kathleen. *Amazing Grace. A Vocabulary of Faith.* New York: Riverhead Books/Penguin Putnam, 1998.

Owen, Nicholas. *Journal of a Slave-Dealer.* London: Routledge, 1930.

Paine, Thomas. "African Slavery in America" (1775). In *Thomas Paine Reader.* Edited by Michael Foot. New York: Penguin, 1987.

Palmer, Colin. *Slaves of the White God.* Cambridge MA: Harvard University Press, 1976.

Parry, K. L. *Companion to Congregational Praise.* London: Independent, 1953.

Parsons, Albert. *John Newton.* London: Church Book Room) 1948.

Pearson, Hugh. *Memoirs of Claudius Buchanan.* Philadelphia: Byington, 1837.

Phipps, William E. *Influential Theologians on Wo/Men.* Washington: University Press of America, 1980.

_____. "John Wesley on Slavery," *Quarterly Review* (Summer 1981).

_____. *Muhammad and Jesus: A Comparison of the Prophets and Their Teachings.* New York: Continuum, 1996.

_____. "The Plight of the Song of Songs," *Journal of the American Academy of Religion* (March 1974).

_____. *The Sexuality of Jesus.* Cleveland: Pilgrim Press, 1996.

_____. *William Sheppard: African-American Livingstone.* Louisville: Geneva Press, 2002.

Pollock, John Charles. *Amazing Grace: John Newton's Story.* London: Hodder & Stoughton; San Francisco: Harper & Row, 1981.

Pope, Alexander. *An Essay on Criticism.* London: printed for W. Lewis, 1711.

_____. *An Essay on Man.* London: printed by John Wright for Lawton Gilliver, 1734.

Pope-Hennessy, James. *Sins of the Fathers.* New York: Knopf, 1968.

Pratt, John, editor. *The Thought of the Evangelical Leaders*. London: Nisbet, 1856.
Pratt, Josiah, editor. *The Works of the Rev. Richard Cecil*. New York: Haven, 1825.

Ramsay, David. *The History of the Independent or Congregational Church in Charleston, South Carolina*. Philadelphia: Maxwell, 1815.
Ransford, Oliver. *The Slave Trade*. London: Murray, 1971.
Reader, John. *Africa*. New York: Knopf, 1997.
Redford, George, editor. *The Autobiography of the Rev. William Jay*. New York: Carter, 1855.
Richardson, Patrick. *Empire and Slavery*. Seminar Studies in History. London: Longmans; New York: Harper & Row, 1968.
Roberts, William. *Memoirs of the Life and Correspondence of Mrs. Hannah More*. Two volumes. New York: Harper & Brothers, 1835.
Rodney, Walter. *A History of the Upper Guinea Coast 1545–1800*. Oxford: Clarendon, 1970.
Romaine, William. *An Essay on Psalmody. A Collection out of the Book of Psalms, Suited to Every Sunday in the Year*. London: n.p., 1775.
Rose, Holland. *The Cambridge History of the British Empire*. Cambridge: Cambridge University Press, 1929.
Rourke, Mary (text), and Emily Gwathmey (pictures). *Amazing Grace in America: Our Spiritual National Anthem*. Santa Monica CA: Angel City Press, 1996.
Routley, Erik. *Hymns and the Faith*. London: Murray, 1955.
_____. *I'll Praise My Maker*. London: Independent, 1951.
Rupp, Gordon. *Religion in England 1688–1791*. Oxford: Clarendon, 1986.

Sawyer, Harry. *God: Ancestor or Creator?* London: Longman, 1970.
Scott, Thomas. *The Force of Truth: An Authentic Narrative*. Repr.: New York: Dodge, 1814. London: printed for G. Keith, 1779.
Sharp, Granville. *A Representation of the Injustice and Dangerous Tendency of Tolerating Slavery, or of Admitting the Least Claim of Private Property in the Persons of Men, in England. In Four Parts*. London: B. White and R. Horsfield, 1769.
Southey, Robert, editor. *The Life and Works of William Cowper*. London: Bohn, 1854.
Stalker, James. "Evangelicalism," in *Encyclopaedia of Religion and Ethics*, edited by James Hastings. New York: Scribner's, 1912. 5:603.
Stock, Eugene. *The History of the Church Missionary Society*. London: Church Missionary Society, 1899.

Telford, John. editor. *The Letters of the Rev. John Wesley*. Eight volumes. London: Epworth, 1931.
Tennyson, Hallam. *Alfred Lord Tennyson*. New York: Macmillan, 1897.
Terhune, Alfred. *The Letters of Edward Fitzgerald*. Princeton NJ: Princeton University Press, 1980.
Thomas, Gilbert. *William Cowper and the Eighteenth Century*. London: Nicholson and Watson, 1935.
Thomas, Hugh. *The Slave Trade*. New York: Simon & Schuster, 1997.

Thomson, James. *Alfred. A Masque. Represented before Their Royal Highnesses the Prince and Princess of Wales, at Clieffden, on the First of August, 1740.* London: printed for A. Millar, 1740.

Townsend, Joseph. *A Dissertation on the Poor Laws.* Repr.: Berkeley/London: University of California Press, 1971; orig. 1786.

_____. *Every True Christian a New Creature: A Treatise on 2 Corinthians 5:17.* London: n.p., 1769.

Trevelyan, George Macaulay. *The American Revolution.* New York: McKay, 1964.

_____. *History of England.* New and enlarged edition. London/New York: Longmans, Green and Co., 1937.

_____. *Illustrated English Social History.* London: Longmans, 1951.

Tyerman, Luke. *The Life of the Rev. George Whitefield.* New York: Randolph, 1877.

Waddington, John. *Congregational History 1700–1800.* London: Longmans, 1876.

Walls, Andrew. *The Missionary Movement in Christian History.* Maryknoll NY: Orbis, 1996.

Watts, Isaac. *Divine Songs: Attempted in Easy Language for the Use of Children.* London: Printed for M. Lawrence, 1715.

_____. *Hymns and Spiritual Songs. In Three Books. I. Collected from the Scriptures. II. Compos'd on Divine Subjects. III. Prepared for the Lord's Supper. With an Essay towards the Improvement of Christian Psalmody, by the Use of Evangelical Hymns in Worship, as Well as the Psalms of David.* London: J. Humphreys for John Lawrence, at the Angel in the Poultrey, 1707.

Wesley, John. *Thoughts upon Slavery.* London: R. Hawes, 1774. Repr. with notes: Philadelphia: Joseph Crukshank, 1774.

_____. *The Works of Rev. John Wesley, with the Last Corrections of the Author.* Fourteen volumes in seven. Third American edition. Edited by John Emory. New York: Carlton & Porter, 1831.

Westermann, Diedrich. *Africa and Christianity.* London: Oxford University Press, 1937.

"Westminster Confession of Faith." See *Humble Advice of the Assembly of Divines.* . . .

Whitefield, George. *Eighteen Sermons Preached by the Late Rev. George Whitefield, A.M. Taken Verbatim in Shorthand, and Faithfully Transcribed by Joseph Gurney; Revised by Andrew Gifford.* Boston: n.p., 1820; orig. London, 1771.

_____. *George Whitefield's Journals* (London: Banner of Truth Trust, 1960) 274.

Wilberforce, Robert, and Samuel Wilberforce. *Correspondence of William Wilberforce.* London: Murray, 1838.

_____. *Life of Wilberforce.* Philadelphia: Perkins, 1839.

Wilberforce, William. *An Appeal to the Religion, Justice, and Humanity of the Inhabitants of the British Empire, in Behalf of the Negro Slaves in the West Indies.* London: Hatchard, 1823.

_____. *A Practical View of the Prevailing Religious System of Professed Christians, in the Higher and Middle Classes in This Country, Contrasted with Real Christianity.* London: T. Cadell, 1797.

Willcox, William. *The Age of Aristocracy*. Lexington MA: Heath, 1976.

Willey, Basil. *The Eighteenth-Century Background*. London: Chatto, 1940.

"William Romaine." In *Dictionary of National Biography*. New York: Macmillan, 1897.

Williams, Eric. *Capitalism and Slavery*. Chapel Hill: University of North Carolina Press, 1994.

Wood, A. S. "The Influence of Thomas Haweis on John Newton." *Journal of Ecclesiastical History* 4 (October 1953).

Wordsworth, William. "Cambridge and the Alps" (1802). Book 6 of *The Prelude, or, Growth of a Poet's Mind: An Autobiographical Poem*. London: Moxon, 1850.

Yancey, Philip. *What's So Amazing about Grace?* Grand Rapids: Zondervan, 1997.

# Index